Joseph Parrish Thompson

American Comments on European Questions

International and Religious

Joseph Parrish Thompson

American Comments on European Questions
International and Religious

ISBN/EAN: 9783337131050

Printed in Europe, USA, Canada, Australia, Japan

Cover: Foto ©ninafisch / pixelio.de

More available books at **www.hansebooks.com**

AMERICAN COMMENTS ON EUROPEAN QUESTIONS, INTERNATIONAL AND RELIGIOUS

JOSEPH P. THOMPSON

FORMERLY OF NEW YORK, AND AFTERWARD OF BERLIN

HOUGHTON, MIFFLIN AND COMPANY
New York: 11 East Seventeenth Street
The Riverside Press, Cambridge
1884

EDITORIAL NOTE.

THE author of the Essays here brought together resided in Berlin from the time when his health broke down in 1871 until his death in 1879. In leaving New York he had expected to lead the life of a scholar, and to prosecute the study of Egyptian antiquities in their relation to the Bible, amid all the advantages which are offered in the libraries, museums, and lecture-rooms of the German capital. But his dominant interest in civil and religious liberty, and in all social movements which involved the discussion of fundamental principles, forbade him to be a recluse; and he responded, notwithstanding the prolonged physical sufferings by which he was hindered, to frequent calls for speeches and essays in different countries where exciting questions were under discussion, and where he believed that the voice of an American familiar with European affairs might help on the deliberations of the friends of human progress. Many of his addresses were widely distributed in different languages. Some of them have permanent value. In this belief, they are offered to those who love and honor the name of a fearless, eloquent, and enlightened advocate of Christian liberty in Church and State. In addition to the addresses several essays are here given, in which the author shows his high estimate of scientific researches, while he steadily upholds the doctrines of the Christian faith.

CONTENTS.

COMMENTS OF AN AMERICAN ON EUROPEAN QUESTIONS.

I.

THE DRIFT OF EUROPE, CHRISTIAN AND SOCIAL.[1]

(From the *Princeton Review*, May, 1878.)

THE stirring events at Rome and Constantinople in the opening of the current year set loose again the tongues of the Cumming school of prophets, — which had been silent since 1871, — and the " times " of Daniel, the seals, trumpets, and vials of the Apocalypse, the beast and the false prophet, the dragon and the scarlet woman, Babylon and Armageddon, the mystic 666, were for the hundredth time paraded as witnesses for the imminent destruction of the world by the second advent of Christ. And, indeed, never before in our time had Christ's warning of the coming judgment such pregnant signs as in these days of widespread commercial depression and bankruptcy, of war, tumult, and suspicion; " wars and commotions, nation against nation, kingdom against kingdom, distress of nations with perplexity, the sea and the waves roaring, men's hearts failing them for fear and for looking after those things which are coming on the earth." But the Europe which has survived all the

[1] Throughout this article, the term Europe is used exclusively for the European continent; Great Britain, with its insular position and distinctive civilization, being left out of account.

political commotions consequent upon the French Revolution, and all the fortunes of war from Austerlitz and Jena to Waterloo and Sedan in the west, and from Silistria to Sebastopol and to Plevna in the east, and that has twice survived the humiliation of the papacy, — in the enforced captivity of Pius VII., and the fictitious captivity of Pius IX., — is not easily to be shaken by forebodings of destruction to religion or the state. Events which have stirred the enthusiasm of prophecy call rather for the sober judgment of philosophy.

Through all the changes of governments, nations, dynasties, institutions, powers, which this eventful century has brought to pass in Europe, two factors have remained constant, — the Church and Civil Society. The relations of these to each other; their several gains, losses, modifications, conflicts; their mutual influences, perils, tendencies, hopes; and the general drift of Europe, Christian and social — are matter of profound philosophic thought, as affecting the future of mankind. Setting aside theories and prejudices, we shall find that convulsions which to the prophetic pessimist had threatened the dissolution of European society, and the end, not only of "Antichrist," but of the Christian dispensation itself, were but the throwing down of the scaffolding behind which Providence had been shaping a new moral and social order. A study of what has fallen and of what has arisen in the place of this, will be a surer guide to the future of society and religion in Europe than any interpretation of Biblical prophecies that lacks their inspiration.

To the philosophic observer the most telling evidence of the advance of Europe in the past fifty years is given in the disappearance of absolutism and the rise of constitutional governments, with a popular element more or less pronounced. Absolutism has vanished from the map of Europe, with the exception of Russia, which remains more Asiastic than European. In the Congress of Vienna (1815), which attempted to adjust the map of Europe to the "balance of power," Great Britain was the only one of the great powers which could with any propriety be said to give the people a voice in the government; and even in Great Britain, at that period, popular representation in parliament was very limited. Austria, Prussia, and Russia were absolute governments. France had indeed the form of a constitution — as with various fluctuations she had had since 1791.[1] But the term " constitution," as used on the continent of Europe during the reaction which followed the Napoleonic wars, should not be taken as synonymous with an active representative government of the people. On the 4th June, 1814, Louis XVIII. had promulgated his *Charte Constitutionelle ;* but this constitution, by the restrictions upon suffrage, conceded the franchise to only 80,000 in a population of 30,000,000 ; and these could vote only for electoral colleges which chose the deputies to the Chamber ; and the presidents of these colleges were appointed by the king. The peers and the judges were created by the king, and could be removed only by his will. In the short interval before the return of Napoleon from Elba, the king had already shown himself as absolute a Bourbon as if no charter had existed.

Of the three smaller powers represented in the Congress of Vienna, Sweden had had a diet since 1809 ; but the government was largely vested in the king and the council of state. In Spain the Cortes had proclaimed a liberal constitution in March, 1812. But almost the

---

[1] See the Constitutions of 14th September, 1791, 24th June, 1793, 22d August, 1795, 13th December, 1799, and the *Senatus-consulte* of the 18th May, 1804. Prussia received a constitution in January, 1850; Austria, her " Fundamental Law " in December, 1867.

first act of Ferdinand VII., in resuming the throne, was to promulgate a decree (May 4, 1814) abolishing the Cortes and all their acts; and soon after the constitution was publicly burned. Portugal, the eighth of the powers which sat at Vienna as the arbiters of Europe, did not have the form of a constitution till 1826.

Among the continental powers in that memorable Congress of 1815 — which marks the beginning of the European cycle now just closed — the secondary power of Sweden was the only one which had a constitutional government representing the interests of the people. In the proposed congress at Berlin in 1878, for the readjustment of the Eastern Question, every power to be represented, Turkey included, is a constitutional government, with the solitary exception of Russia. In that fact lies the political progress of Europe from Waterloo to Plevna. That one fact chronicles the revolutions of France from kingdom to kingdom, to republic, to empire, to commune, to republic; the vicissitudes of Spain under dynasties, domestic and foreign, republican manifestoes and civil war; the emancipation of Italy, and her unification in Rome through the overthrow of the temporal power of the Pope; the insurrections of 1848 in Germany; the abortive insurrection of Hungary; and the subsequent humiliation of Austria, and her reconstruction after Königgrätz. That fact is the biography of Stein, of Thiers, of Prim, of Cavour, of Deak, of Bismarck. Much more is it the chronicle of Mazzini and Kossuth, of Victor Hugo and Karl Blind, and of the thousands of nameless patriots who, in the struggle for popular freedom, suffered in the dungeons of Florence, Rome, Naples, Venice, and the fortresses of Austria, Germany, and France, or toiled in exile in England and America — some of whom are now honored in the parliaments of Versailles, Buda-Pesth, Rome, Berlin, though to most liberty came only with

death. Forty years ago Silvio Pellico's story of his imprisonment moved the civilized world to horror of Austrian despotism in Lombardy. Even in Spain, so familiar with the cruelties of political and clerical absolutism,
this refinement of tyranny was spoken of with a shudder.
To-day both Italy and Austria are free to develop themselves under parliamentary institutions, and the name of
Silvio Pellico adorns a street in the heart of Milan,
adjoining the grand "Gallery of Victor Emmanuel."
When in 1815 at Paris the sovereigns of Russia, Prussia, and Austria signed that memorable convention, the
" Holy Alliance," by which they declared their purpose
of governing according to " the sublime truths taught by
the eternal religion of the Holy Saviour," they spoke of
themselves as " delegated by Providence to govern three
branches of the same family, Austria, Prussia, and Russia," and declared that " looking upon themselves, with
regard to their subjects and their armies, as fathers of a
family, they will govern them in that spirit of brotherhood with which they are animated for the protection of
religion, peace, and justice."

This pompous declamation was put forth after the
downfall of the first Napoleon, when " legitimacy " was
made the salvation of Europe. Since the overthrow of
the third Napoleon there has existed an unwritten compact between the Emperors of Russia, Germany, and
Austria, providing for·a certain community of interest
and of action in the affairs of Europe ; yet not even the
Czar of all the Russias would have the audacity to-day
to proclaim himself, in the ear of Europe, the vicegerent
of Providence for establishing the political and moral
order of the continent. It is far more likely that the
Czar will be compelled to follow the Sultan in granting
parliamentary institutions and political reforms. He is
perhaps even more sensitive to the opinions of the press

and of parties, and more apprehensive of popular demonstrations, than are the sovereigns of constitutional states. Come what may, in the modification of civil society in Europe, personal absolutism is at an end, from the Bay of Biscay to the Sea of Marmora. Hereditary sovereigns may cling to the fiction of "divine right," and, like the King of Prussia, may crown themselves in token of a direct commission from heaven ; a usurper may take advantage of some popular commotion to install a despotism ; but the principle of constitutional government and popular representation are too deeply planted to be displaced by any personal ruler, however cunning or bold. A Louis XIV., a Frederick the Great, a Napoleon Bonaparte, is no longer a possibility to European society. "*L'État c'est moi*," is as obsolete as the famous bull "*Unam sanctam*," which declared that "every human creature is subject to the Roman Pope, and that none can be saved who doth not so believe."

It would be a rash inference from the repudiation of absolutism, that society in Europe is tending to republicanism. Outside of Switzerland and France there can hardly be said to be in any country of Europe a strong popular movement toward a republic ; and in France it is too soon to determine whether the republic is definitively established by the national will, or is a temporary expedient between the rivalries of monarchical and imperial factions. Hitherto, the experience of republicanism in France has not been of a character to recommend the republic as a model to other nations of Europe. And, unhappily, the United States have utterly lost in Europe that influence for republican institutions which was so potent in the first half of the century. A costly civil war, heavy taxation, official corruption, high prices, the depression of industry and trade, the strifes of parties and classes, and, worst of all, a weakness for evading and repudiating debts, have estranged the liberals of Europe from the American republic, and have dispelled the illusion of the common people, that America was the paradise of the workingman. In countries which have already secured general suffrage, a popular legislature, and a responsible ministry, the liberals would have little to gain by substituting for the orderly succession of a constitutional sovereign the quadrennial strife of parties for a change in the executive head of the government. Liberal progress must lie rather in the reform of laws and of local institutions, than in substituting the name of a republic for the reality of a representative government. And as for the masses, who are chiefly concerned about wages and taxes, the social democracy they crave is as far removed from a republic as is republicanism from absolutism. The one point made sure, — the displacement of absolutism by popular constitutional government, — names and forms are of secondary consequence to the future of free institutions in Europe.

Now that absolutism in the state no longer blocks the stream of progress, the drift of Europe is strongly toward the emancipation of civil society from ecclesiastical control. Autocracy had always in the papacy either a jealous rival or a vigorous ally; and in either case the effect upon popular liberty was the same. If the papacy was jealous of a prince, it was that the Pope coveted a more absolute power over prince and people; if the papacy upheld a prince, it was that spiritual despotism might be strengthened through political absolutism. An immediate effect of the abolition of the temporal power of the Pope is that the head of the Roman Church no longer takes rank with sovereigns in discussing and determining the political affairs of Europe. No Catholic power, even, now thinks of inviting the Pope to send a legate to a conference upon the Eastern Question, nor of looking to Rome for advice, much less for authority, upon any question of a political character.

To an absolute sovereign a strong alliance with the Pope could be worth an army for keeping his people in subjection; but a constitutional sovereign finds it more important to court the favor of his people, even by forfeiting the good-will of the papacy. This was the honest choice of Victor Emmanuel, and the nation ratified it by a homage to his memory never exceeded in the obsequies of a king. Since by the syllabus and the assumption of infallibility, Pius IX. set the papacy in antagonism to all that distinguishes modern society, there has been a marked disposition, even in Catholic countries, to free political society from ecclesiastical control. This is shown in measures for the suppression or regulation of monasteries and ecclesiastical corporations, for withdrawing education from clerical influence, and for bringing the church under allegiance to the state. The Italian clings to the church of his fathers, and would not have this shorn of its glories; he is proud of the papacy as a symbol of the world-supremacy of Rome; yet he will suffer no meddling of priests in politics, and no dictation from the Vatican to the Quirinal. This curtailment of clerical interference in political affairs is not due to any abatement of political pretensions on the part of the Catholic hierarchy. Indeed, the Vatican Council enhanced these pretensions to a degree that necessitated a conflict of sovereignty with every government which would have its own authority respected by its subjects; and the proclamation of the infallibility of the Pope stripped every official of the church of the last remnant of personal independence, and transformed him into an agent of the papal will for subjecting governments and peoples. To the state, as a " moral person," bound to follow justice and right, a certain ethical guidance from the teachers of religion is normal and needful. In times of national peril this influence has been most salutary in the United States; and there it has almost always been a leading power for freedom, integrity, and humanity. So long as the Roman Catholic Church shall stand, there will be thousands of its adherents in every land who will blindly obey the priest in politics and at the polls. Even in a republic this is one of the perversities of freedom itself. But clerical control in political affairs is henceforth doomed in Europe by the same causes which have banished absolutism from the state.

The relative decline of privileged orders and class prerogatives in the scale of European society, if less marked, is hardly less significant than the overthrow of absolutism and of clerical domination. Princes and prerogatives still hold their place in books of heraldry and court calendars; but in critical times it is the word of a minister, the vote of a parliament, the result of an election, • that Europe waits to hear. Peoples are more than princes, parties than potentates. Since the French Revolution leveled all social distinctions, the attempt has been made again and again to reinstate in France an aristocracy either of birth as under the monarchy, or of preferment as under the empire; but, notwithstanding a Frenchman's innate affection for a title or a bit of ribbon, there is a charm in the motto " Liberty, Equality, Fraternity," which no prerogative can lay. Any aristocracy that may be built up in France can be but a children's card-house against the popular institution of the ballot-box. In Germany the cheapness of a " von " has long been matter of ridicule; and the fortunes of war and the creation of the empire have so reduced the number of petty princes, that there are scarcely enough of these remaining to supply royal families with eligible suitors. Two of this class, with little beyond their titles to recommend them, were married in February at Berlin to princesses of the imperial family. The occasion brought together the aristocracy of Germany; and the visible splendors of the festival, the popular regard for the emperor and the crown prince, and the amiable qualities of the princesses, drew the eyes of the capital and of Germany with a curious sympathy toward this royal spectacle; yet all the while people were thinking and talking of what Bismarck should say the next day in parliament upon the Eastern Question, in answer to an interpellation by the orator of the people. The princes serve for ornament — something to be gazed at; the parliament is looked to when anything is to be done.

In the struggle of the sixteenth century with the papacy, Luther looked to princes for countenance and support, and it was the league of princes that at last secured the Reformation to Germany. But in the struggle of to-day with Ultramontanism, the Emperor of Germany has looked not to a confederation of princes against Rome, but to his ministers and to parliament. The scales are turned. Bureaucracy and patronage in Prussia are yielding to direct representation and local autonomy. In Italy rank and title still serve to tickle the national vanity; but the spectre of the republic stands behind the aristocracy, ready to advance at any moment when the prerogative of birth should be asserted against the rights of manhood. Even in Spain nobility has been cheapened by the intrigues of factions, and in Austria by the jealousy of Hungary. Whatever the form of society, there must be some provision for the natural love of distinction and display. Democracies are not exempt from this infirmity of human nature. But European society has already reached a point where the table of affairs is provided and ordered by government as purveyor to the people, though sovereigns and princes may be retained to do the honors, or as lay figures to lend a historic costume to the feast.

This brings into prominence the drift of European society toward national unity. As the map of Europe was settled by the Congress of Vienna in 1815, the central belt from the North Sea to the Mediterranean, between the seventh and the twentieth degrees of east longitude, was divided into forty-eight distinct sovereignties for Germany and Italy alone. Of these, eight belonged to Italy and forty to Germany, including Austria. Seven different titles of sovereignty were represented in Germany: kaiser, king, elector, grand duke, duke, prince, landgrave, and city ; in Italy, king, pope, grand duke, duke, and the little republic of San Marino. These divisions gave occasion to unhappy domestic rivalries and contentions, and to mischievous foreign alliances. Germany and Italy were always open to invasion, and could at any time be made the battle-ground of Europe, through the alienation of petty states from each other, and the impossibility of a truly national sentiment under such territorial and political restrictions. Now this belt is occupied by two great nations, — a united Germany, a united Italy, — each based upon representative institutions, and pursuing with undivided aim its own industrial and political development, and the harmony of the two guaranteeing the peace and order of Europe. In Italy the national unity is simple and absolute. There is a single parliament representing the whole people, and all minor sovereignties have disappeared before the one constitutional king. In Germany, though the unity of the people is real and cordial, finding its appropriate expression through the " Reichstag," yet the unity of the empire is a bit of complicated patchwork. The " Bundesrath," which has both an initiative and a determinative voice upon measures of parliament, represent twenty-five local sovereignties ; and the empire embraces four kingdoms and sundry duchies which still keep up their own interior administration. But the centripetal force of the empire preponderates more and more year by year, and the German people have become a nation with the consciousness of a new life upon their own soil and a new function in the politics of Europe. At the same time the humiliation of France through personal misrule has brought out a fresh assertion of the national spirit, which is the most hopeful sign of vitality and growth which France has given since her first revolution. This rise of nationality in Europe marks the advance of the people from subjection to sovereignty. Political Europe is no longer a group of sovereigns, with territories and subjects as appendages to their rank and power; it is a family of nations whose organic life finds expression through the state. Even the stringent military service which so many states now exact serves as a badge of citizenship, and enhances the life of the nation by the cost of its defense. The soldier's calling, which by turns has been the badge of feudal servitude, of despotic rule, of mercenary subjection, is now the mark of national unity and equality in burdens which the state imposes upon itself through the forms of law, and, with honest though mistaken motives, for the common weal. In the fact that war is no longer the game of princes but the defense of nations, Europe finds hope of peace.

That we have not sooner introduced popular education as a token of progress in European society is due to the fact that this is both cause and effect ; and the contrasts of education upon the continent of Europe leave one in perplexity as to how far public education has stimulated political and social progress, and how far this progress, resulting from other causes, has encouraged public education. Americans of wide reading and travel no longer

harbor the illusion — once the stock of Fourth of July
oratory — that monarchs fear the spread of intelligence
among their subjects, and that republics alone favor the
general diffusion of knowledge. But so long as politicians
in the United States who aspire to the presidency indulge
in such idle boasting, it is worth while to show how idle
and pernicious it is. To-day nearly all the monarchies
of Europe are in advance of the United States, in requiring that every district within their dominions shall maintain at least one public school, and in making the attendance of children at school obligatory up to a certain age,
and through a prescribed course of study.[1] The century has not seen a sovereign more impregnated with the
vice of absolutism, more averse to conceding a constitutional government, more set in the notion of personal
government by divine right, than Frederick William III.
of Prussia. He was one of the signers, if not the framer,
of the " Holy Alliance" — one of the famous " three
kings," who, though they made an ostentation of laying
their crowns at the feet of Christ, were far from approv-
ing themselves to history as " the wise men " of their .
time. But after the bitter humiliations which Prussia
had suffered from Napoleon, Frederick William III.
looked for recovery to the intellectual elevation of the
nation, and openly said, " Though we have lost territory,
power, and prestige, still we must strive to regain what
we have lost by acquiring intellectual and moral power ;
and, therefore, it is my strong desire and will to rehabil-
itate the nation by devoting the most earnest attention
to the education of the masses of my people." Univer-

---

[1] Attendance upon the primary school, or its equivalent in private education, is compulsory in Prussia, Austria, Sweden, Denmark, Italy, Spain, and Portugal. Those who have not access to
the school laws of these several states will find an excellent summary in the *Cyclopædia of Education*, by Kiddle and Schem.

sal and obligatory schooling and universal and obligatory military service have made Prussia the leader of Germany, and Germany the arbiter of Europe. The theory that the citizen exists primarily for the state, and therefore the state must see to it that he is duly trained for all the services and duties which the government may exact of him, has made of political society in Prussia an intelligent machine, highly organized and wondrously effective, but still a machine, in which the care bestowed upon each particular part is made subservient to the working of the whole. The introduction of parliamentary institutions with popular suffrage, within the past thirty years, has given a new impetus to the education of the masses in Prussia, by enhancing their political importance ; but it should not be forgotten that the theory of an absolute sovereign " educating the masses of his people " for the service of the state wrought out a more thorough and universal system of popular education than has been secured in the United States under the republican theory of the personal importance of the individual citizen.

Another popular illusion in the United States concerning education is worth correcting here, — the assumption that education is the one panacea for the evils of society, the one qualification for active participation in government. That an average number of voters can be more relied upon to vote intelligently if they can inform themselves by reading than if obliged to take all opinions at second hand will readily be granted ; yet the intelligence of a voter may depend quite as much upon what he reads as upon the fact that he can read at all. Hence there was little to be hoped for from general public education in Austria, when, by the concordat with the Pope in 1855, the whole system of instruction was placed under the supervision and control of the clergy of the Roman Catholic Church. So, if the " workingman " in the

United States reads only newspapers and pamphlets which teach that capital is his enemy, that a division of property is his right, and that it is the duty of the state to provide him with money, land, and home; or if the "granger" at the West reads only that banks, railways, and other corporations are oppressors of the farmer, and that government is bound to see that his produce is conveyed to market at rates below cost, his loans obtained below the normal rate of interest, and his debts paid in a "legal tender" below par; — then to what extent has reading made him an intelligent voter, or lifted him above the Austrian or the Spaniard whose tuition is in the hands of his priest? But though we cannot deify education as the "savior of society," or find an exact measure of the intelligence and prosperity of a country in the percentage of its population who can read and write, nevertheless there is in popular education this grand element of hope for the future of society: that by reading, a broad free avenue is opened for the diffusion of knowledge, and knowledge, like light and air, once set free, diffuses itself. Hence the increase of popular education in Europe is both a sign and a promise of the renovation of political society. It may still be true in Austria, in France, in Spain, and even in Italy, that the apathy induced by long periods of repression, the stagnation of thought and inquiry within the Catholic Church by dogma and authority, and the limitations imposed upon the press by tyranny, tradition, or timidity, have caused the tangible fruits of popular education to fall below the legal provision made for it; yet every new disclosure of the popular will, and notably just now in France and Italy, shows that knowledge is spreading itself by its own light, and that light carries health and vigor to political society.

For the old notion that ease and security in govern-

ment demanded that the people should be kept in ignorance has succeeded the doctrine that the enlightenment
of the people is the true support and defense of the state.
Every government in Europe has openly declared for
popular education as an obligation of the state to its citizens. Even the government of Turkey thirty years ago
gave official encouragement to the schools of the various
religious communities agglomerated within the empire,
and in 1869 made a spasmodic effort to establish a general school system. And though this, like so many reforms in Turkey, has hardly gone beyond a project on
paper, the bare project was a concession to the principle
of popular education as the preserver and not the peril
of the state. And Russia, too, within the last decade,
has attempted to give universality to that system of primary instruction which had hitherto prevailed chiefly in
great cities and in favored central districts. This accession of the Russian government to the promoters of popular education by the state encourages the hope that the
Czar is preparing a constitutional government for his
subjects by preparing them to appreciate and administer
a representative system.

Leaving Turkey out of the question, with the exception
of Belgium, France, Holland, and Russia, every state in
Europe now makes attendance upon the primary school
— or its equivalent in private education — obligatory
upon all children within a fixed term of years. The zeal
of Austria for general education was quickened by the
disaster of Königgrätz, which led to the reorganization
of the empire, of the military system, and every department of the public service. The control of the clergy
over the public schools was greatly abated, and primary
instruction was made compulsory between the ages of six
and fourteen. In Denmark, the compulsory school age
is from seven to thirteen, and attendance is enforced by

fines. All Germany has now followed the example of
Prussia in making the school obligatory. In Greece,
school attendance is obligatory from five to twelve; in
Italy, from six to fourteen, enforced by fine. In Portugal, " every year the study commission publishes a list of
all children of school age. The names of those parents
who fail to have their children registered are read by the
minister from the pulpit, and a list of them is nailed to the
church door. Upon repeated offenses, fines are imposed.
In the same manner, regular attendance is enforced."[1] In
Spain, Sweden, and Switzerland, attendance on the primary school is compulsory; and the Russian government
has lately applied the system of compulsory attendance
to the schools of St. Petersburg by way of experiment.

In Italy, the transition from the political tyranny of
Bourbon, Hapsburg, and Pope to the constitutional government of Victor Emmanuel has been so recent and rapid
that the system of compulsory education has not yet
brought forth its legitimate results, has not indeed been
thoroughly set in order. Recent statistics show that in
Italy there are in the schools but 70 in 1,000 of the whole
population, whereas in Denmark there are 135 in 1,000,
in Germany 152, and in Switzerland 155. France, which
has not adopted the compulsory system, nevertheless has
at school 131 in 1,000 of her population, a marvelous increase since forty-five years ago. M. Guizot broached
the scheme of public primary schools under the direction
of the state. There are now in France upwards of 50,000
such schools, with more than three and a half million
scholars.

In those countries where a school age is not fixed and
made obligatory by law, it is made obligatory upon com-
munes, corresponding to a school district in New England,
to establish primary schools either at the cost of local tax-

[1] Kiddle and Schem, *Cyclopædia.*

2

ation or by grants from the public treasury. And thus everywhere in Europe it is settled that the education of the people is a care of the state, and a primary education is brought within the reach of all, and in many states enjoined upon all. Thus, with absolutism abolished, clericalism curbed, caste and privilege curtailed, and education established, the cause of the people is fast being identified with European society.

Apart from schools, the democracy of Europe have had a training by experience which has both enlightened and sobered them. They have learned that society cannot be reconstructed in a day; that, while political equality may be secured by law, social equality is a thing impossible to the nature of man; that reform is better than revolution; that theories of socialism and pronunciamentos of democracy cannot avail against the laws of trade and of labor that grow out of the wants of society, and that represent not organized forces to be controlled by authority, nor the collective will of the community to be determined by the majority, but only the statistical agglomeration of myriads of individual wills; in a word, the people are learning that liberty is a growth requiring time and care, and due regard to soil and climate and surrounding conditions; that it may even grow best around and upon the whole framework of society, till it shall be strong enough to drop this and stand alone. In some conditions, liberty will thrive best if grafted into the old stock, drawing from this a vigor, tone, and flavor which one could not hope for by uprooting the old and planting anew.

Such is the better part of the education which the democracy of Europe have been learning since 1848. Few of the German revolutionists of that day would care to change the present order of things in Germany, where progress is assured under law, and the voice of the people is becoming more potent in parliament. Few of the Italian republicans of that time would care to overthrow the constitutional monarchy, if this shall continue to be administered in the good faith of Victor Emmanuel. The Paris commune did not represent the true democracy of France; and the elections of 1877 showed how the people have been sobered to a respect for order as the guaranty of liberty. Upon such a basis of experience popular education may erect a social structure that shall be enduring.

Parallel with the liberation of political society and the advance of popular education, the continent of Europe has witnessed also that industrial progress, and the consequent equalization of opportunity to the workingman, which in the last half century have been so remarkable in England and the United States. This enormous material development has not indeed been to the masses of society an unmixed good. Later on we shall show wherein the material civilization which the nineteenth century boasts of necessity entails upon society evils hardly known to the Middle Ages. Every new application of science to the arts of life, every new invention substituting machinery for manual labor, must bear hard upon classes of workmen until society shall have increased its demand for the products of the new manufacture, and the workmen shall have learned to earn more with the machine than they once earned without it, or shall have taken up new occupations no less profitable than the old. But notwithstanding these drawbacks, the material progress of modern times has brought its most substantial benefits to the masses of society, and has tended especially to equalize their condition in respect of the comforts of life and of opportunities for advancement. With industry, prudence, and sobriety, the wages of the workingman enable him to share the comforts and enjoyments that were once possible only to the rich; while the increased facilities of education, travel, and other means of culture raise his children to a par with the nobility of former times in the means of personal improvement. The science of political economy, which concerns itself with the material prosperity of the nation, and seeks to enhance the comforts of society and of all its members, is a constant witness for the consideration which human life has attained in the view of philosophy and of the state. The abolition of slavery and serfdom; the growth of co-operation and arbitration between capital and labor; the care of legislation for health, safety, and comfort in mines and factories, and in the dwellings of laborers; the sensitiveness of governments to taxing the necessaries of life or laying burdens upon the common people; the stupendous scale upon which governments and people encourage competitive expositions of industry and trade — these all show that labor, much more than the *man*, whom labor represents, has come to a position of influence, and even of honor in society, hardly dreamed of a century ago. "Industrial development" and "social amelioration," once the watchwords of a few philanthropists and reformers, are now incorporated into the legislation of every civilized people.

That astute critic of society, H. Taine, has characterized this altered state of things in his comparison of old Italy with the new.[1]

"Three quarters of the labor of humanity is now done by machinery, and the number of machines, like the perfectibility of processes, is constantly increasing. Manual labor diminishes in the same ratio, and consequently the number of thinking beings increases. We are accordingly exempt from the scourge which destroyed the Greek and Roman world — that is to say, the reduction of nine tenths of the human race to the condition of

---

[1] Taine's *Italy: Florence and Venice,* chap. vi.

beasts of burden, overtasked and perishing, their destruction or gradual debasement allowing only a small number of the *élite* in each state to subsist. Almost all of the republics of Greece, and of ancient and modern Italy, have perished for want of citizens. At the present day, the machinery now substituted for subjects and slaves prepares multitudes of intelligent beings.

" In addition to this, the experimental and progressive sciences, having finally embraced in their domain moral and political affairs, and daily penetrating into education, transform the idea entertained by men of society and of life ; from a militant brute who regards others as prey and their prosperity a danger, they transform him into a pacific being, who considers others as auxiliaries and their prosperity as an advantage. Every blade of wheat produced and every yard of cloth manufactured in England diminishes so much the more the price I pay for my wheat and for my cloth. It is for my interest, therefore, not only not to kill the Englishman who produces the wheat or manufactures the cloth, but to encourage him to produce and manufacture twice as much more.

" Never has human civilization encountered similar conditions. For this reason it is to be hoped that the civilization now existing, more solidly based than others, will not decay and melt away like the civilizations which have preceded it." [1]

The facts thus far presented would seem to indicate that political society in Europe is already beyond the drifting period, and has reached a stable if not a finished state of order, freedom, and equity ; that it is no longer a privileged artificial construction, but a human institution reposing upon the rights and liberties of the people. With constitutional government, parliamentary representation, popular suffrage, religious liberty, universal education, the enfranchisement of labor, equality of

---

[1] This does not hold absolutely. The whole civilized world is now suffering from over-production, and of course work and wages decline with the falling off in demand. Men can only eat and wear so much, and *too* much makes waste and trouble. Still, the drift of M. Taine's argument is sound.

rights and of opportunity — even woman having an un-
impeded "right to labor," to teach, and to talk — what
is wanting to that which in America has always been
held up as the ideal of democratic society? Alas for
that ideal, when each successive step towards its realization seems to put farther off that perfection of humanity
which social theorists had promised through revolution
and reform! One specific after another has been administered to the body politic, — constitution, parliament,
education, suffrage, liberty, have all been tried, — yet
the pessimist finds only symptoms of deterioration that
threaten decay and dissolution. That European society
is far from sound, that it has yet chronic evils to contend
with, and occasionally exhibits violent and alarming
symptoms, lies upon the surface. This is indeed a sign
of the crisis through which political society everywhere
is passing. But there is nothing in all this to qualify
the view that the general drift of Europe is toward a
better state of things, social and Christian. Some of the
evils which remain, formidable as they are, it is within
the power of society itself to throw off, or at least to
hold in check, by its own action. Others belong to the
ineffaceable elements and conditions of human existence,
and these society can but hope to mitigate, though to
keep them under control may demand an incessant warfare for its own life.

It is a great advance to have secured freedom of conscience and have liberated civil society from priestly
domination. But *how* free the human mind from that
tendency to superstition, that love of religious mystery,
which shows itself even in cultivated circles and in the
most enlightened times — which, for instance, for the
miracles of the Middle Ages would substitute the fantasies of modern spiritualism? It is a great advance to
have secured freedom of scientific thought — to have

reached an ago in which Secchi, as Director of the Observatory of the Roman College, could openly teach, as in harmony with religion, the very doctrines of nature for which Galileo was condemned. But with this triumph over dogmatism and bigotry, *how* to deliver the human mind from that skepticism which, in its reaction from superstition, is a tendency hardly less fatal to the search for truth ?

Now, these two tendencies, superstition and skepticism, divide in almost equal proportions the masses of European society. With the spread of general intelligence in the community, Roman Catholicism seems to address itself more and more boldly to the element of superstition in human nature, and to demand of its adherents a more absolute submission of reason and will to dogma and priestcraft. It was in the very face of peoples who were thought to have come to their majority by the institution of constitutional government and popular education, that the first ecumenical council since the Reformation — heedless of the progress of three hundred years — put forth dogmas more arbitrary and absurd than those which drove Luther to revolt. And the same pontificate which promulgated the immaculate conception of the Virgin, the infallibility of the Pope, and put its ban upon modern society and the state, received an unprecedented homage of gifts and pilgrimages from lands reputed to be free and enlightened, and witnessed also the revival of superstition and imposture on the stupendous scale of the pilgrimages to Lourdes, La Salette, and Marpingen.

On the other hand, the infidelity of the eighteenth century had died of inanition, as all purely negative skepticism must. The spirit of inquiry cannot long sustain itself upon *un*belief. In some lands that era of infidelity was succeeded by an earnest revival of the religious spirit under various forms from Methodism to mysticism. But the progress of physical research has revived the skeptical tendency in the form of materialism. And the materialism of a school of evolutionists is more dangerous than the infidelity of the Encyclopædists, in that it does profess to meet the yearning of the human spirit for the Why and Wherefore of things, and in denying a personal God does not leave the universe an utter blank, but finds in Nature enough to originate and to satisfy beings that are no longer conscious and accountable spirits, but agglomerated and dissolvable molecules. A most ominous tendency in European society is that of higher minds to dissociate philosophic and scientific thought, and of common minds to dissociate social reform from religion, as something quite outside alike of the intellectual and the practical in human life. And this calamity is heightened by the absence of any intelligent and persuasive religious zeal, whether in the university, the church, or the family.

With such indifferentism in the mass of its constituency, Protestant Christianity is feebly aroused against superstition and materialism. Now that the Turk is down, there is no place for a conflict of true and false religions, as when the Teutonic knights subdued the pagan Prussians, or the knights of Castile and Aragon drove out the Moors from Spain. Now that Protestantism and Catholicism have settled into their equalized positions with princes and peoples, the battle of the Reformation, as between a true and a false Christianity, cannot be renewed. Sects find too little encouragement, either from the laws or from the tastes and habits of the people, to stir the zeal of denominational propagandism in European society. And so it has come to pass that Christianity, which should be the leader of society in ever-broadening lines of light, liberty, and love, seems to stand apart as a spectator of the contest between superstition and materialism for the control of the newly-emancipated peoples.

In Germany, it may be hoped that this indifferentism is but a passing phenomenon. Till within a few years the dogmas and usages of the national church were made obligatory in domestic and official relations, and even enforced by the police. The tyranny of ecclesiasticism over opinion engendered in the hearts of multitudes a hatred of the church. By degrees a legal emancipation from forms will reconcile many to the faith. At bottom there is in the hearts of the German people a sentiment of religion, which often shows itself in contradiction to a speculative skepticism, and which skeptics themselves allow, by separating faith from philosophy and making religion purely a matter of feeling. This sentiment, under wise direction, may yet be set in action against the current of materialism.

In the political philosophy of De Tocqueville, there is in democracy a logical tendency to pantheism. This he would counteract by reviving the principle of authority as this is impersonated in the Roman Catholic Church. Forty years ago, in reflecting upon the relations of modern society to religion, he had the sagacity to write that " our posterity [here having France especially in view] will tend more and more to a division into only two parts — some relinquishing Christianity entirely, and others returning to the Church of Rome." [1] Sooner, perhaps, than De Tocqueville anticipated, ultramontanism and materialism have seemed to verify his prediction. Relying upon the superstitious element in human nature, ultramontanism works the machinery of democracy for the restoration of spiritual despotism. And no combination more potent for the destruction of liberty could be devised than the infallibility of the head of the church

[1] *Democracy in America*, vol. ii. book i. chap. vi.

backed by a *plébiscitum* — that invention of Napoleon for using the hands of the democracy to forge the chains of the empire. While superstition would crush society from above, materialism would explode it from beneath. The scientific materialism which serves the evolutionist as a speculative theory of the universe becomes in the common mind a social materialism for the practice of life. And such materialism is not only hostile to this or that institution of society, but would reduce society itself to anarchy by taking away those supreme motives without which it is impossible for human society to hold together — responsibility and hope. Without responsibility in the individual and in the whole, responsibility to authority, to law, to justice, civil society is an impossibility; and the atomic theory of man, which denies personality and resolves consciousness and conscience into mere physical or phenomenal experiences, leaves no place for responsibility.

Without hope, which is essentially a moral sentiment, society would stagnate, and man revert to the troglodytes from which the evolutionists would have us believe that he sprang. But hope is impossible to a mere equation of chemical elements subject to inexorable physical laws. To some extent, superstition and materialism will counteract each other in their effects upon the masses; but the just-budding liberty of Europe will be crushed between them, unless the gospel of Christ shall intervene with its wise and benignant authority on the one hand, and its large and loving liberty on the other.

However serious may be the perils to society from superstition and materialism, the source of these mischiefs lies in human nature; and society, in its organic capacity, can do nothing against them except by legal restraints upon imposture and fanatical excesses, and by a wise combination of ethics with physics in the training of the public schools. History teaches that forms of superstition and skepticism pass away with time ; and though we may not hope to eradicate the spirit of either — which, indeed, at bottom is one and the same — we may be confident that each succeeding form of superstition, each recurring phase of skepticism, though as threatening as the giant shadows of the Alpine mists, will melt as the day advances, or vanish when we cease to put our own doubts and fears between them and the sun.

But there is one peril to European society more formidable than these, which society has imposed upon itself, and now hugs in the delusion that its safety lies in this very danger. The one common curse and woe of the leading nations of Europe is the military system, which maintains enormous standing armies and holds every man directly or indirectly to duty as a soldier. In every great state, the army on a peace establishment is reckoned by hundreds of thousands, in war by millions ; the military appropriations form the largest item of the yearly budget ; science and invention are taxed for the production of more effective implements of war ; agriculture, industry, trade, are crippled by the withdrawal of young men in their prime from the field, the factory, the shop, to the barrack and the camp ; the training of the family and the school must be surrendered to the discipline of arms ; and the one lesson of law and of morals drilled into every man is that to be ready to fight is the first duty of the citizen, and to make every man fight is the first right of the state.[1] Germany set the example of universal compul-

---

[1] As an offset to this, it must be admitted that to boorish young men, such as miners and field hands, the army serves as a school — training them in habits of cleanliness, order, obedience, and expanding their knowledge of men and of the world. And it must further be admitted that the cost of suppressing the rebellion in the United States, through the lack of trained and efficient troops at the first,

sory military service, and Sadowa and Sedan are memorable witnesses to its efficiency. Germany pleads her geographical position as the necessity for adhering to this system, and for maintaining her large standing army. But France might plead her geographical position, open to invasion from Germany and England. Italy is vulnerable on the side of Austria and of France; Austria on the side of Italy, of Germany, and now of Russia or her satellites on the Lower Danube. Every nation uses the argument of Germany and pleads her example. Every nation is expending more and more upon its armament, and is increasing its public debt. Statesmen are at their wits' end to secure a revenue without aggravating the people; yet none dare nor will propose a congress for mutual disarmament, in the interest of national prosperity and of international peace. But unless this shall be effected, then, before the close of the century, Europe will witness one of three things — universal bankruptcy, sporadic revolutions against taxes and conscription, or a general war to relieve popular discontent, give occupation to armies, and win reprisals for filling bankrupt treasuries. Whichever of these ways society shall enter upon, the end is anarchy or despotism, alike the ruin of free institutions. Mons. P. Broca, in reminding the French scientists of the troglodytes as their first progenitors in the arts of life, said: " Barbarous no doubt they were, but are not we also barbarous in some degree, we who can only settle our differences on the battle-field. They were not acquainted with electricity or steam, they had neither metals nor gunpowder; but wretched as they were, and with only weapons of stone, they carried on against nature no mean struggle; and the progress they slowly ef-

exceeded the cost of a standing army for a generation. Still a large standing army is a constant burden to society, a temptation to war, and a danger to liberty.

fected with such efforts prepared the soil on which civilization was hereafter destined to flourish." [1] But the civilization for which those scarcely human beings contended against nature now employs its highest intellectual and material forces in fighting against man!

But the most formidable prospect to European society is the tendency of democratic civilization to crush the individual in the effort to raise the masses. The American doctrine has been, Give every man liberty, education, and the opportunity to rise, and there will be universal contentment and prosperity. This doctrine seemed sound and sufficient so long as there was plenty of land, plenty of work, plenty of trade, and plenty of money. But now that years of stringency in the money market and the labor market have made land a burden and trade a loss and work a drudgery, it is recognized that individual freedom and universal equality do not create a paradise. Worst of all, the equality of the many presses down the liberty of the individual. One man being "as good as another," each man finds that the liberty and equality which make him of so much more account to himself make him of less account to society. He is but a single atom among millions of like atoms, and his neighbors have no scruple about jostling him out of place or even crushing him out of existence. The democracy which made its chief boast the emancipation of the individual from the "paternal care" of government, and asked only freedom for every man to make his own way, now turns about and offers to surrender all individuality to centralized power in the state, invoking government to supply work, to fix its hours and its wages, to create trade and money, to furnish capital and abolish interest, and instead of levying taxes to pay them in the form of

---

[1] Address to the French Association for the Advancement of the Sciences, at the Havre Congress, 1877.

largesses. Democracy has insisted upon the right of every man to the fruits of his own labor, enterprise, skill, or luck. But now the individual who has laid up capital must divide with the many, and the workingman is no longer at liberty to make his own terms for hours and wages, but shall be allowed to work only upon such conditions as the many have prescribed. In seeking the elevation of the masses, democratic civilization has incited vastly more aspirants for higher places than it can create places to be filled. It has overlooked the unchangeable law of nature, that society can exist only on the condition of subordinate places and a division of classes. No legislation, nor education, nor combination can alter this law. Though all the operatives may be equally competent to run the factory, there is room for but one superintendent at a time ; that every poor man may have cheap coal, somebody must mine it ; if cities are to be kept healthy, somebody must sweep the streets. In digging away old institutions in order to " level up " a mound upon which all society shall stand on an equal footing, there is danger of digging a pit into which many shall fall deeper than ever before. In Europe this danger is greater than in the United States.

" The magnitude of states, the development of industry, the organization of the sciences, in consolidating the edifice, prove detrimental to the individuals who live in it, every man finding himself belittled through the enormous extension of the system in which he is comprised. Societies, in order to become more stable, have become too large, and most of them, in order the better to resist foreign attack, have too greatly subordinated themselves to their governments.

" Moreover, in order to become efficacious, industry has become too subdivided, and man, transformed into a drudge, becomes a revolving wheel. It is sad to see a hundred thousand families employing their arms and thirty superior men expending their genius in efforts to increase the lustre of a piece of muslin.

" For these evils there are palliatives, perhaps, but no remedies, for they are produced and maintained through the very structure of the society, of the industry, and of the science upon which we live. The same sap produces on the one hand the fruit, and on the other the poison ; whoever desires to taste one must drink the other." [1]

The mischiefs of contemporary civilization in depressing the individual by attempting to raise the masses, and in spreading discontent by fostering expectations which society cannot fulfill and the realization of which would render civil society impossible, are more serious and imminent in Europe than in America. By the tradition of centuries, and by experiences yet fresh in the memory of the present generation, the masses in Europe impute all their grievances to the oppressions of government. Their experiment in self-government is too recent to have weaned them from this prejudice. To the workingman in Europe, the government is still what the rain-doctor is to the African — at once the author of all mischiefs, and the only possible deliverance from them. The " hard times " are charged upon the government, and the remedy is to be found in surrendering all power to the " social democrats." This feeling is aggravated by the ill-timed attempts of governments to repress socialistic discussion by force of the police — a course which is sure to provoke a day of reckoning. It will be long before the commonalty of Europe outgrow their hereditary suspicion of the officers of law as their natural enemies. For evils inherent in democratic civilization no remedy has been found by any political philosopher, nor even by any lady novelist who has yet appeared. Happily in the United States there is yet hope that all

---

[1] Taine's *Italy : Florence and Venice,* book iv. chap. vi.

social mischiefs as they arise will be palliated by the sober second thought of the people, and by a speedy change of times. But in Europe every social evil is made more formidable by the attempt to organize the masses for a political action which would be destructive of society itself, as communism in France and social democracy in Germany. In the last resort, society must and will save itself from anarchy even by military despotism. The United States may yet save to mankind the principles of political liberty and legal equality by demonstrating that these do not deprive a people of common sense and common honesty.

II.

PAPARCHY AND NATIONALITY.[1]

(From the *British Quarterly Review*, 1875.)

AT the meeting held in St. James's Hall, London, on the 27th of January, 1874, it was resolved, " That this meeting unreservedly acknowledges it to be the duty and right of nations to uphold civil and religious liberty, and therefore deeply sympathizes with the people of Germany in their determination to resist the policy of the ultramontane portion of the Church of Rome ; " and at the responsive meeting held in the Rath-Haus at Berlin, on the 7th of February, this expression of sympathy from England to Germany was construed as " a pledge that the two nations will in the future stand firmly together in the manly struggle for the civil and religious freedom of peoples." Both these resolutions assume that, in the recent measures for counteracting ultramontanism, the government of Germany, and especially that of Prussia, is upholding civil and religious liberty, and contending for the rights and liberties of the people ;

---

[1] *Ultramontanism: England's Sympathy with Germany, as expressed at the Public Meeting held in London on January 27th, 1874; and Germany's Response ; with the Ecclesiastical Laws of Prussia, &c.* Edited by the Rev. G. R. Badenoch, LL. D.

La Liberté Religieuse en Europe depuis 1870. Par E. de Pressensé.

The Vatican Decrees, in their bearing on Civil Allegiance: a Political Expostulation. By the Right Hon. W. E. Gladstone, M. P.

3

and therefore that the ecclesiastical conflict in Germany is of common concern for Christendom, and notably for free nations such as England and the United States — in one word, this is a case of the solidarity of modern society. If this assumption is true, the question, why should England be called upon to sympathize with a great successful military power like Germany in her internal conflicts, is already answered : for the real question is not whether Germany is great or small, strong or weak, but is she just and right? No nation is great enough or strong enough to disregard the judgment of mankind and the verdict of history upon her actions. The highest military power must stand before the moral tribunal of just men. Moreover, the conflict in Germany is not one of numerical nor of military strength, but of moral forces which group themselves respectively about two essentially antagonistic and irreconcilable ideas, — the universal supremacy of the Pope, and the independent sovereignty of the nation. In this view the conflict is historical ; it was necessary ; it is a conflict of fundamental political and ethical principles ; and it can admit of no compromise. To comprehend it and to measure it there is need of a calm intelligence to be exercised in investigating facts and in evolving principles, without regard to national or ecclesiastical theories and prejudices on the one hand, or to claims of sentiment and of sympathy on the other.

In the current statements of this conflict far too much prominence has been given to the Roman Catholic Church, and even to the Pope himself, as one of the contending parties. It is not the Roman Catholic Church in faith, order, or worship, that is in question, but the attitude of the hierarchy of that church toward certain laws and measures of civil government, and the relative sanctity of the civil and the ecclesiastical oath. It is not the Pope as the head of the Latin church that is assailed, nor Pius' IX. in his proper personality, or in his administration of church affairs, but the assumption of the Pope to define the functions of the state, and to enjoin his will upon all rulers in Christendom, on the ground that " every one who has been baptized belongs to the Pope in some way or other."[1] Though Pope and Emperor are in open controversy, and the one is the representative of the Romish Church, the other of an evangelical dynasty, yet when stripped of all personal and doctrinal elements, the contest remains, in its whole substance and strength, as the historical and inevitable conflict between the claims of ecclesiastical prerogative and the sphere and scope of civil power.

In his speech of March 10, 1873, in the Prussian House of Lords, Prince Bismarck defined the position in the following terms : —

" In my opinion, the question with which we are occupied is falsified, and the light in which we view it is likewise false, when it is represented as a question of church or of confession. It is really a political question ; it has nothing to do with the struggle of an evangelical dynasty against the Catholic Church — though some would persuade our Catholic fellow-citizens that this is the issue ; it does not enter into the strife between faith and unbelief; it is concerned only with the immemorial conflict of authority, — old as the human race, the conflict between kingship and priestism [König-thum und Priester-thum, royalty and hierarchy]; that contest of power which is older far than the appearing of our Redeemer in the world; that contest of power in which Agamemnon lay at Aulis with his seers, which there cost him his daughter, and hindered the departure of the Greeks ; that contest of power which, under the name of the wars of the popes with the emperors, filled the history of the Middle Ages, down to the disintegration of the German empire. . . . In my view it is a falsifying of politics and of his-

[1] Letter of Pius IX. to the Emperor William, August 7, 1873.

tory when one regards His Holiness the Pope exclusively as the
high-priest of a confession, or the Catholic Church chiefly as a
representative of churchdom. The papacy has ever been a
political power which, with the greatest audacity and with most
momentous consequences, has interfered in the affairs of this
world ; which has striven after such encroachment, and held
this in view as its programme. That programme is well understood. The goal which, like the Frenchman's dream of an un-
broken Rhine boundary, floats before the papal power, the programme which, in the time of the mediæval emperors, was near
its realization, is the subjection of the civil power to the ecclesiastical ; a high political aim, an endeavor which, however, is as
old as humanity, since there have always been either shrewd
men or actual priests who have put forth the pretension that
the will of God was more intimately known to them than to
their fellows, and that upon the ground of this pretension they
had the right to rule their fellows ; — and that this position is
the basis of the papal pretension to sovereignty is well known."

That position and that pretension are indeed the historical ground of the present conflict in Germany between the civil government and the Roman hierarchy.
The old battle for sovereignty between the civil and the
ecclesiastical power, left by the " Holy Roman Empire "
as an inheritance to the Germany of the Reformation,
was again left as a drawn game or an armed truce at
the Peace of Westphalia ; and through the culmination
of two forces then evolved — ultramontanism now enthroned in the Vatican, and nationalism now realized
in the Empire of Germany and the Kingdom of Italy —
is at length precipitated to what should be its final issue
between Paparchy and Nationality. For a historical
date of this contest for supremacy in Germany, it is
enough for our present purpose to take the bull of Gregory VII. excommunicating Henry IV. (*Beate Petre*,
Apostolorum Princeps, etc.) A. D. 1075.[1]

[1] Magnum Bullarium Romanum, i. pp. 27–29. See also in Eisenschmidt, Römisches Bullarium, i. pp. 9–16.

Bismarck, who has the rare faculty of compressing a principle, a history, a philosophy, into a proverb for the people, in his speech of May, 1872, in the imperial Parliament, after the Pope had declined to receive Cardinal Hohenlohe as the ambassador of Germany, in answer to an interpellation as to the intentions of the government toward the Pope, said pithily, " *We are not going to Canossa*, either bodily or spiritually." Henry III. had won the right of nominating the Pope, and had made German authority supreme at Rome; Gregory VII. summoned his son before the papal court at Rome, to answer for offenses against the church. The scales of power had already turned. From that independence of control which the Pope had claimed as necessary to his functions as " the common Father of the Faithful," it was an easy step to that universal supremacy which he asserted as the vicegerent of God. Henry IV., smocked and barefoot in the snow, imploring absolution of the pitiless Hildebrand, may represent only the personal humiliation of a weak and vacillating sovereign, who had alienated both princes and people from the empire which his father had raised to the height of its power. In this view, the incident of Canossa is of no more significance to the present ecclesiastical conflict in Germany than the deposition of three rival Italian popes by Henry III.; for though the contests of personal power between the popes and the emperors of the Middle Ages affected by turns the preponderance of the church and of the state, that which concerns this discussion is the conflict of principles, or of claims put forward under the guise of principles.

But the struggle between Gregory VII. and Henry IV. had this universal significance, — that the Pope then gave a concrete practical expression to the doctrine that, as the vicar of God, and intrusted with the keys of heaven and hell, the Roman pontiff has supreme and

indisputable dominion over all the rulers of this world.
In a second bull of excommunication against Henry IV.
(A. D. 1080), Gregory invokes the apostles, Peter and
Paul, in these words : —

"Now, I beseech you, O most holy fathers and princes, cause
that all the world may understand and know that if ye are able
to bind and loose in heaven, ye are able upon earth to give and
to take away empires, kingdoms, principalities, marquisates,
duchies, countships, and the possessions of all men, according to
the deserts of each. Often, indeed, have ye taken away patri-
archates, primacies, archbishoprics, and bishoprics, from the evil
and unworthy, and have bestowed these upon men of true piety.
If, then, ye judge spiritual things, what must not be believed of
your power over worldly things? And if ye judge the angels
who rule over all proud princes, what can ye not do to their
slaves?" [1]

The pontiff thus reinforces his own authority by all
the hierarchies of heaven, and, as the successor of Peter,
assumes to wield upon earth the invisible powers and dignities attributed to the apostle in his beatified state.
Gregory would have the world believe that all things in
heaven were at his beck to enforce his excommunications
on earth, and with this array he divests Henry of his
crown, absolves his subjects from their allegiance, and
threatens with excommunication any and all who shall
acknowledge Henry's authority. It is not the act alone,
but the ground and the manner of this papal utterance

---

[1] "Agite nunc, quæso, Patres et Principes Sanctissimi, ut omnis
Mundus intelligat et cognoscat, quia si potestis in cœlo ligare et sol-
vere, potestis in terra Imperia, Regna, Principatus, Marchias, Duca-
tus, Comitatus, et omnium hominum possessiones pro meritis tollere
unicuique et concedere. Vos enim Patriarchatus, Primatus, Archi-
episcopatus, Episcopatus, frequenter tulistis pravis et indignis, et re-
ligiosis viris dedistis. Si enim spiritualia judicatis, quid de sæculari-
bus non posse credendum est? et si Angelos dominantes omnibus
superbis Principibus judicabitis, quid de illorum servis facere potestis?"

that stamps it as the historical precedent of the present struggle between the Pope and the Emperor of Germany. It is of this very bull of Gregory VII. that Mr. Bryce has said : " Doctrines such as these strike equally at all temporal governments, nor were the Innocents and Bonifaces of later days slow to apply them so." [1] But Gregory did not content himself with words. By denying to the civil power and to secular patrons the right of ecclesiastical investiture, and threatening with his anathema any ecclesiastic who should acknowledge a temporal or laical right of patronage or of confirmation in his benefice, Gregory not only severed the papacy from all dependence on the empire, but provided the elements of revolution within the empire itself. He aimed at the centralization of spiritual power in the person of the Pope, but would also retain in every abbey, in every cathedral chapter, in every bishopric, a fulcrum for the leverage of the spiritual power against the temporal.

The shrewdness and firmness of Hildebrand in grasping the independence of the papal see, and in asserting the bishopric of Rome to be universal and absolute, prepared the way for the audacity of Innocent III. in claiming to be the arbiter of Christendom in all disputes among princes and peoples — a claim of virtual supremacy in temporal affairs, by the plea that it was " his province to judge where sin is committed, and his duty to prevent all public scandals." Already had Gregory VII. conceived the comparison of the apostolic and royal dignities to the sun and moon as the chief lights that rule the world; but Innocent pressed this analogy to the relative position of these powers. Writing to the Emperor of Constantinople, he says : —

"Thou shouldest know that God created two lights in the firmament, the sun and the moon — that is, he created two dig-

[1] *The Holy Roman Empire*, 4th ed. p. 161. Gladstone, p. 41.

nities, the papal authority and the kingly power. But the former, which is set over the days, *i. e.*, the spiritual things, is the greater; that set over the things of the flesh is the smaller; and there is the same difference between popes and kings as there is between the sun and the moon."

And in plain prose Innocent made the civil power as truly a reflection of the spiritual, and its tributary, as is the moon of the sun. Englishmen must ever blush to remember how audaciously this subordination of the King to the Pope was paraded by Innocent, in the bull in which he accepts the submission and vassalage of King John, and vouchsafes to England the protectorate of Rome. In that bill the pontiff declares that both kingship and priesthood are established within the church — to the end that the kingdom may be sacerdotal and the priesthood royal; that as every knee must bow to Christ, of things in heaven and things on earth, and things under the earth, so should all obey and serve the vicar of Christ on earth — that there may be one fold and one shepherd; and hence temporal kings are not to be acknowledged as having rightful authority, unless they study to serve with true devotion this representative of Christ's kingly and priestly power.[1]

Audacious as were these assumptions of Innocent III., they were capped by the more audacious acts of Gregory IX. and Innocent IV. in excommunicating Frederic II.,

---

[1] "Rex Regum et Dominus dominantium, Jesus Christus, Sacerdos in æternum secundum ordinem Melchizedek, ita Regnum et Sacerdotium in Ecclesia stabilivit, ut sacerdotale sit Regnum et Sacerdotium sit regale, sicut in Epistola Petrus et Moyses in lege testantur; unum præficiens universis, quem suum in terris Vicarium ordinavit; ut sicut ei flectitur omne genu cœlestium, terrestrium, et etiam infernorum, ita illi omnes obediant et intendant, ut sit unum ovile et unus Pastor. Hunc itaque Reges sæculi propter Deum adeo venerantur, ut non reputent, se rite regnare, nisi studeant ei devote servire." — Eisenschmidt, i. 25.

and in finally deposing him from his imperial and kingly
authority by decree of the General Council of Lyons
(A. D. 1245). The life-long struggle of Frederic with the
papacy, — covering more than thirty years and the reigns
of four popes, — like the struggle of Henry IV., rises
above the incidents of personal ambition and official rivalry to the dignity of a conflict of principles, a contest of
the spiritual and temporal powers which, then personified
respectively in Pope and Emperor, are no less hostile and
vigorous to-day, though the Pope is stripped of all temporal sovereignty, and the empire, stripped of the titles
" Holy " and " Roman," is confined within the boundaries
of Germany proper, and rests upon a representative constitution and universal suffrage. Indeed, in reading the
controversy between Frederic II. and Gregory IX.,[1] one
can almost imagine himself reading the correspondence
of the Emperor William of Germany with Pius IX., and
finds enough to justify the saying of the emperor in his
letter of February 18th to Earl Russell, that the duty is
devolved upon him of "leading the nation once more in
the war maintained in former times, for centuries long,
by the German emperors, against a power whose domination has never in any country been found compatible with
the freedom and the welfare of nations." Though Pius
IX. cannot wield against the present Emperor of Germany the weapon of excommunication that his predecessors used so often and so effectively against Frederic
II.,[2] yet he has found a substitute in apostolical denuncia-

[1] See in Von Raumer, *Geschichte der Hohenstaufen und ihrer
Zeit.* b. iii. pp. 416–444.

[2] For the titles and the substance of these numerous bulls, the
reader is referred to the admirable compendium of Dr. A. Potthast,
Regesta Pontificum Romanorum, — a prize work of the Berlin Academy, — in which every official document of the popes, from A. D. 1198
to 1304, is catalogued in the order of its date, and is cited by its title,
with a summary of its contents and a reference to historical sources.

tions that are just as telling with the mass of German adherents of the papacy. In effect, Gregory's greater excommunication went no farther in inciting the Catholic
hierarchy and laity of Germany to a contemptuous disregard of their emperor and his laws than do the denuncia-
tions of Pius IX., though, of course, the language of excommunication was more formal and precise. Gregory
absolved all subjects of Frederic from their oath of allegiance, threatened with the papal interdict any city,
castle, villa, or neighborhood that should harbor him, for-
bidding the celebration, either publicly or privately, of
any offices of religion during his stay; threatened with
excommunication all who should assist Frederic, either
with or without arms; and enjoined it upon all patriarchs,
archbishops, and bishops in Germany, without delay, to
proclaim this excommunication and anathema with ring-
ing of bells and illuminations in all cities, castles, and villages throughout their dioceses.[1] This open, high-handed
attempt of the Pope to incite in Germany an insurrection
of the spiritual power against the temporal is feebly imitated in the warning of Pius IX. to the Emperor William, that " the measures of his government against the
religion of Jesus Christ have no other effect than that of
undermining his majesty's own throne." But the Pope
of to-day uses the weapons at his command with the same
arrogance as the haughtiest of his predecessors used the
thunders of excommunication; and the Emperor complains that leaders of the Romish Church in Germany
are organizing rebellion against the state : —

" To my deep sorrow, a portion of my Catholic subjects have
organized for the past two years a political party which endeavors to disturb, by intrigues hostile to the state, the religious
peace which has existed in Prussia for centuries. Leading
Catholic priests have, unfortunately, not only approved this

[1] See in Eisenschmidt, i. pp. 35–39.

movement, but joined in it to the extent of open revolt against existing laws."

It is the same old endeavor of the papacy, unaltered in spirit or intent by all the changed conditions of society.

From the excommunication of Frederic, so haughtily proclaimed by Gregory IX., it was but a step to his deposition by Innocent IV.— a logical step in the line of papal assumption. In presence of the 140 prelates assembled in the Council of Lyons, and assuming the assent of the council, without even condescending to take their suffrages, the Pope delivered this solemn judgment, " to be had in everlasting remembrance : " —

" Reciting the offenses of Frederic against the church, and the fatherly admonitions and ecclesiastical censures through which it had been sought to reclaim him, Innocent declares ' that the Emperor had imitated the obduracy of Pharaoh, and had stopped his ears like a viper ; [1] ·that he had wrested from the church its possessions, and oppressed the clergy with taxes, and brought their office into contempt; while to show his own contempt for the papal excommunication, he had openly consorted with heretics ; ' most of all — and this is the last specification, as being worst of all — ' he had built neither churches nor cloisters, but had rather persecuted and destroyed them.' Then, by virtue of his authority as the vicegerent of Jesus Christ, and as empowered by Him, in the person of the apostle Peter, to bind or loose upon earth, Innocent declares ' that because of his iniquities the emperor has been set aside by God from the sovereignty of which he has proved himself so unworthy, and is stripped of all his honors and dignities, which judgment the apostolic see doth now pronounce and enforce, absolving all from their oath of allegiance to him, threatening with excommunication all who shall in any way acknowledge or uphold him as emperor or as king ; and summoning the electors of the empire to choose at once a successor to its now deposed and anathematized head." [2]

---

[1] " Pharaonis imitatus duritiam et obdurans more aspidis, aures suas — monita — despexit."

[2] Nos itaque super præmissis, et compluribus aliis ejus nefandis

What gives to this act a universal interest is the assumption upon which it was grounded, that the Pope is the representative upon earth of Jesus Christ, and is empowered to interpret and to enforce the will of God against all temporal rulers, in the supreme and sole interest of the Catholic Church. The papacy, at first dependent upon the empire, then coördinate with it, gradually achieved its independence of the temporal power; next exercised its spiritual sovereignty in opposition to civil powers upon their own soil; and finally asserted its absolute suzerainty, by Divine appointment, even to the extent of dethroning kings and emperors, and of parceling out their power and their territory as fiefs of the Holy See. It only remained for Boniface VIII., in his famous bull " *Unam Sanctam*," to declare it for the teaching of the gospel, that —

" The Pope has two swords, the spiritual and the temporal; the one to be wielded by the church, the other for the church; the one by the priesthood, the other by kings and soldiers, but this only on the hint or the sufferance of the priest. One sword, however, must be under the other, and the temporal authority must be subject to the spiritual power. As saith the Apostle, ' there is no power but of God: the powers that be are ordered (*i. e., set in order*) of God;' but they would not be in order unless one sword were under the other, and also unless excessibus cum fratribus nostris, et sacro Concilio deliberatione praehabita diligenti, cum Jesu Christi vices licet immeriti teneamus in terris, nobisque in B. Petri Apostoli persona sit dictum; quod cumque ligaveris super terram, etc. — memoratum Principem qui se imperio, et Regnis, omnique honore, ac dignitate reddidit tam indignum, quippe propter suas iniquitates a Deo ne regnet vel imperet, est abjectus suis ligatum peccatis, et abjectum, omnique honore, et dignitate privatum a Domino ostendimus, denunciamus, ac nihilominus sententiando privamus." Here follow the absolution of subjects from the oath of allegiance, the denunciation of allies and supporters, and the decree for the election of a new emperor. T. i. p. 87; Eisenschmidt, i. pp. 39-52.

the lower could be lifted by the other. If the temporal power goes astray, then must it be rectified by the spiritual ; if such a power ill-treats those that are under it, it has a judge in the higher spiritual power ; but this which is highest of all can be judged by God only, not by any man, as saith the Apostle ; he that is spiritual judgeth all things, yet he himself is judged of no man. . . . Wherefore do we declare, proclaim, decree, and determine hereby that every human creature is subject to the Roman Pope, and that none can be saved who doth not so believe."

Small credit is due to Pius IX. and the Vatican Council for having formulated the syllabus and infallibility as dogmas of the church ; for here we have, almost six centuries before, all the anathemas of the one, and all the arrogance of the other. These reminiscences will suffice to establish our first point : that the controversy now waged between the imperial government and the Roman hierarchy in Germany is deeply rooted in the historical incompatibility of the pretensions of the papacy with the autonomy of the state. Much as England is beholden to precedents, she has largely outgrown her historical antecedents, while her insular position and her world-wide commercial intercourse have helped her free development ; whereas Germany is still a land of traditions, forms, and usages — a land in which " that which hath been is now, and that which is to be hath already been." It would be impossible to reproduce in England the ecclesiastical quarrels of Henry VIII., or to revive the severities of Elizabeth against the Catholics ; but in Germany the seeds of the old quarrel between the temporal and spiritual powers still live, and Germany is compelled to do to-day what England sought to do in 1581, by the bill " to restrain her majesty's subjects in their due obedience." And with the same literal truth it may be said of Germany, —

" A sort of hypocrites, Jesuits, and fragrant friars have come into the realm, to stir up sedition. . . . When fair means have done no good, and behind our tolerance there come in these emissaries of rebellion and sedition, it is time to look more strictly to them. They have been encouraged so far by the lenity of the laws. We must show them, that as the Pope's curses do not hurt us, so his blessings cannot save them. We must make laws to restrain these people, and we must prepare force to resist violence which may be offered here or abroad." [1]

This ready analogy introduces our second point : that the present ecclesiastical conflict in Germany was inevitable. The heritage of the empire of the Middle Ages, it takes up the unfinished conflict of the Reformation, under the necessary conditions of modern society. Philip the Fair of France had met the towering impudence of Boniface with ridicule and contempt. The Pope had written to him, " Know thou, that thou art subject to us both in spiritual and in temporal things ; " had denied him the disposal of ecclesiastical offices and benefices, and required him, in case of vacancy, to guard the revenues of the same for successors duly appointed, adding, " Whoever shall otherwise believe and do, the same shall be deemed a heretic." To this Philip answered, —

" Philip, by the grace of God, King of France, to Boniface, who gives himself out for Pope, little or no greeting ! Know thou, O supreme fool, that in temporal things we are not subject to any one ; that the disposal of vacant churches and benefices belongs to us of royal right ; that the revenues of the same belong to us ; that all our bestowments of the same, past or to come, are valid, and shall stand, and that we will manfully defend their possessors. If any think otherwise, we will take them for fools and idiots." [2]

[1] Speech of Sir Walter Mildmay, *D'Ewes' Journals*, 1580, 1581, quoted by Froude, *Hist.* vol. xi. ch. xxviii.
[2] Eisenschmidt, i. 104, 105.

In this scornful defiance Philip had all France at his back; and the anathemas and excommunications that Boniface heaped upon him were met by protests from all the estates of the realm. To-day, one sees in France ultramontanism triumphant over the old Gallican independence, and hears an archbishop, who had contested the proclamation of infallibility, now requiring his clergy to accept the dogma, with the implicit obedience of the soldier to his superior. In May, 1872, E. de Pressensé wrote in the " Revue des Deux Mondes : " —

" Before the proclamation of the infallibility of the Holy Father there existed in France a liberal Catholicism ; this accepted modern society, and that separation of powers which is its essential condition. Such a Catholicism, no doubt, exists in the minds and hearts of individuals, but its partisans cannot speak as heretofore; they are condemned to silence or to ambiguities ; the encyclical of the infallible Pope no longer permits extenuating commentaries. It is certain that the doctrine of the later encyclicals tends to destroy completely the distinction between civil society and religious society. The ultramontane reaction which has commenced under our eyes is the putting in operation of that which was decided upon at the Council of the Vatican ; this is the real *campaign of the interior* which Rome has now begun."

How much this pregnant phrase signifies, Pressensé tells us in these words : —

" France enfeebled, is exposed to a new peril, no less grave than those she has gone through with. The foreigner has seized her provinces; and now come those who would have her abandon her moral patrimony, that most incontestable fruit of the glorious movement of 1789 — the lay character of the modern state. The French Revolution has had no result more sure than the secularization of social society. But it is in France, after her disasters, that ultramontanism has found the most favorable ground for engaging in the contest against modern society."

This contrast of the subservient French Catholicism of to-day with the defiant Gallicanism of Philip the Fair, or even with St. Louis IX.'s milder assertion of the independence of the king and the national church, shows how far from dead, either in letter or in spirit, are the pretensions of Rome to the universal control of society in temporal as in spiritual affairs; and the picture which this intelligent and impartial witness gives of the origin and the endeavor of the ultramontane reaction in France, should be seriously pondered by all who imagine that in Germany Bismarck has got up a quarrel with the Romish Church for political ends of his own. " Whence has arisen that formidable agitation which troubles all states if not from the Council of the Vatican ? . . . Papal infallibility is nothing but the speaking-trumpet (*le porte-voix*) of the Society of Jesus, for fulminating its anathemas against all liberty, civil and religious." [1] It is Rome that has opened in every land " a campaign of the interior," a contest with society itself, in the bosom of Germany, of Austria, of France, of Italy, of Brazil, of Switzerland, and of England as well, where a " Catholic first and an Englishman afterwards," is the cry of the Ultramontanes !

But to return to the logical development of this irrepressible conflict. After the bold resistance of Philip of France to papal domination, Germany so far recovered from the blow inflicted upon Frederic II. and his house, that in 1338 the imperial electors assembled at Rhense resolved to maintain the honor and dignity of the empire against the encroachments of Rome, and refused to submit their choice of emperor to be ratified by the Holy See. Emperor no less than pope held his office by divine right; but this gain to civil independence was igno-

---

[1] E. de Pressensé, *La Liberté Religieuse en Europe depuis 1870*, pp. 443, 444. See, also, Gladstone, p. 11.

miniously bartered away in the next century by the
Hapsburg Frederic III., for the sanction of the court of
Rome. And so the contest between the dual powers of
Pope and Kaiser, now rival, now reconciled, each claiming to be independent of the other by the same divine
prerogative, yet each dependent upon the other for human recognition and support; each by turns exercising
over the other an authority well-nigh exclusive, yet each
professing to act only within its distinctive sphere, and
to concede to the other, though with changeful and contested boundaries, its appropriate functions and powers;
both struggling for the highest dominion within their
reach, and neither yielding save on compulsion; this
contest between will as law and faith as authority, that
lies in the very dualism of man's nature as belonging to
the temporal and the spiritual, and in the duality of
spheres and institutions as adapted to these, continued
to vibrate from the throne to the altar, and from the
altar to the throne, till the Reformation gave to both
powers a shock that compelled each to look to its own
foundations, regardless of the fate of the other.

Already the scandal of the great schism had shaken
the reverence of princes and people for the Holy See,
and had accustomed men to look upon the papacy more
in the light of a rival and intriguing political power than
of a supreme spiritual sovereignty. And now the dis-
graceful exposures of nepotism and profligacy at Rome,
and of venality in the disposal of the most sacred rights
and offices of the church, and also of the pardoning
grace of the gospel itself, had roused Germany to a revolt against the authority of the Pope even in spiritual
things. The old contests of Rome with the personal
spirit and strength of individual German emperors paled
before this new struggle with the conscience of the nation, stirred with the most vital concerns of the church,

4

of the faith, of the soul itself. Here was the personal
soul, armed with faith in a personal God, resisting any
intervention between itself and its Maker other than the
mediation of Christ as taught in the Gospels, and confirmed by spiritual experience.

With the Reformation, in its doctrines, its measures,
its results, we have here nothing to do. From its beginning with the Theses of Luther against Tetzel, to its
termination with the Catholic restoration and the religious Peace of Westphalia, it concerns us only as a new
epoch in the time-worn conflict of the temporal and
spiritual powers.

Had the Reformation been allowed to have its way as
a revolt of the people against corruption and tyranny in
the church, and finally against the Roman curia as the
fountain of this corruption and the centre of this tyranny, it could hardly have stopped short of its logical
issue in the separation of church and state, and in the
repudiation by both of the authority of Rome. In that
event the papacy might have been finally driven from its
position of spiritual dictatorship in temporal affairs.
But, as it proved, the papacy not only survived the popular revolution that at first threatened to sweep it away,
but regained much of the territory that it seemed to
have lost, expanded its activity into new regions of conquest, and consolidated its spiritual power within the
church in determined hostility to society itself; for
Rome, like Russia, knows well how to bide her time, —
if she seems to recede, it is only to recuperate her forces,
and since she never loses sight of her goal, she counts
upon time and opportunity to make even defeats and
hostile treaties conduct her to it.

The causes of the halting of the Reformation were
threefold : first, the necessity felt by the reformers themselves of making alliances with princes in order to se-

cure to Protestantism a footing as a political power; second, the fear of political revolutions, which led other princes to form a league with the Pope for the preservation of their own dominions; and, finally, that tendency in human nature, and especially in communities of men, to a reaction from an intense and exciting public movement — a tendency sure to be favored by the excesses of enthusiasts in the movement itself. All these causes combined to modify and restrain the Reformation in Germany, the spring of the whole movement; Luther required the aid of powerful nobles and princes ; Charles V., who had first thought to play with Luther against the Pope, and who tantalized the Protestant princes with promises of reform, at length made pact with Leo X. to put down heresy in Germany if the Pope would support him in Italy against France ; and the excesses at Münster and the peasants' war made all men desirous of more quiet times. But the definitive close of the Reformation in Germany — when Protestantism passed from the condition of a movement against Rome into one of the orders of society — dates from the Peace of Westphalia in 1648, after a civil war between Protestants and Catholics had desolated the land for thirty years. And it is at this point that we take up again the thread of the relation of the papacy to the civil power.

The Peace of Westphalia was in reality nothing but an armed truce between powers, neither of which could boast a victory, but which must stop fighting if they would save their existence. It established a *modus vivendi*, upon the basis of confessional toleration, but it neither dissolved church and state, relegating each to its distinct and independent sphere, nor defined the authority of each in relation to the other, but left the ecclesiastical and civil powers to adjust themselves by traditions, treaties, concordats, and incongruous mixtures

of civil and canon law. As before the Reformation,
princes continued to juggle or to joust with popes according to their political interests. With the fate of
such puppets we have here nothing to do ; but from the
chaos of the Reformation there emerged two hostile principles whose fate involves to-day the fate of our modern
civilization. A compromise between principles of ethics
or systems of politics which are irreconcilable in their
own nature entails a conflict upon after generations.
Sooner or later, such a compromise must be broken, and
where the compromise is between a free movement that
trusts to light and evidence and a hide-bound system
that insists upon precedent and form, it is the tendency
of the latter — having a sort of hereditary compactness
suited to aggression — to push itself and grow, till its
encroachments compel the former to arouse to self-de-
fense. Now at the period of the Reformation we find
the old notion of a universal paparchy incorporated in
the order of the Jesuits — " who claimed for the church
an unlimited supremacy over the state, and made the
existence of a government, and the allegiance paid to it,
to depend on the application of its power to the interests
of the Catholic Church." [1]   On the other hand, the
struggles in Germany for religious life and for political
rights had begun to develop that sentiment of nationality
which shapes the political divisions and orders the political life of the modern state. The first of these principles
has culminated at Rome in the dogma of infallibility ;
the second has culminated in Germany in the realization
of a true integral union and political life of the nation,
and again also in the kingdom of Italy ; and these antagonistic principles have come to an inevitable collision,
whose focus is in Germany.

[1] Ranke, *History of the Popes*, part ii. bk. vi., " Ecclesiastico-
Political Theory."

It may be alleged, however, that from an early day a national life was developed in France and in Spain in subordination to the papal supremacy. But as to France, the sentiment of nationality was there nurtured by the earlier Gallicanism of her clergy, — episcopal against papal supremacy, — and the volcanic eruption of nationalism in her revolution overwhelmed the Roman hierarchy as hostile to the state. Moreover, France, however passionate in her own nationalism, has not respected nationality as the unit of state organization ; but by invasion and intervention, by lust of conquest or of control, has violated in others the self-same principle which she asserted for her own political existence. At the present, in the chaos of the forms of national life in France, one sees how far the life itself has been depressed through that Catholic training which now substitutes pilgrimages for patriotism. And who would think of quoting Spain, the field of provincial rivalries, for an illustration of the modern idea of the nation as the normal unit of the political state ? — Spain, in the days of her prosperity, the creature of the papacy for exterminating the Protestant heresy by the Inquisition and the Armada ; now, in her adversity, a warning of what the paparchy would make of any and every nation.

By the nation, in the conception of political philosophy, is meant a people of like spirit, language, and aims, united in one political body, upon the same soil and under the same institutions. Fiore, in his " Nouveau Droit International," defines a nation by " communauté du sang, de langue, d'aptitude, et une affinité de vie civile, de temperament, de vocation." Mr. David Dudley Field, in his " International Code," says, " A nation is a people permanently occupying a definite territory, having a common government, peculiar to themselves, for the administration of justice and the preservation of in-

ternal order, and capable of maintaining relations with
all other governments." This body, whatever the political form under which it is organized as a state, possesses
in its own nature the supreme attribute of sovereignty,
and this sovereignty of the nation is independent, complete, and absolute. "It is *suprema potestas;* it is subject to no external control, but its action is in correspondence with its own determination. It is inalienable; it
is indivisible ; it is irresponsible to any external authority ; it is comprehensive of the whole political order. In
its own sovereignty, and in its own free spirit, the polit-
·ical people is to mould its own political life, and to embody in it its own ideal, and to apprehend in it its own
aim."[1] This is the conception of the nation which modern society has evolved, and by which the political map
of Europe is now to be constructed, in contradistinction
to the "Holy Roman Empire," the "Holy Alliance,"
and the notion of the "balance of power." Upon no
condition can such a nation admit a power that is not in
and of itself, yet claims to be above itself, and by an infallible authority from God to supervise, to condemn, or
to resist its laws. The conflict between nationality and
paparchy was inevitable, and is irreconcilable. One or
the other must go under. Had Bismarck brought on
this conflict for some passing policy, he might incur the
censure of history. But Bismarck did not originate it in
Austria, in Switzerland, in Brazil, nor yet in Germany.
As Mr. Seward with slavery, he had the sagacity to see
that the conflict was "irrepressible ; " but with more
boldness than Seward he seized the enemy by the throat,
and will not let him go. This is no forced collision, no
politician's quarrel.

A comparison of the territorial and numerical strength
of the Romish Church in Europe with what it was at the

[1] Mulford, *The Nation*, chap. viii.

Peace of Westphalia will show that there is as much call to-day for resistance to her devices and encroachments as there was at the era of the Reformation ; — that Rome has not changed with the times, nor learned to abate one whit of her pretensions, nor lost any of her old *penchant* for political conspiracies. Unfortunately the materials are scanty for a close and accurate comparison, especially in the statistics of population two hundred and fifty years ago.

If we examine the map of Europe at the beginning of the sixteenth century, from an ecclesiastical point of view, we find the whole continent, and the British Isles as well, divided into ecclesiastical provinces, and these again into archbishoprics and bishoprics, the only marks of diversity being toward the East, where dioceses of the Greek and Armenian churches displace the Roman Catholic. The boundary lines are those of provinces and dioceses, and the map is dotted all over with symbols that distinguish sees and cloisters.[1] And these territorial divisions were far from being conventional, for the mere convenience of ecclesiastical administration ; they often represented principalities and powers having a vested inheritance in the soil, and a voice in political affairs. Indeed, throughout Germany the bishops had become more conspicuous as secular princes than as ecclesiastical superintendents, and in this character they had a relative independence of the Roman curia, which sometimes made them quite serviceable to the Emperor in his quarrels with the Pope, — though the ecclesiastical instinct commonly guided them to Rome.

[1] The ecclesiastical cartography of Europe, in successive centuries, is by no means complete. Enough has been done, however, by Von Spruner, in his *New Historical Atlas*, published by Perthes, in Gotha, to furnish the more prominent data for such a comparison as is here attempted. See also Wiltsch, *Kirchliche Geographie und Statistik ;* Neher, *Kirchliche Geographie*, and C. v. H. Aloys, *Katholische Kirche.*

Sixty years later the map of Europe shows us the tokens of Roman Catholic occupation well-nigh effaced in the northern and middle countries of the continent; bishoprics and cloisters, either sequestered by the state or appropriated to another faith; Protestants having a recognized and legal existence in France; and the Reformation gaining head even in the peninsulas of Spain and Italy. Protestantism was now at its height — just, indeed, turning to the ebb, while the flood-tide of the counter-Reformation, destined to overflow so much of the reformed territory, was already setting in. It is impossible to give with accuracy the popular strength of the Protestant and the Romish elements, for there are no census returns of that period by which to estimate the two confessions; and the rule acceded to at the Peace of Augsburg, *cujus regio ejus religio* — that each state should follow the religion of its head — would, of course, disfavor any discrimination in matters of faith among subjects of the same government. But, taking only the broad territorial view, we find all Scandinavia Protestant; all Northern Germany, not excepting the chief cities and towns of Polish Prussia, to-day the seat of ultramontanism; nor the Rhine provinces, nor that very Paderborn in Westphalia where to-day the Roman hierarchy openly defies the Prussian government; we find Protestantism strong in Bavaria, where to-day the Ultramontanes threaten to control the King and the Parliament, and to disband the German Empire; we find Protestantism prevalent in Bohemia and in Hungary, and almost universal in Austria, where " all the colleges of the land were filled with Protestants; and it was said to be ascertained that not more, perhaps, than the thirtieth part of the population had remained Catholic." [2] The condensed summary which Ranke gives of the tri-

[1] Ranke.

umphs of Protestantism is marked by his characteristic clearness, thoroughness, and candor : —

" In short, from east to west, and from north to south, throughout all Germany, Protestantism had unquestionably the preponderance. The nobility were attached to it from the very first ; the body of public functionaries, already in those days numerous and important, was trained up in the new doctrine ; the common people would hear no more of certain articles, such, for instance, as purgatory, or of certain ceremonies, such as the pilgrimages ; not a man durst come forward with holy relics. . . . The confiscation of church property was energetically carried on. . . . Protestant opinions had triumphed in the universities and educational establishments. The teachers in Germany were all almost without exception Protestant ; the whole body of the rising generation sat at their feet, and imbibed a hatred of the Pope with the first rudiments of learning. Such was the state of things in the north and east of Europe ; in many places Catholicism was entirely exploded, in all it was subdued and despoiled. While it was struggling to defend itself, the Calvinistic system, an enemy still more formidable than Lutheranism, rose against it in the west and south. . . . Protestantism embraced the whole range of the Latin church ; it had laid hold on a vast majority of the higher classes, and of the minds that took part in public life ; whole nations clung to it with enthusiasm, and states had been remodeled by it." [1]

For a moment the fear seems to have been entertained at Rome that all would be lost ; — at least if we must understand the Venetian ambassador to the curia, Paolo Tiepolo, in his report on Rome in the times of Pius IV. and V., to reflect the rumors and apprehensions current during his sojourn at the capital ; and this was his testimony : —

" Speaking only of those nations of Europe which not only used to obey the Pope but also followed in every particular the

[1] Ranke, *History of the Popes*, bk. v., " First Period of Counter-Reformation."

rites and usages of the Roman church, celebrating public worship too in the Latin language, it is notorious that England, Scotland, Denmark, Norway, Sweden, and, in a word, all the countries of the north, are alienated from it. Germany is almost wholly lost, Bohemia and Poland are in a great degree infected, the low countries of Flanders are so corrupted that, notwithstanding all the efforts of the Duke of Alva to remedy the evil, they will hardly ever return to their original healthy condition; and lastly France, by means of these morbid humors, is all replete with confusion, so that it appears nothing remains to the Pope intact and secure but Spain and Italy, with some few islands, and with those countries possessed by your Serenity in Dalmatia and in Greece." [1]

But in the middle of the seventeenth century the ecclesiastical map shows us not only Italy, Spain, and Portugal as dependencies of Rome, and France a strong Catholic power, though tolerating Protestantism within her bosom, but Bavaria, Austria, Bohemia, Hungary, Poland, and several of the minor states of Germany, restored to their allegiance to the curia, and that territorial preponderance secured to the Romish Church which it has retained to this day. The reforms in practice and in discipline which the Council of Trent had introduced, together with the rigor of dogma which it had enjoined, the tact and resolution of Pope Paul IV., the dissensions among Protestant princes and the leaders of the reform, the league of Catholic princes with one another and with the Pope for mutual defense and help, and the exhaustion consequent upon long years of war, had all contributed to this result. "In Germany the reaction had been measureless. Protestantism was repulsed with as much energy as it had before swept onwards. Preaching and doctrine contributed to this, but infinitely more was done by policy, commands, and open violence." [2]

---

[1] Quoted by Ranke.   [2] Ranke, *ut sup.*

But with this period, as with that from Hildebrand to the Reformation, we are concerned only as its results affected the hereditary struggle between the spiritual and temporal powers, and this especially with reference to Germany. If for a moment papal authority reeled under the strange, wild blows of popular revolt, so different from a passage-at-arms with an emperor, it gradually recovered itself, and opposed to the reform not only the personal prerogative of the Pope as the vicar of Christ, but this authority organized more compactly and firmly in the church itself, which now presented one solid, united front.   In the Council of Trent the extreme view of papal authority prevailed, Pope Pius IV. overriding the remonstrance of the Emperor and of France, and not the unity of the church alone, but the unity and supremacy of her authority in her divinely constituted head, being the principle that ruled in all its decrees.   Those decrees themselves were to be interpreted by the Pope, and the extent of reforms was reserved for his decision.

Again and again in the council was it asserted that the authority of the Pope was indisputable and inviolable ; and that by appointment of God he was above all emperors and kings.   If Pius IV. was too sagacious to hazard the newly-recovered powers of the curia by reviving openly the struggle with temporal princes for permanent sovereignty over their subjects, he did not hesitate to seize the occasion of the council for making his sovereignty more immediate and absolute over the entire hierarchy, the bishops being severally sworn to obey the decrees of Trent and to obey the Pope as their master. But the claim of universal jurisdiction was not one whit abated, though held in abeyance for its opportunity. We see it again enforced by Clement VIII., when in presence of the assembled cardinals and a multitude of spectators before St. Peter's, King Henry VI. of France,

in the person of his ambassador, prostrated himself at
the feet of the Pope to receive the absolution that should
confirm him in his throne; and this claim was pressed
with the old shameless impudence by Paul V., with his
fanatical assertion of " the power of the keys," and by
Gregory XV. with his magnificent ambition to subdue
the world to the church.

On the other side, the political convulsions and the
politico-religious wars of the Reformation had secured to
the Protestant princes of Germany a degree of territorial
independence and of personal sovereignty which relieved
them in part of vassalage to the empire, and prepared the
way for that distinctive state and national development
which marks our modern civilization. Thus arose the
principle of an independent nationality as the successor
of the Holy Roman Empire — which was now reduced
practically to a German kingdom — in contesting the
claim of a universal paparchy. The Peace of Westphalia
may be said to have crystallized these two forces into permanent antagonism. The war brought nothing to an
end excepting the resources of the country, and the peace
established nothing beyond the somewhat vague admission of the equality of confessions, or the recognition by
each party of the right of the other to exist. Against
this recognition Innocent X. protested, demanding the
restitution of all Catholic rights, privileges, and possessions, as these had stood before the Reformation, that is,
he would efface all the conquests of Protestantism by a
stroke of the pen, refusing to concede to Protestants anything of ecclesiastical possessions or to enter into treaty
with Protestant princes. The Peace of Westphalia he
declared to be null and void, vacating it by his absolute
prerogative.[1] Against this, however, the parties to the

---

[1] The bull " Zelo domus Dei," dated November 26, 1648, published
January 3, 1651 : — " Ipso jure nulla, irrita, invalida, iniqua, injusta,

peace had provided, declaring beforehand that no regard should be had to any one, whether of ecclesiastical or political station, within or without the empire, who should oppose its articles.[1]

So stood the powers, civil and ecclesiastical, in 1648 — on the one hand, the idea of the state as an independent, self-sufficient organism, which brings within its scope all the functions and interests of society, judicial, political, industrial, educational, and religious; on the other hand, the idea of the church as centred in Rome, and from that seat of inalienable and indivisible authority issuing to the faithful in every land laws paramount to all temporal authority whatsoever, and holding such authority under control and rebuke by virtue of a divine prerogative. The first idea, so counter to tradition, to prejudice, and to usage, had for its development but little adventitious help, and must rely mainly upon the slowly-maturing processes of time; whereas the second, for its support and propagation, used the order of Jesuits, which had arisen for this very purpose, and which had already.been a chief agent in restoring to the Pope so large a portion of the spoils of the Reformation. Jesuitism is the despotism of intolerance. The Reformation had assailed the Catholic unity; Jesuitism would resist the Reformation by intensifying that unity through the subordination of all persons, parties, interests to the head of the church. Protestantism in Germany had contended for spiritual

damnata, reprobata, inania, viribusque et effectu vacua, omnino fuisse, esse, et perpetuo fore. . . . Articulos præfatos aliaque præmissa, potestatis plentitudine penitus damnamus, reprobamus . . . cassamus, annullamus, viribusque et effectu irritamus, vacuamus."

[1] "Non attenta cujusvis seu Ecclesiastici seu Politici, intra vel extra Imperium, quocunque tempore interposita contradictione vel protestatione, quæ omnes inanes et nihil vigore horum declarantur." See in Gieseler, iv. 1, note 18.

freedom; Jesuitism insisted upon the annihilation of self-will, and its absorption in the will of a superior, who should be reverenced, not on the ground of his wisdom or his goodness, but as the official representative of God. Protestantism had revived reason as a judge in matters of faith; Jesuitism made diversity of belief a sin, and would enforce dogma by authority. Protestantism made much of conscience as a criterion of duty; Jesuitism made of religion a power, the triumph of which was the end to be had always in view, and which must be secured by any and every means, even by the sacrifice of conscience itself.[1] The principles of Jesuitism are wholly irreconcilable with the modern conception of society and of the state, and must come into collision with that theory of national autonomy whose germ was in the Protestant factors of the Peace of Westphalia. To the realization of its grand and startling conception of a universal paparchy, Jesuitism brought the discipline of an army and the missionary zeal of the Apostolic age. It sought to control all orders and functionaries within the Catholic Church, to control people and princes through education and diplomacy, and to win over the pagan world by baptism and the sign of the cross.

The spirit of liberty is essentially unproselytizing; it trusts to liberty, light, and truth. But Jesuitism means propagandism; and hence, while the spirit of national liberty awakened at the Reformation has advanced only by natural causes against traditional hindrances and political jealousies, the spirit of Jesuitism has maintained unresting and unswerving activity, and under all changes and conditions has kept in view the putting all things under the feet of the Pope, and then, that the Pope himself

---

[1] E. de Pressensé, *La Liberté Religieuse en Europe*, p. 11; see, also, *Der Jesuiten Orden*, von D. Johannes Huber, and *Geschichte der neusten Jesuitenumtriebe in Deutchland*, von Wolfgang Menzel.

should also be subject unto the power that put all things under him, that this order may be all in all. The national element has had upon its side those industrial and economical causes and laws which, under the free spirit of Protestantism, further the growth and prosperity of a nation. Thus, within our own century, there has been in Prussia a perceptible growth of the Protestant population. On the authority of Hassel, in the year 1817 there were in Prussia 6,370,480 Protestants, and 4,023,513 Catholics ; [1] by the census of 1867, the Protestants or Evangelicals in Prussia numbered 15,596,380, the Catholics 7,950,753. Various causes, such as war, emigration, and the like, may have contributed to change the ratio between the Protestant and Catholic populations, but the relative increase of the former is a marked fact of the past fifty years. Yet Prussia has been preeminent for adhering with fidelity to the principle of confessional equality. There Catholics have had equal rights with Protestants, and larger donations from the public treasury.

This freedom of worship and this favoritism of support accorded to the Catholics have of late years been improved by a remarkable activity in the multiplication of religious orders, foundations, and institutions in Prussia, especially under the lead of the Jesuits and their missions. In Prussia, between the years 1852 and 1861, the number of convents increased from 79 to 185, at the rate of 15 per cent. yearly.[2] About the same period there was a marked increase of convents in other coun-

[1] *Handbuch der neusten Erdbeschreibung*, von Gaspari Hassel, und Cannabich; bearbeitet von D. G. Hassel, 1819. By the same authority, in 1817, the Roman Catholics of Europe numbered 95,000,000, including Greek and Armenian adherents; the Protestants 47,000,000, the Greek Church in Europe 32,000,000, the Mohammedans 3.600,000, and the Jews 2,060,000.

[2] Hausner, *Vergleichende Statistik von Europa*, 1865.

tries of Europe. In France, for instance, there were 4,750 in 1862, against 2,592 in 1847, an increase of 137 every year. In Belgium in 1859 there were 994, against 430 in 1830. Throughout Germany during this period the number of these ecclesiastical orders had so increased that there was a member of some order for every 481 Catholics in the population; and it was a fact of much significance that the superiors of most of these orders, having absolute authority over the membership, were foreigners, residing either at Rome or in France, and naturally hostile to German ideas and to German unity. The facility with which these orders were multiplied in Prussia, and the privilege accorded them of establishing separate schools for the training of priests, apart from the universities with their rigorous examinations, — a privilege contrary to the whole educational policy of Prussia, — shows with what fidelity the Prussian government had adhered to the Pact of Westphalia; how even more than just Prussia had been in securing to her Catholic subjects the full measure of liberty accorded to Protestants. In Prussia for a century there have been no "Catholic disabilities." Jews and dissenters have labored under disabilities, legal and political; for the Peace of Westphalia secured confessional equality only to Roman Catholics, the Lutherans, and the Reformed or Calvinists; and notwithstanding the famous saying of Frederic the.Great, that "in Prussia every man shall get to heaven after his own fashion," dissenters from these three recognized confessions have had no help from the state, but rather hindrance, in their heavenward pilgrimage. But Roman Catholics have had only help — recognition, money, privilege, place, power; they have been satisfied with their position, and have made good use of their opportunities.

For more than fifty years past the greater part of the

Lutherans and the Reformed in Prussia have been combined in one church, known as the Evangelical — this and the Roman Catholic being the privileged churches, with the exclusive countenance and support of the state ; and of this countenance in the way of official dignity and consideration, and this support in the way of substantial endowments and grants, during this century the Romish Church has had the lion's share.

Meantime the idea of nationality had been slowly crystallizing itself out of the ferment of wars, revolutions, compacts, and policies which the Napoleonic era had stirred in the whole continent. Prussia had suffered under long humiliation; Germany had been divided into hostile camps; poets, visionaries, revolutionists, socialists, diplomatists had made abortive attempts at German unity — now under the fiction of a republic, and again under the hardly less fictitious shadow of an empire. But at length the man arose who could divine the true solution of the problem — who had the courage to attempt this, and the sagacity to accomplish it. Prince Bismarck is one of those rare men who combine prescience and providence in respect of events with an intuition of men and of motives, and an executive will equal to any emergency. It may be questioned whether he has a policy, either in the higher sense of a pronounced system of administration, or in the inferior sense of expediency in management. His state-craft is not of the order so much approved in England and in the United States, that works by a definite programme or platform of ideas and measures ; nor of the fashion of France, that seeks to govern by a theory without regard to facts ; but with a keen outlook upon events, and a foresight of tendencies, he is quick to seize or to shape whatever may serve his immediate purpose, and resolute to bring both men and things within the scope of his

5

plan without prematurely unveiling it. This habit of
using events, men, occasions for his underlying purpose,
causes him sometimes to appear variable in his methods
and in his relations to parties — now conservative, now
liberal ; now conciliating the Catholic hierarchy, and
now ruling it with an iron hand. But this mutability is
only the eddying on the surface; the deep undercurrent
moves steadily onward. The key to Bismarck's politics is given in these words — devotion to the unity of
Germany as the supreme good of Germany herself, and
as the best guarantee of the peace and prosperity of
Europe. Bismarck saw that the ideal of one Germanic
nation — the dream of her poets, the aspiration of her
patriots, the vague longing of her people — was not to
be attained through any combination of German politics, as these stood when he came into power. No artificial bund, no conventional empire, could make a united
Germany. It was necessary first to remove from Germany the incubus of Austrian supremacy — a domination narrow, selfish, bigoted in proportion as it was weak,
and, in a measure, alien ; and next it was necessary to
emancipate Germany from the traditional superiority of
France, and to secure her against the dread of French
invasion. To this end he saw that the first requisite was
strength — the actual material strength of arms, and the
moral strength that comes by victory. Reversing the
motto, "in union is strength," he sought union by
strength; first strong, then united and free. Germany
must have a leader strong enough to inspire her confidence, to hold her adversaries in check, and to command
the respect of all European powers. And this leader
could be found only in Prussia ; Prussia reacting from
the humiliations of more than half a century, to emulate
the days of the great Frederic ; Prussia, organized into a
camp, and drilled to her last man ; Prussia, equipped

with the best weapons, officered by the best generals, and, above all, led by the soldier-king, who had the confidence and affection of the truly national army which he had done so much to form and to discipline.

Whether Bismarck planned, provoked, or precipitated the wars with Austria and with France, must, perhaps forever, lie buried with the mysteries of diplomacy; it is enough that the displacement of these two powers was necessary to *his* conception of a united Germany ; that he foresaw the contingency of these conflicts, was on the alert for both, and was prepared at every point when the moment came. And with each stroke of victory he made a stride for unity, creating the North German Bund out of the triumphs of Königgrätz, and annealing the German empire in the furnace in which the dross of the French empire was consumed.

The question of religion did not enter at all into the wars of 1866 and 1870. These were wars for German nationality — to free Germany from foreign dictation, and to combine all the states into one nation. Though the constitution of the German empire, like the constitution of the United States, expressly reserves to the several states certain prescriptive rights, and though the imperial government at Berlin, like the national government at Washington, is a government of limited powers, yet there is now a *Germany*, with its emperor, its parliament, its army, its navy, its postal service, its code and courts, its diplomatic corps, its national policy — a constitutional empire with an hereditary sovereign in the person of the King of Prussia; an empire with a population of forty-one millions, in the heart of Europe, capable of defending itself against any enemy without, and of dictating peace to its neighbors. In a word, here is the idea of nationality realized in a people of one language, one country, one government, one policy, one destiny.

The German empire, as such, has no religion. Its
constitution has no provision concerning churches or confessions — these are left under the jurisdiction of local
laws in the several states. And yet the creation of this
empire has been the occasion of an ecclesiastical controversy in Prussia, that seems almost to threaten a religious war. This state of things, however, was not planned
by Bismarck, and does not seem to have been appre-
hended by him, until the ultramontanes had openly
manifested their hostility to the empire. Perhaps the
severity of his measures is due, in part, to the fact that
he awoke a little too late to the real and pressing danger
of the case; yet even should we allow the criticism of
Von Arnim and his friends upon Bismarck's earlier indif-
ference or leniency toward the usurpations of Rome, we
must still concede to the chancellor the merit of sincerity in his consideration for the German Catholic bishops down to the time of their concerted hostility to the
German empire. We incline, however, to the opinion
that Bismarck's sagacity was not at fault in declining
Von Arnim's counsel, but that upon broader grounds he
was reluctant to enter the arena of politico-ecclesiastical
strife; and it is an open secret that the emperor sought
to avert such a strife by any means consistent with the
dignity and authority of the state. In any case the
contest began on the other side. While the principle of
Nationality was striding toward its consummation in
Germany, the principle of the Paparchy, as embodied in
Jesuitism, had already triumphed at Rome, in the pro-
mulgation of infallibility and the indorsement of the syllabus; the one subjugating the Catholic hierarchy to the
absolute will of the Pope, the other setting the papacy
in open and irreconcilable hostility to modern society.
Between this usurping paparchy and the nationality almost simultaneously perfected in Germany and in Italy,

a collision was inevitable. Bismarck did nothing to bring it on, and could do nothing to avert it. The times and tendencies were stronger than he. The truce of Westphalia was at an end; the unsettled conflict must break out anew; the battle between the spiritual and temporal powers must be fought over upon the soil of the Reformation. So far was Bismarck from crippling the Roman hierarchy in Germany as a means of resisting papal usurpation, that at first he sought rather to strengthen the hierarchy in its relations with the Prussian state. This fact the publication of the Von Arnim correspondence has fully revealed. Before the meeting of the Vatican Council, the bishops of Germany assembled at Fulda — the tomb of the Holy Boniface — and issued a pastoral, in which they virtually repudiated the programme attributed to the ultramontanes : —

" A general council never did and never can establish a dogma not contained in Scripture, nor in the apostolical traditions. A general council never did and never can proclaim doctrines in contradiction to the principles of justice, to the rights of the state and its authorities, to culture and the true interests of science, or to the legitimate freedom and well-being of nations. Neither need any one fear that the general council will thoughtlessly and hastily frame resolutions which needlessly would put it in antagonism to existing circumstances, and to the wants of the present times ; or that, in the manner of enthusiasts, it would endeavor to transplant into the present times, views, customs, and institutions of times gone by."

The government of Bavaria early took alarm at the prognostic signs of the Vatican Council, and the theological faculty of Munich reported to the government that the syllabus, if accepted by the council, either in its original negative form or in the positive redaction of Father Schrader, must lead to serious changes in the relations between the church and the state. Count Von

Arnim, who represented Prussia at Rome during the council, was of the same opinion, and recommended to his government some active intervention in the council, or a remonstrance with the Pope in person ; but Bismarck steadily refused to meddle with the council, or to attempt a moral coercion in respect to any of its decisions, and adhered to the policy of sustaining the German bishops in the opposition to ultramontanism, which they had foreshadowed at Fulda. When these bishops all succumbed to the ultramontane majority in the council, and came back to Germany to proclaim infallibility as a dogma, and to carry out the teachings of the syllabus, it was not Bismarck but THEY that had changed. Nevertheless, they would have been allowed in peace to hold the new dogmas, had they not set out to use these, and suffered themselves to be used, as instruments against the lawful authority of the state, and especially against the empire, so soon as this came into form.[1]

From the moment that the victory of Königgrätz expelled Austria from the field of German politics, and placed a Protestant power at the head of a new German confederation, the ultramontanes began to show their hostility to Prussian ascendency and to the scheme of a Germanic empire. So bitter, intense, and powerful was that hostility in Bavaria, that her government came within one of refusing to join the Northern States in the war with France.[2]

Ultramontanism was already a political power organized to uphold the paparchy, even at the cost of the Fatherland. The proclamation of Napoleon at the opening of the war showed that he counted upon the neutral-

---

[1] See note on Count Von Arnim, at the end of this article.

[2] It was literally by a bare majority of one, that the Bavarian House voted to make common cause with the rest of Germany.

ity, if not the coöperation, of the South German States; and the ultramontane press gave him reason to suppose that he could depend upon the sympathy of those states with Catholic France against Protestant Prussia. The peril of that internal discord which had so often made Germany the battlefield of Europe, led Bismarck to urge at Versailles the consummation of German unity, while the fires of patriotism were aglow with victory ; but this empire at once became the mark of ultramontane hate through the press, the pulpit, and the party of the Centre in Parliament[1] — a hatred now organized in the " Catholic Unions," that set the church above the state. But in assailing the empire they touched the apple of Bismarck's eye, since both his policy and his patriotism subordinate Prussia itself to Germany. His view is broad enough for an empire.

Now, this feature of Bismarck's politics is distasteful to Prussians of the " old line." The bureaucratic system, in which day by day and year by year each subordinate officer worked out his prescribed details, and government went on like an automatic machine, was to these high conservatives the perfection of the state ; and they were at first scandalized at the notion of an imperial chancellor who would govern not by red-tape but by personal ideas and forces, would make of government a living power animated and pervaded with his own spirit, would assert strength of will against the stolid routine of facts and precedents, would set the larger interests of Germany above the traditions of Prussia, would remodel the Prussian Foreign Office, the Ministries of War and of Marine, and even the interior economies of Prussia, to meet the new conditions of the empire; and, worst

---

[1] For proof of the hostility of the ultramontanes to the empire, see *Geschichte der neusten Jesuitenumtriebe in Deutschland*, von Wolfgang Menzel.

of all, who would even invoke the fickle and perilous support of the people and the press. "Baggage-master" is
the title given on American railways to the official who
superintends the luggage-vans and sees that all luggage
is duly ticketed and cared for, and fitly delivered; but
"baggage-*smasher*" is the epithet he sometimes receives
when, in the hurry of quitting one station for the next,
he pitches out luggage in a promiscuous manner, careless
of damage to trunks or to toes. So, when this new master took things in hand, in the hurry of movement from
Düppel to Königgrätz, from Königgrätz to Sedan, from
Sedan to Paris, it was no wonder that old-fashioned,
slow-coach conservatives were startled at the way in
which the luggage of traditions and precedents was tossed
about; and certainly a good deal of lumber and trump-
ery was smashed as the new imperial train got under
way. But ready as Bismarck was and is to bend or
break everything to his own quick, imperious, and resolute will, he did not lay hands upon the Roman hierarchy until they had assailed the empire with intrigue,
and had defied the laws. If now he has pitched them
over with seeming violence, it is because the train must
move on ; and this train of events is impelled by a power
higher than the chancellor, higher and stronger than any
man.

The time has fully come when the question must be
settled for the whole future of society, Whether each
nation shall make its own laws, rule its own subjects, determine its own policy, subject only to the law of justice
within and to the comity of nations from without, or
whether an ecclesiastical power shall be recognized as
higher than all governments, and competent to dictate,
to revise, and even to annul their acts by the personal
will of a man who claims to be the infallible medium
and expounder of the will of God ? To understand the

question as it lies in Germany, one has but to ask himself whether the Parliament of Great Britain and the
Congress of the United States shall pause on the eve of
every act to inquire, Will this be approved or allowed by
the Pope of Rome?

Some affect to think that there is no longer reason to
fear the aggressions of Rome; that Bismarck exaggerated
the danger to Germany from ultramontanism, and appealed to political fears and religious prejudices to cover
his ambitious designs; that he, in fact, restored the papacy to vitality, and converted infallibility from a theological juggle into a political weapon, by the consequence
he gave to what he himself has pithily styled, "The
Church of the Vatican." But in reality the personal
power of the Pope within the Romish Church was never
so immediate nor so absolute as it is to-day. Wherever
the movement of modern society has unhinged the Roman
Catholic Church from the state, it has thrown the hierarchy into personal dependence upon the Pope. The bishop
who can no longer fall back upon a powerful prince or
patron to support his independence receives implicitly
the mandates of Rome. And the doctrine that the Pope
is the supreme and infallible autocrat of the church and
of the world, which in the Middle Ages was the ambitious assumption of individual pontiffs, is now obligatory
as a dogma of the church upon every true Catholic. All
faith and all authority are centred in him, and the whole
hierarchy hangs upon him, and is the instrument of his
will. Ten years ago, speaking as for the Pope, Dr.
Manning put into his mouth these words: —

" I acknowledge no civil power; I am the subject of no
prince; and I claim more than this — I claim to be the supreme judge and director of the consciences of men, of the
peasant that tills the fields and of the prince that sits upon the
throne; of the household that live in the shade of privacy and

the legislator that make laws for kingdoms ; I am the sole, last
supreme judge of what is right and wrong." [1]

If, ten years ago, this seemed a rhetorical extrava-
gance, to-day one must accept Dr. Manning's testimony
that "the Holy See is ultramontane, the whole episco-
pate is ultramontane, the whole priesthood, the whole
body of the faithful throughout all nations, excepting
only a handful here and there, of rationalistic or liberal
Catholics — all are ultramontanes. Ultramontanism is
Popery, and Popery is Catholicism." [2]

This compact, unified power, seeking always its own
supremacy, is ready in France to ally itself with legiti-
mists or imperialists ; in Germany, with social democrats
or with Polish revolutionists ; in Spain, to bless the Car-
list banditti ; in the United States, to work by free
schools or against them ; and in every land, whether
through the laws, behind the laws, under the laws, or
over the laws, to seize its own opportunity.

The conflict, which we have seen to be historical and
inevitable, involves the profoundest political and ethical
principles, and admits of no evasion or compromise.
There are three theories of the constitution of human society in relation to government and religion, or to state
and church. The first is the theory that, inasmuch as
the divine is superior to the human, the spiritual to the
physical, the eternal to the temporal, all the institutions of society should be ordered and controlled with
respect to man as a religious being — that is, the church
should direct human society not only in matters of faith
and morals, but in education, in laws, in government.
This was the theory of Rome in the Middle Ages, and it
· is now revived in the syllabus. The second theory is,

---

[1] Sermon in the Pro-Cathedral, Kensington, *Tablet*, October 9,
1864.

[2] *Sermons on Ecclesiastical Subjects.*

that man exists for the state; that the state has a demand upon the subject for his supreme allegiance, and should train and govern him for its own service alike in peace and in war; and, therefore, all the interests of society, material, political, educational, religious, must be subjected to the rule of the state. This was the theory evolved by the Protestant states of the Reformation, and which has since obtained in Germany.

The third theory is, that man is the true centre about which all else should revolve; that both state and church should exist for man, be administered by his will, and in such way as shall best promote his welfare. This is the view of civil society in the United States, and is, to a growing extent, the practical condition of society in England.

The first two of these systems have come into collision in Germany. We have no sympathy with either as a system for modern society, but in the conflict between the two we plant ourselves unhesitatingly on the side of the second, upon grounds of Scripture, of reason, and of experience; the more freely, that in Germany the theory of state supremacy and state supervision does not meddle at all with the dogmas of the church, nor with modes of worship; does not interfere in the least with confessional freedom; but only insists that the allegiance which is demanded of every subject shall be rendered by priest as well as laic, that the obedience to law which is required of every citizen shall be rendered by the highest ecclesiastic as well as by the meanest boor, and that the scientific preparation exacted of every servant of the government shall be made also by the clergy under its pay.

The contending systems bring the paparchy into open conflict with the ruling power in the state; but underlying the latter is also the nation just waking to the consciousness of a new life. Now, as between these two the teachings of Christ and the Apostles leave us but one choice. The New Testament requires that the Christian shall be a loyal subject of the government under which he lives. "Let every soul be subject unto the higher powers. For there is no power but of God: the powers that be are ordained of God: whosoever therefore resisteth the power, resisteth the ordinance of God." [1] Such is the general principle; and there are also special injunctions which may be recommended to the Pope as successor of the holy Apostles Peter and Paul, in preparing his next instructions for the faithful in Germany. The first is from Peter: "Submit yourselves to every ordinance of man [*i. e.*, every institution of government among men, ἀνθρωπίνῃ κτίσει] for the Lord's sake: whether it be to the king, as supreme; or unto governors, as unto them that are sent by him for the punishment of evil doers, and for the praise of them that do well. As free [*i. e.*, be loyal, not in the servile spirit of fear, but in the free spirit of Christian love], and not using your liberty for a cloak of maliciousness [not making your privileges in the church a cover for Jesuitical plottings against the state]. Honor all men. Love the brotherhood. Fear God. Honor the king." [2] The second is from the instructions of Paul to Titus for the regulation of the faithful in Crete: "Put them in mind to be subject to principalities and powers, to obey magistrates." [3] Like all the injunctions of the Bible, these precepts are given in broad general terms, without the limitations and qualifications of ethical philosophy; but it is enough that some of them were given under the bloody rule of Nero. Now

---

[1] Romans xiii. 1, 2. The Apostle here lays down the broad doctrine of the sovereignty of the existing government, the government *de facto* is the government *de jure* — this as opposed to anarchy. He does not here consider the abstract right of revolution.

[2] 1 Peter ii. 13–18.   [3] Titus iii. 1.

it is impossible to find in the New Testament any injunctions of obedience to organized ecclesiastical power,[1] like those here given of obedience to civil government. It is not ecclesiastical authority, nor a corporate ecclesiastical institution, but the personal God and the individual conscience in its direct personal relations with God, which is set over against an unrighteous demand of the civil authority in that crucial motto of Peter, " We ought to obey God rather than men ;"[2] and in the teaching of Christ, " Render unto Cæsar the things which are Cæsar's, and unto God the things which are God's." Of conscience as an ecclesiastical corporation, or of conscience as an imputed or a vicarious faculty, determined and exercised by one for another, the ethics of the New Testament have no knowledge. Peter knew of a conscience within himself that should obey God rather than man, but he never demanded a conscience in others that should obey *himself* officially, or his ecclesiastical successors, rather than submit to " the king as supreme." This discrimination between conscience as a personal faculty by which each soul determines for itself questions of right and duty, and conscience as an obligation imposed by external authority, is vital in a case of collision between the civil and the ecclesiastical powers. The civil government cannot claim to rule the conscience. The subject has the right to protest in conscience against what he deems an unjust or an immoral law; has the right to decline to obey what he deems an unrighteous law, and to accept and suffer the penalty of disobedience. Society must recognize this right as one that may be necessary to its own deliverance from an unjust law or a

---

[1] No scholar would think of quoting as parallel Heb. xiii. 17, which reads strictly, " Follow your leaders," with a dutiful respect and deference to their teaching and example.

[2] Acts v. 29.

tyrannical government; society cannot afford to ignore
that protesting conscience which has made patriots glorious and martyrs immortal; which has displayed such
moral heroism and effected such wholesome reform; —
least of all could Germany afford to obliterate that right
of a protesting conscience which Luther consecrated to
her emancipation, when he said, " *Hier stehe ich! Ich
kann nicht anders; Gott hilf mir.*"

Shakespeare, as ever, has here given us the finest
philosophical distinction in the fewest possible words.
" Every subject's duty is the king's; but every subject's
soul is his own." [1] Conscience and Christianity make
loyalty to government a duty; yet, as between soul and
state, there can be no question that a man must be loyal
to his own soul at whatever cost. The personal conscience, even when deluded, should be treated with ten-
derness; and though society must protect itself against
a fanaticized conscience, it should not assail the faculty
to remedy its morbid conditions. But a factitious conscience which puts forward obligation to an ecclesiastical
authority within the state or without it as higher than allegiance to the state, society cannot afford to parley with,
nor to recognize as entitled to any concession. Such an
antagonistic sovereignty would annihilate social order.

Here reason stands by the New Testament in teaching
that, in a collision between the state and any organized
ecclesiastical power, the higher allegiance is due to the
state. Some form of civil government is indispensable
to the existence of human society. Without this all is
anarchy. But there is no form of church organization
the maintenance of which is essential to human society,
however important religion as a soul-faith may be to
social order; and the assertion of sovereignty in affairs
for an ecclesiastical authority is a constant menace to

---

[1] *King Henry V.*, act IV. scene 1.

that organic condition of society which we call the state. The claim of a divine prerogative vested in a person or a power apart from the constituted government to supervise that government and its laws, to define the limits of obedience, and to absolve subjects from allegiance, is destructive of all order and authority in the state, and must reduce society to anarchy. The instinct of self-preservation is for the civil power against the clerical.

Experience justifies this teaching of Scripture and of reason. The worst tyranny the world has seen, the most atrocious persecutions that history records, have sprung from ecclesiastical power, or from the temporal power as wielded by and for the spiritual. The civil power tyrannizes or persecutes from motives of interest or expediency; but the ecclesiastical adds to these that most terrible weapon of cruelty — the claim of a divine warrant for extirpating its enemies as the enemies of God. Who would not rather take his chances as a Christian under the bloody Diocletian, than as a Christian reformer under the remorseless Alva? No inquisition was ever invented in the service of the civil power alone.

Upon every ground, then, of Scripture, of reason, of society, of history, and of humanity, we are moved to side with the civil against the ecclesiastical power, in a conflict for sovereignty within the state. The harshest measures of the civil power in resisting ecclesiastical encroachment are a far less evil than is the bare possibility of ecclesiastical supremacy over the state. In the state, or rather in the community as ordered through the state, there is always a tendency to reaction from severe measures when the danger that provoked these is over. The state justifies its severities by the plea of self-protection. But the ecclesiastical power justifies its persecutions by the pleas of protecting and propagating the faith, and of executing a divine prerogative of judgment — and such motives suffer no modification nor relaxation. Formulated in the doctrine of infallibility, and incarnated in the person of the Pope, they are forever irreconcilable with the autonomy of the nation, and can rest only with the destruction of modern society. It is at this point that Prussia has planted herself in opposition to the paparchy; and though her own theory of church and state is far from perfect, and her ecclesiastical legislation in some particulars is not to be commended, yet in resisting ecclesiastical encroachment upon civil rights, she is maintaining the cause of nationalism, and defending interests common to society throughout Christendom.

The contest between Protestantism and Romanism, in respect of faith and discipline, may be safely left to the pulpit, the university, and the press. With such matters the recent ecclesiastical legislation of Prussia has nothing to do. Protestantism would but weaken itself, and would confess the weakness of its own principles and position, by invoking the arm of the state to protect it against the spread of the Roman Catholic Church; and the Prussian government would weaken itself by espousing Protestantism as against Catholicism through its Ministry of Worship, or by legislating against any particular sect or confession. In laws affecting the rights, the duties, the liberties of subjects, no government can show ecclesiastical favoritism without weakening the tie of allegiance to itself. This the Prussian government has not done. Its recent legislation was not Protestant in its motive, but political. Protestantism would be too narrow a basis for the defense of the state and the nation against the paparchy. This is of no less moment for the unbeliever and the Jew. Rightly considered, the Prussian ecclesiastical laws are a defense of Catholics themselves, in the freedom of their faith and worship, against a Roman dictation that would destroy their independence as Germans, and obliterate their consciousness of nationality. As Mr. Gladstone has pithily said, " Individual servitude, however abject, will not satisfy the party now dominant in the Latin Church : the state must also be a slave." [1]

But why not determine the contest in Prussia by the immediate separation of church and state — which to an English nonconformist and to an American Christian of whatever name would be its ready and proper solution ? Because the people do not wish that solution ; are not ready for it ; really stand in dread of it. Trained as the Prussians are to dependence upon a state provision for religion, accustomed to the impartial support of both the Evangelical and the Roman Catholic churches from the public treasury, and constitutionally averse to sudden and radical changes, they have no desire to dissolve the connection between church and state. The Roman Catholics are not willing to relinquish the revenues they derive from the state, nor the hope of political ascendency in some change of the ministry ; and Protestants fear to dissolve the existing relation of the church to the state, lest, on the one hand, rationalism or socialism should control a large proportion of the parochial property of the Evangelical Church ; and, on the other hand, Romanism should become too formidable through wealth and organization no longer subject to state control. No statesman would venture to force a dissolution of church and state in the present state of public opinion. Cavour's maxim, " A free church in a free state," does not mean that the church should be free to conspire against the state. Tenacious as we are of church independence, and confident as we are of the resources of liberty in a fair and open field, we will not blind ourselves to the

[1] *The Vatican Decrees*, p. 40; also p. 32.

fact that Germany, threatened with the revengeful hatred of France, with the envy of Austria, with the jealousy of Russia, and having at Rome an implacable enemy who teaches millions of her subjects that to disobey her laws is their duty to God — that, thus circumstanced, the new composite empire of Germany is in a very different condition for experiments of " the largest liberty " from England in her insular position, or the United States beyond the Atlantic. Moreover, " let not him that girdeth on his harness boast himself as he that putteth it off," and the United States may yet learn that, to cope with the political schemes and encroachments of the Roman hierarchy, liberty must equip herself once more as for the final conflict with slavery.

We must therefore judge Prussian legislation not by English theory nor by American practice, but by the condition of Prussia herself. And what is that condition ? In respect of intellectual freedom (*Freiheit des Geistes*), Prussia is in advance of England and the United States, especially in the sphere of theology. Here she knows nothing of that tyranny of the press and of public opinion, which, in more democratic communities, satisfies the craving of human nature for some form of arbitrary power. But in respect of freedom of political action, and of that institutional freedom which has grown old in England, and with which the United States were born, Germany until a very recent period has stood where England was two hundred and fifty years ago. The reason of this tardiness of development in Germany is fitly expressed by Mr. Freeman : " On the Teutonic mainland, the old Teutonic freedom, with its free assemblies, national and local, gradually died out before the encroachments of a brood of petty princes. In the Teutonic island it has changed its form from age to age ; it has lived through many storms, and it has withstood the

attacks of many enemies, but it has never utterly died
out."[1] Keeping this distinction in view, one must judge
the recent ecclesiastical legislation of Prussia by the
England of Elizabeth's time, as to its motive and necessity, and as to the theory of state control in church
affairs — though there has been nothing in Prussia so
arbitrary nor so severe as the Act of Uniformity, and no
attempt to coerce any man in respect of his faith. This
will help us to account for a legislation which we could
not at all points defend : the exigency is one in which,
as in time of rebellion, the preservation of the larger liberty of society requires the seeming or temporary restriction of the liberty of the individual and the particular.

It is not necessary here to enter upon a minute exami-
nation of the new ecclesiastical laws.[2] The policy that
dictated them, the principle that underlies them, and the
spirit that animates them are more relevant to this discussion than are forms of expression or modes of execu-
tion. Now the motive of these laws is not to restrain
the liberty of conscience, of faith, or of worship ; not to
interdict, nor to control the Roman Catholic Church as a
religious confession and communion ; not to enforce uniformity of belief or of worship, nor to exalt one church
above another, nor to interfere in any wise with the interior spiritual discipline of the churches ; but their sole
purpose is to defend the nation against the political action of a hierarchy that would destroy both its unity and
its sovereignty. The hierarchy excommunicated Catholic
teachers for refusing to teach in the state-schools the in-

---

[1] *The Growth of the English Constitution*, p. 18.

[2] In illustration of the legislative policy of Prussia respecting
church affairs, the reader may refer to the recent ecclesiastical laws,
and to an exposition of the same, contained in the volume named
at the head of this article, entitled *Ultramontanism : England's
Sympathy with Germany*.

fallibility of the Pope as an article of faith ; the government hereupon withdrew from the clergy the old privilege of supervising the confessional teaching in the public schools ; and when the bishops were contumacious
against this just and reasonable measure, the government
insisted that, as beneficiaries of the state, the bishops
should give proofs of their loyalty. Finding that semina-
ries for the training of priests, supported by grants from
government, were controlled by ultramontanes from Italy,
and used for denationalizing the priesthood and making
them partisans of Rome against the state, the government
now requires of the clergy, as of all officials in the bureaux
of state, a preparatory training in a state gymnasium and
university, i. e., a good literary and scientific education ;
and also, as preliminary to induction into the clerical
office, it requires evidence of such education, of good
character, and of loyalty to the state. To guard against
abuses of power the ecclesiastical reformatories are placed
under state inspection. It is forbidden to use church discipline for political ends, or for the injury of any one in
his person, his property, or his liberty ; and for the protection of the inferior clergy, there is a right of appeal to
a state tribunal against the oppressions of ecclesiastical
power. One may also withdraw from a church without
censure or damage by notifying the proper authorities.
Such is the general scope of these laws. Many of their
provisions are directly for the protection and the enlarge-
ment of liberty ; and of the code, as a whole, it must be
said, though some of its demands and penalties are much
too stringent for our times, yet its plea of political necessity is sound and sincere.

Roman Catholics are barred from complaining of this
legislation ; first, because laws concerning the clergy, similar to those of Prussia, have long existed in Oldenburg
and in other German States by compact with the Pope,

and what the papacy has assented to in one part of Germany cannot be "against God and the church" in another; and, secondly, as Archbishop Manning knows well enough, should temporal power be restored to the Pope, no teacher or preacher would be allowed within the Papal States except under far more stringent conditions from the Holy See, and any departure from those conditions would be visited with penalties far more severe than those of Prussian law. But the precedents and *animus* of Roman Catholic legislation, though it should shame Romanists into silence touching "the persecution" in Prussia, could furnish no apology for religious persecution, if such there were. Religious persecution there is none, though political proscription and penalty are inflicted in ways that violate the English and American sense of religious liberty. As patron and paymaster of the church the Prussian government has the legal right to make regulations for the education and the induction of the clergy, precisely as the Parliament of Great Britain has reasserted its right to legislate for the Church of England, to regulate public worship within the church, and to create a judge of ecclesiastical causes. Indeed it may be fairly said, that the Public Worship Bill comes much nearer than the Prussian ecclesiastical laws to trenching upon private judgment and liberty of conscience. The Prussian laws do not touch the Roman Church in its worship or its internal economy; they deal with the church only at points where it comes into external relations with the state; they provide that the clergy whom the state supports shall be Germans by birth, shall be intelligently and liberally educated, and shall be loyal to the government. Upon the Prussian system of church and state — a system by which the Roman hierarchy have largely profited, and which they still desire to retain — these laws are strictly defensible.

It is to be regretted that the penalties of criminal offenses must needs be applied for the enforcement of such wholesome regulations. We do not fancy the imprisonment of bishops for the technical offense of adhering to old concessions and usages against laws made since their own induction into office. Yet we would not waste much sympathy upon men who cling to the revenues of their office, but refuse to comply with the reasonable conditions upon which those revenues are granted ; men who assail the laws and government of their country, at the dictum of a foreign potentate, and fight the hand that feeds them.

For the principle at stake we wish Prince Bismarck well through with the controversy which the ultramontanes have forced upon him, which the times demand of him, and in which he is the representative of social order and civil liberty. We have sometimes suspected that he had not taken into account the pertinacity of religious stubbornness, especially when the will has assumed the office of conscience. The violent declaration of the Catholic Union at Mayence against the German empire, and the attempt upon his life, engendered in this atmosphere of religious hate,[1] show how earnest is the power with which he is contending. The cause of nationality is in his hands, and he cannot falter. To compromise would be to fail. The nation cannot ask consent of the Pope to be. When Austria, Catholic in court and people, attempted a wholesome reform of her

---

[1] " And blessed shall he be that doth revolt
From his allegiance to an heretic ;
And meritorious shall that hand be called,
Canonized, and worship'd as a saint,
That takes away by any secret course
Thy hateful life."

Cardinal Pandulph, the Pope's Legate, to King John. — *King John*, act III. scene 1.

school-laws, the Pope anathematized the movement, and required his bishops to resist it as a crime against the church. In his reply of May 9, 1873, Count Andrassy expressed his regret that "the encyclical should have pronounced a condemnation of things that belong to the sovereign domain of state legislation;" and he added, "if the clergy do not obey the laws which have been enacted and sanctioned, the government will consider itself bound to protect the rights of the state, and is convinced it will be able to compel respect for the law." Could the Austrian minister have done less? But the note of Count Andrassy contains the very principles of Bismarck's legislation, and the ultramontanes may yet drive Austria into the Prussian measures of defense. For a nation to allow such interference with its internal legislation would be to vacate sovereignty. The old historical struggle for supremacy has reached its last stage, a struggle between paparchy and nationality, the syllabus and society. Inevitable, fundamental, the conflict must now be uncompromising and final. Happily, Prince Bismarck has found a way to the end, by vacating the sees of recusant bishops, and turning over the administration of affairs to the congregations acting under advisement from the state. The process may be slow, but it will be sure; the result, a Catholic Church in Germany that is not of Rome; a German Catholic Church, privileged, though not established, by the state, and so far popularized as to effect within the church itself the triumph of nationality over paparchy. To that triumph all Christian nations should give their sympathy, —

"And from the mouth of *England*
Add thus much more, — that no Italian priest
Shall tithe or toll in our dominions ;
But as we under heaven are supreme head,
So under him, that great supremacy

Where we do reign, we will alone uphold,
Without the assistance of a mortal hand :
So tell the Pope : all reverence set apart
To him and his usurp'd authority." [1]

NOTE. — The publication of official letters, written by
Von Arnim from Rome during the council, was the first
open step in that diplomatic quarrel which has given to
the count such an unenviable notoriety. Von Arnim is
one of the most gifted, accomplished, versatile, and brilliant men that the Prussian diplomatic school has produced ; and three years ago his advance by gradual preferment to the highest post in the empire seemed assured.
But he sacrificed his opportunity through pride of opinion
and an imperious will that would brook no contradiction
nor restraint. Admitting that he had a clearer insight
than Bismarck into affairs at Rome, and that the policy
he then urged has been justified by subsequent events,
this surely would be no disparagement to Bismarck's
sagacity. Von Arnim was sent to Rome on purpose to
ferret out the intentions of the ultramontanes, and to
suggest measures for thwarting them. But when he had
advised Bismarck of the tendencies at Rome and had
proffered his suggestions, his responsibility for the policy
of his government was at an end, and his duty was to
carry out the instructions sent from the Foreign Office.
Though Von Arnim's counsel was not followed in all
particulars, his ability was recognized, and he was re-
warded by being sent to Paris upon the delicate and responsible mission of representing the new German empire
directly after the war. Here again he seems to have had
a policy that he thought wiser than the policy at Berlin,
to have attempted to dictate to the chancellor, then to

[1] *King John,* act III. scene 1.

have appealed to the king against the policy of the chancellor, and finally to have acted upon his own responsibility, regardless of the views of the Foreign Office. For this he was rebuked — no doubt in terms somewhat irritating to one of his haughty spirit — and was finally recalled.

He now sought to make political capital for himself out of his differences with the chancellor. It was discovered that important papers were missing from the archives of the embassy at Paris, and the publication of Von Arnim's letters from Rome gave rise to the suspicion that a similar misuse would be made of the Paris correspondence. Of some of these missing papers Von Arnim declared himself ignorant; a few he restored, but others he retained, on the plea that these were private papers, necessary to his own vindication, and he refused to admit any claim of the Foreign Office, either upon the papers or upon himself as their custodian.

With regard to semi-official papers, a margin of discretion must be conceded to an ambassador. The practice of the English Foreign Office is to number these in the regular order of correspondence, but to indorse them "separate," so that they do not enter into the archives of the embassy. But in the case of Von Arnim, the papers being duly registered, it could not be left to him alone to decide upon their character. The Foreign Office was clearly a.party in the case. Had he frankly submitted the papers to a court, agreeing to abide by its decision, there would have been an end of the matter; but, after fruitless negotiations, the Foreign Office had no resource but to bring the affair to the notice of the judiciary. From that point all the steps were by the order of the court, and in conformity to the laws. The domiciliary visits, the imprisonment of Von Arnim without bail, and without an open hearing, were con-

trary to English procedure; but, stern and absolute as
the Prussian code and its executors may appear, the
Prussian courts may be trusted to administer the law im-
partially, without personal or political bias.

Whatever may be the final judgment upon Von Arnim's action, thus much has been gained for the future
of diplomacy in Germany. Persons connected with the
diplomatic service are admonished to be upon their guard
against official indiscretions, and are reminded of their
amenability to their superiors and to the laws. The dis-
graceful practice of publishing diplomatic papers for
personal ends — a practice that might easily disturb the
peace of nations — has received a salutary check. And,
best of all, the power of the law to deal with all offenses,
without respect of persons, is triumphantly vindicated.
Bismarck has demonstrated that the law can reach an
archbishop or an ambassador, as well as an assassin.

But to return to the Von Arnim correspondence from
Rome ; it is not so clear that in this the count was wiser
than his chief. He may have been warped by influences
around him, and have shared the excitements and passions of the hour; whereas Bismarck could survey the
whole field of Germany and of Europe. As yet there
was no German empire ; and Bismarck was true to Prussian traditions in pledging support to the bishops in their
loyalty to their own government. This whole matter is
put at rest by the testimony of the eminent Bavarian
statesman who now represents Germany at Paris.

Prince Hohenlohe, in a speech at Kulmbach last October, returning thanks for his election to the Reichstag,
said, —

"Great astonishment had frequently been expressed, that a
statesman of such acuteness as Prince Bismarck did not see the
approach of the conflict with the church, and did not betimes
make preparations for it. He gladly embraced the opportunity

of stating that he did not share this view. In April, 1867, he himself (Prince Hohenlohe, then being prime minister of Bavaria) issued his circular to the foreign powers, giving a warning which was not listened to ; and some months afterwards he had an opportunity of frequently and fully discussing the matter with Count Bismarck. He knew, therefore, with what earnest and ever-increasing anxiety the chancellor beheld the approach of the conflict, the importance of which he did not underrate. At that time — namely, in September, 1869 — he himself had received the refusal of Austria and France to take any action ; and in view of this refusal of the two chief Catholic powers, what could have been done by Bismarck, the chancellor of the mainly Protestant North German Confederation, and himself, the minister president of comparatively small Bavaria, to prevent that concentration of ecclesiastical power which afterwards found expression in the council by the definition of the dogma of papal infallibility ? "

This testimony vindicates Bismarck upon every point raised, either by the ultramontanes or by Von Arnim, whom they have taken into their alliance. It shows that he foresaw the evil that ultramontanism was preparing for Europe ; that he sought to save the Catholic Church in Germany from the' clutches of the Jesuits, and to avert a collision between the church and the state ; and not till the hierarchy assailed the empire did he strike the blow so long deferred.

III.

THE ARMAMENT OF GERMANY.

(Read before the Association for the Reform and Codification of the Law of Nations, at its meeting at the Hague, September, 1875.)

THE following questions were put forth by the General Secretary, touching a proportionate reduction in the armaments of European nations.

1. What is the armament, by land and sea, of the nation to which you belong, and what, also, according to your information, are the armaments of the other European nations?

2. What proportion of such armament, in the case of each nation, do you consider necessary to its internal security?

3. What proportion do you consider necessary to its external security?

4. Do you consider it desirable that there should be a proportionate reduction in the armaments of European nations, and whatever may be your opinion, will you give the reasons for it?

5. Is a proportionate reduction practicable; and, if so, to what extent?

6. By what methods may such a reduction be accomplished?

As a resident of Berlin, I have prepared a brief reply to these questions with regard to Germany; and though I cannot presume to speak with the authority of an official statement, nor to represent adequately the tone of German sentiment and the demands of German nationality, in military affairs, I shall hope to speak in candid sympathy with the national life of Germany, while giving the judgment of an impartial observer upon the practicability of reducing her armament.

The total fighting force of the German empire may be estimated roundly at 1,700,000 men; this includes the navy and the two classes of reserves of the army, the Landwehr and the Landsturm. The standing army in time of peace, consists of 438,831 men, and 96,875 horses, at a yearly cost of 359,434,000 reichsmarks; being about an average of 900 reichsmarks, or 300 thalers per man. This army is organized with 469 battalions of infantry, 465 squadrons of cavalry, 300 campaign batteries, 29 battalions of fort artillery, 18 battalions of pioneers, and 18 battalions of service corps. No attempt is made to classify the men by race or religion; and it is the uniform opinion of officers, that in spite of the present fervor of ecclesiastical differences in some sections, Catholics and Protestants would fight side by side, with equal zeal, against a foreign foe, — so overpowering is the sentiment of loyalty to the fatherland and the strength of army discipline and *esprit de corps.*

This standing army of the German empire is an increase upon the sum total of the standing armies of the several states that now compose the empire, as these stood before the war with France in 1870; and the number of the army and the yearly appropriation for its support were fixed, at the last session of parliament, for the term of seven years — just overlapping the septennate of Marshal Macmahon. The increase of the standing force of the country was urged by the necessity Germany is under of maintaining her newly-acquired boundaries, her national unity, and her independent position in Europe;

and also by a vague apprehension of impending danger. The appropriation for the term of seven years was voted — against what some would make the strict construction of the constitution — under the pressure of public opinion, which demanded some permanent guarantee of peace. By the constitution the duration of any one parliament is limited to three years, and each parliament has absolute control over the supplies and subsidies of the empire during the term of its own existence. The government had sought to withdraw the army appropriation from the chances of the yearly budget; not leaving it open to be canvassed at every session of parliament, but having it definitively fixed as to amount, for an indefinite term of years. This would have been equivalent to a vote of unlimited confidence. Now, there was no unwillingness of the majority to repose this confidence in the government; but many scrupled at assuming to bind future parliaments by forestalling their prerogative; and others, like the English Commons of old, were jealous for the hard-won right of controlling the purse-strings. But the great financial and industrial interests of the country insisted that its military defenses should not be exposed to the whims and fluctuations of parliamentary majorities; and on demand of the press and the people, the army estimates were voted finally for seven years, as a compromise between government and parliament. Commerce and Industry said, Give us security, and we will pay the cost.

At the same time new regulations were made for the reserves, so that directly upon being called out, these will be incorporated with the regular army, and even the landsturm, ordinarily reserved for a last defense against actual invasion, may now be moved from place to place, and not kept simply each detachment for the protection of its own district. Hence, in case the new rule of war concerning combatants and non-combatants, proposed at Brussels and to be revived at St. Petersburg, should be adopted by the Great Powers, Germany, when threatened with invasion, could enroll in the regular army her entire population capable of bearing arms, and among men under fifty-five would have neither non-combatants nor irregulars. These reserves are made up of men who have had the discipline of the army in their youth, and are of course far superior in training to a volunteer militia.

The standing army of Germany is constantly kept up to the highest point of drill, and by field manœuvres is made familiar with the operations of war. It is in readiness to be put in motion on the shortest notice; and the exigencies of the military service are studied in the construction of railways and other public works. From all this it is evident that Germany is doing nothing, and intending nothing, toward a proportionate reduction of her army in the interest of peace.

Yet it would be wrong to infer that the Germans are a belligerent nation and preparing for a career of imperial conquest. The people are decidedly averse to wars of ambition or of invasion, and the government is not likely to seek occasion for a foreign war; though if danger threatens from without, both people and government will do energetically whatever the interests and the safety of Germany may seem to require.

So far the first question: the armament of Germany is upwards of 400,000 men equipped for war, with every facility for arming, at short notice, at least four times that number, trained to the use of arms.

The second question is, What proportion of such armament is necessary to the internal security of the nation? Of course a foreigner can only guess at a reply; but I would say at a venture, that, in the absence of any foreign intervention to provoke dissension among her people, one tenth of her present army — say 40,000 men — should suffice for the internal security of the German empire. I know this estimate will be received with incredulity by the average German citizen, and with amusement by German statesmen and military men ; but it is really a complimentary recognition of their growth in self-government, for a citizen of the United States who has lived among them for years, to say that forty million Germans could now be trusted to govern themselves with as little military force as forty million Americans require for their internal security. The Germans are not belligerent among themselves ; they are not addicted to insurrection ; they are exceedingly well trained in the habit of obedience to the laws ; they have now an outlet for political fermentation in free constitutional parliaments, imperial and local; and the traditions of the Thirty Years' War, and the lingering effects of that war in retarding the political and industrial development of the nation, have induced a chronic aversion to civil war as a remedy for any evils, real or imaginary. Even the excitements of church politics in the past three years have not roused a spirit of martial combat. The people do not need to be governed by awe of a military force, and a very small army should suffice for any extraordinary emergency of the public peace. Indeed, the internal dangers and disturbances of Germany would lose much of their importance, save for the apprehension of foreign dangers that might give to any domestic disquiet a purely factitious consequence.

To the third question, What proportion of the armament of Germany is necessary to her external security ? I answer, the WHOLE of it, every man, every horse, every ship, every gun, as matters now are with respect to armament upon the continent of Europe. If Europe is to live in the constant expectation of war, and in a state of enormous and incessant preparation for war, then Germany must be, and will be, armed as she is. The statesmanship of every continental people is now largely devoted to the means of national defense; to the strengthening of fortifications and the efficient organization of the army; the diplomacy of every nation is on the alert for the probabilities of war; the interior economy of every nation is taxed more and more for the military branch of the public service; the inventive genius of every people is occupied with the improvement of weapons of destruction. Lying in the centre of Europe, with powerful neighbors upon all sides, who are emulating her own military system, Germany must keep up that system to the highest point of efficiency and of readiness, for her own external security. Alone she cannot, dare not, set the example of reducing her armament or slighting her preparations for war.

Till revenge, jealousy, ambition shall be disarmed throughout Europe, Germany must have her body-guard of 400,000 men, her life-guard of 1,700,000. Whenever you urge upon her statesmen the policy of reducing her armament, the answer is, " Give us another geographical position." No other country is so exposed to be simultaneously attacked by formidable powers upon all sides. No other country so needs a wall of fire to be to her what the channel is to England, the ocean to the United States.

Nevertheless, in answer to the fourth question, it is most desirable that there should be an early reduction in the armament of Germany, upon a scale of proportion with other nations, that should keep all relatively in the same position as at present for maintaining their external security. For this opinion there are two weighty reasons. (1.) The enormous drain of a universal mili-

7

tary conscription upon the industrial life and resources
of the nation ; and (2.) The fact that a large standing
army is a temptation to war, and is liable to seek occasion for war, to justify its own existence.

In one view, no doubt, the maintenance of a large,
well-equipped army, by any country, favors peaceable relations with other nations. However restless and belligerent a nation may be, it will hesitate to attack another
that is known to be always ready for vigorous and decisive warfare. A nation well armed may count upon a
certain immunity from insult or attack from abroad.
But there are limits to the restraint that one nation can
impose upon others by exhibiting the strength of its armament. That very armament may be taken for a menace or a taunt ; it may excite jealousy or fear, and
provoke combinations for its overthrow : or the spirit of
bravado, which in human nature answers to the crowing
propensity in the cock, may excite two military nations
to peck at each other for a fight that shall determine
which is master of the walk. The history of war shows
that a great standing army incites as much warfare as it
forefends. The nations that are now vieing with each
other in their military systems, and in the inventions
and munitions of war, will hardly rest satisfied till actual collision in the field shall have settled the question
of superiority. Hence the external security of each nation would be better assured by a proportionate reduction
of the armaments of all.

That the internal peace and prosperity of each nation
demand such a reduction of its own armament, is too
obvious for argument. The drain of a large army upon
the resources of a country is constant and depleting. In
Austria the army consumes 19.83 per cent. of the whole
income of the state ; in Germany 26.14 per cent. ; in
Russia 36.33 ; in Italy 17.92 ; in France, with the navy,

30.91 ; in Great Britain 30.95 ; in Denmark 28.24 ; in Sweden 32.15 ; in Norway 29.17 ; in the Netherlands 27.23 : making for these ten states an average of 28.01 per cent. of income consumed in arming against each other. But this is not all. It is one of the commonplaces of political economy, that the soldier, while consuming yearly the fruits of the labor of others, and at their cost, adds nothing to the productive resources of the country, unless by the fortune of war he may annex something to her territory. And furthermore, the term of compulsory military service, as in Germany, comes to young men at a time when it seriously interferes with their training for other occupations in life. Many a young man will testify, " I might have been other than I am, or been in business for myself, but just as I was getting forward, I had to go into the army, and in my three years of service I lost not only my place, but what qualification for business I had previously acquired, lost my opportunity of advancement, and now must begin again at the bottom of the ladder." Thus the army service becomes to many a serious obstacle to business, to marriage, to all that men cherish for themselves in life, and to that free development of the individual which tends to the highest mean of national good. This is felt seriously by many in Germany, who nevertheless submit to the present military system as a political necessity, and would defend it from motives of patriotism.

But it should be said with equal frankness, on the other hand, that for many, also, the course of obligatory military service is a salutary discipline, and has an elevating influence. This is true, for example, of the more ignorant of the peasantry and of the mining population, who gain in the army notions of order, of cleanliness, and of regularity, to which they were strangers ; and who, by coming in contact with men of a higher grade,

and by moving from place to place, undergo a civilizing
process that is much to their advantage in after life. As
to officers, it will be admitted that there is no higher
school of men and manners than that provided in the
Prussian army. Loyalty to king and country, culture in
literature and science, chivalry and magnanimity of
mien, though not without a certain pride of caste, place
these officers among the picked men of the kingdom.

As a rule, the people of Germany are proud of their
army, recognizing the great services it has done for the
nation, and being also identified with it by many personal ties. By the constitution of the empire, personal
military service is made obligatory upon every citizen,
and by act of parliament it is unlawful for the press to
call in question this fundamental organic provision, or to
cast reproach upon the nation's defense. The people ac-
quiesce in a seeming necessity, but they groan under the
taxes, and the personal and domestic privations, to which
this system subjects them; and should a long peace make
the necessity of the military system less obvious and imperative, the murmurs of tax-payers would soon become
audible, and might even grow formidable.

And in this lies the risk of a large army being urged
on to war by a popular clamor against its costly *inertia.*
That a distinctive war party exists in Germany, I see no
evidence; nor do I imagine that any statesman would
venture to advocate a policy of war, as the key to his
administration. Among younger officers, zealous for
chivalrous exploits and impatient for promotion, there is
often talk of war as approaching or desirable; but as a
rule, old and experienced officers are slow to plunge their
country into war — possibly a school of politicians may
fancy that to take the initiative in a foreign war, when
the aspect is threatening, is the surest road to victory,
safety, and peace. But there is no party in Germany

that openly avows this policy, nor could such a party or policy find favor with the people, except in some manifest emergency.

But a protracted peace must tend to undermine the conviction that a great standing army is a necessity of the state ; and history warns us that burdensome taxation for the support of an army may provoke popular revolt, and then such revolt be pleaded as a pretext for a great standing army as an internal police. There are no present signs of such a peril to Germany ; but the peril lies in the very provision made to guard against it. Upon all these grounds, therefore, a reduction of the armament should recommend itself to statesmen.

This leads to the concluding questions, Nos. 5 and 6, which, for brevity, may be treated as one : " Is a proportionate reduction practicable ; and, if so, to what extent ? And by what methods may such a reduction be accomplished ? " A reduction is practicable only upon the condition that some other expedient than war be clearly set before the people, that shall give an equal assurance that the interests and honor of the nation shall be faithfully preserved. The only expedient capable of this is arbitration. But to induce a military nation to have recourse to arbitration as a substitute for war, confidence must first be inspired in arbitration as practicable and equitable ; and such confidence will be of comparatively slow growth, as the result of experience. Arbitration is not likely to be accepted at wholesale, as an abstract principle, but can be recommended in detail, by clear and tangible cases.

Now there are two classes of cases which can be hopefully recommended to all nations as matter for arbitration.

(1.) Disputes concerning territory or property. The first of these are in a certain sense international, since questions of boundary affect the whole community of nations. Hence, with special propriety, such cases could come before an international tribunal.

Experience has shown that the forcible settlement of boundary leaves cause of rankling, dispute, and retaliation in the future, and thus becomes a costly and uncertain mode of settlement: while the example of great nations testifies that, in such cases, arbitration would be accepted with dignity and satisfaction.

As to property, we have reached an age of civilization when a war risking thousands of lives and the morals of a nation, simply for money, could hardly justify itself to the moral sense of Christendom ; and now that the whole resources of commerce and banking are available for the peaceful adjustment of such disputes, arbitration is their obvious remedy.

(2.) Questions affecting persons. By the comity of nations, or by special treaties, many questions concerning persons are already provided for by peaceable methods. As a rule, questions concerning ambassadors, emigrants, refugees, criminals, neutrals, are disposed of by some specific agreement or by public international law. A principle so widely accepted might well be extended to cover all manner of cases concerning persons.

There would then remain only a class of questions lying within the vague region of national honor. But the more practical and substantial questions being already provided for on terms of peace, and the habit being established of adjusting these peaceably, the class of problematical questions would diminish in number, and by degrees would come to be referred to the same category of arbitration. Step by step this grand consummation may be gained.

A growing help in this direction is the influence of international congresses for the advancement of knowledge and the improvement of society. I know it has been wittily said that every great international exhibition has

been followed by a great war. Yet it were vain to deny
that the intercourse promoted by such occasions favors a
peaceable disposition among the nations. In the recent
Geographical Congress of Paris, a German geologist,
whose name is honored throughout the scientific world,
presided over one of the sessions, with the same apparent
welcome that was accorded to every representative of
foreign nations; German travelers recounted to admiring
audiences their explorations in Africa; German authorities were quoted with commendation; and prizes were
awarded to German societies and savans, with the hearty
courtesy and impartiality that marked the whole pro-
ceedings; and when, in that vast concourse, one heard
the Russian, the German, the Hollander, the Swede, the
Belgian, the Englishman, the Frenchman, the Italian,
the Hungarian, each in his own tongue pay tribute to
the commonwealth of science; when one heard the vice-
admiral of France, president of the congress, instance
its assembling as one of the conquests and tokens of
peace, and saw the marshal-president of France and the
heir to the throne of Russia assisting at the congress
with the personal interest and attention of its more active members, one could not but feel a loftier inspiration
for humanity, — the pulse of that inner life, which not
all the savage surgery of war has been able to exhaust
nor permanently to enfeeble.

The Geographical Congress taught that the physical
globe belongs to man, for community of exploration, of
discovery, of development, of utilization, for the behoof
of human society. In this it was our fit auxiliary. But
this association teaches the higher lesson that human society itself belongs to man; — a community of nations,
girded with the armament of justice, ordered and perfected by equal and universal law — arbitrating the
claims of every member and conserving the welfare of
the whole.

IV.

THE INTERCOURSE OF CHRISTIAN WITH NON-CHRISTIAN PEOPLES.

(Presented at the Conference of the "Association for the Reform and Codification of the Law of Nations," at Bremen, September, 1876.)

IF by the "*Reform* of the Law of Nations," in the title of the association, is meant not only the rectification of errors and abuses, but an intelligential advance in principles and methods in the ever-widening field of national intercourse, then, in no department of our work could there arise a question at once so urgent and so comprehensive as that of the principles which should govern the intercourse of Christian with non-Christian peoples. This is indeed a question of reforming the law of nations, in the literal sense of forming it anew. It covers all the methods and aims contemplated by this association, — philosophic, philanthropic, and practical. Since I proposed this topic to the favor of the council, three months ago, three events of no common significance have occurred to give it point and urgency.

(1.) At the very moment when the people of the United States were celebrating the centennial of an independence based upon the natural rights of men, and were exhibiting the progress of the world in the arts of peace, a frightful outbreak of Indian cruelty and revenge raised anew the question of the treatment of aborigines by a Christian nation, in respect of territory, possessions, and protection.

(2.) The brutality reported of the Turks in Bulgaria raised throughout Europe a cry for the intervention of the Christian Powers, upon grounds of humanity and religion, — thus bringing the fervor of humane impulse and of religious enthusiasm into one of the most confused problems of international law.

As a side-light upon this problem it is worth recalling, that just seventy years ago Napoleon wrote to his brother Joseph concerning the insurrection in his Neapolitan kingdom, " I am glad to see that a village of the insurgents has been burnt.[1] . . . You should order two or three of the large villages that have behaved the worst to be pillaged ; it will be an example, and will restore to your troops their gayety and desire for action." [2] Burning, pillaging, shooting, hanging, Napoleon justified by the laws of war ; saying " there is nothing sacred after a conquest." [3] But we must remember that it was one of his mottoes, that " What a nation most hates is another nation." [4] It is a long advance from the *sang froid* with which Napoleon ordered such severities in Naples, to the shudder with which Europe reads of them in Bulgaria ; yet we cannot forget how recently an English commander whom none would charge with inhumanity ordered the burning of Ashantee villages as a punishment and a warning. The same retribution has been inflicted just now in Dahomey. These hints will suffice to show how far Christendom yet is from unanimity as to what constitutes brutality in war, or what measure of brutality would justify protest and intervention in the name of humanity.

(3.) In pleasing contrast with these aggravating events,

[1] Letter to Joseph, April 21, 1806.
[2] Letter to Joseph, July 30, 1806.
[3] Letter to Joseph, March 31, 1806.
[4] Letter to Joseph, August 9, 1806.

appeared at the same time an invitation from the King of the Belgians, for a congress of African travelers and explorers to meet at Brussels and take the initiative for the civilization of equatorial Africa by a system of scientific stations and commissarial depositories to be established under an international commission; — that is to say, the opening of the vast interior of Africa to intercourse with the civilized world should not be left to the enterprise of travelers, the caprice of adventurers, the cupidity of monopolies, nor the rivalry of separate nations, but should be made the common cause of Christendom, under well-ascertained principles of international law, regulating the approaches of civilized peoples to the rude tribes of the Nile, the Niger, and the Congo.

At the opening of this unique conference, on the 13th of September, his majesty said, " Le sujet que nous réunit aujourd'hui est de ceux qui méritent au premier chef d'occuper les amis de l'humanité. Ouvrir à la civilisation la seule parti de notre globe où elle n'ait point encore pénétré, percer les ténèbres qui enveloppent des populations entières, c'est, si j'ose le dire, une croisade digne de ce siècle de progrès ; et je suis heureux de constater combien le sentiment public est favorable à son accomplissement." He invited the conference to discuss and determine " les voies à suivre, les moyens à employer pour planter definitivement l'étendard de la civilisation sur le sol de l'Afrique centrale ; " and he suggested the following points as worthy of special attention : —

1. " Désignation.précise des bases d'opération à acquérir sur la côte de Zanzibar et près de l'embouchure du Congo, soit par conventions avec les chefs, soit par achats ou locations à régler avec les particuliers.

2. " Désignation des routes à ouvrir successivement vers l'intérieur et des stations hospitalières, scientifiques et pacificatrices à organiser comme moyen d'abolir l'escla-

vage, et d'établir la concorde entre les chefs, de leur pro-
curer des arbitres justes, désintéressés, etc.

3. "Création, l'œuvre étant bien définie, d'un comité
international et central, et des comités nationaux pour
en poursuivre l'exécution, chacun en ce qui le concernera,
en exposer le but au public de tous les pays et faire au
sentiment charitable un appel qu'aucune bonne cause ne
lui a jamais addressé en vain."

In proposing my theme to the council, I had barely
anticipated these noble wishes of his majesty the King of
the Belgians.

The framing of regulations for a closer intercourse
with non-Christian peoples is the fit work of an association for the reform of the law of nations ; and it is with
the hope and the request that the present conference
will appoint a commission to give effect to this suggestion, that I venture to submit an essay toward principles
of international law, to govern the intercourse of Christian with non-Christian peoples.

This classification is the best that the subject admits
of. One could not say " pagan " peoples, since not only
are Mohammedans the fiercest of iconoclasts, but the
Chinese and Japanese, who fall within the category of
" non-Christian " peoples, resent such epithets as " pagan " or " heathen." Neither could one classify these
last as " uncivilized ; " since China and Japan have a
fair title among civilized nations. But inasmuch as
modern international law was born of Christian sentiment in Grotius, and now obtains throughout Christendom, the division is fair between Christian and non-
Christian peoples. Moreover, since all authorities agree
that international law can take effect only between communities organized as nations or states, and since roving
hordes and societies united *sceleris causa* are not recognized as states, I have purposely avoided the terms

" state " and " nation," and have used " peoples " as including tribes, because my object is to ascertain the
principles that should govern Christian nations — that
do acknowledge a law among themselves — in their intercourse with all sorts and conditions of men, whether
within the family of nations or still without its pale.

In this view the theme is broader and deeper — at
once more comprehensive and more radical — than that
which the Institute of International Law last year submitted to a commission, viz. : " The Applicability of the
European Law of Nations to the Nations of the East ; "
— a topic which is ably discussed by Sir Travers Twiss,
in the " Law Magazine and Review " for May, 1876,
with special relation to African slave states. That inquiry has reference to the ripeness of the nations of the
East for admission into the general community of International Law. Turkey was formally received into that
community by the treaty of Paris of 1856, the seventh
article of which declares that " the Sublime Porte is admitted to participate in the advantages of the public law
and concert of Europe ; " and this association numbers
among its vice-presidents distinguished representatives of
Turkey, Egypt, and Japan.

But my inquiry has reference to the ripeness of Christian nations for some concert of principles that shall govern their intercourse with all non-Christian peoples ; not
how far such peoples are qualified to accept the law of
nations as it is, but whether Christian nations can agree
upon certain just and equal rules of dealing with non-
Christian peoples under all circumstances and conditions
of intercourse with them. In other words, in what form
shall Christian peoples put the law of nations before
non-Christian peoples whom they would educate up to its
level, and finally win to its authority? This question
I shall not presume to answer to the extent of formu-

lating principles as rules of action, but shall content myself with an essay toward such principles.

The subject divides itself into five categories.

1. *Territory.* Upon what principles should Christian nations deal with non-Christian peoples in the acquisition of territory found in their occupation ?

2. *Commerce.* What principles should regulate the commercial intercourse of Christian with non-Christian peoples ?

3. *Humanity.* How far may Christian nations interfere in the affairs of non-Christian peoples to regulate or restrain their doings in the interest of humanity ?

4. *Public peace and order.* To what extent may Christian nations undertake the police of the world, with a view to public safety and order ?

5. *Religion.* To what extent and upon what grounds may Christian nations interfere with non-Christian peoples in matters of religion ?

Under each of these heads I will briefly state the law of nations as it is, and point out particulars in which improvement or advancement seems to be called for ; ending with a summary of the principles upon which such reform should be based.

I. OF TERRITORY. In countries so organized and advanced as Turkey, China, and Japan, the acquisition by foreigners of a right of domicile and of title to land is obviously within the scope of treaty negotiation, though it may happen, as with the opening of the five ports in China in 1842, that the privilege of residence, property, and commerce is first extorted by force of arms. But in countries held by aboriginal tribes, or by sparse and feeble communities, the policy of territorial acquisition has varied with the notions, the temperament, the opportunities of discoverers or colonists from abroad. There is indeed a semblance of international law to reg-

nlate such acquisition. The Pope would not now presume to parcel out heathen nations as the spoil of their
Christian conquerors ; Queen Victoria would not renew
the commission of Queen Elizabeth to Sir Humphrey
Gilbert, " to discover such remote heathen and barbarous
lands, countries, and territories, not actually possessed
by any Christian prince or people, and to hold, occupy,
and enjoy the same, with all their commodities, jurisdic-
tions, and royalties ; " nor would the Puritan or the Fifth
Monarchy Man now plead the Hebrew conquest of Ca-
naan as a divine warrant for exterminating the heathen
or reducing them to slavery.   Still, in acquiring the
territory of aborigines, civilized men have too often put
policy and power before justice, and have overlooked the
idea of any right or title of the aborigines to the soil they
occupied.   And even where there is a disposition to do
justly by the aborigines, two principles, each having the
authority of great names in public law, come into conflict, and require to be reconciled by more clear and positive rules.

The first principle is that occupation or actual possession creates a presumptive right of property in the soil.
If there be a precedence among rights, then it would
seem that long-time occupation should give the first claim
to territory : — that, however valid the right of discovery
may be against subsequent explorers, or other nations
within the concert of public law, this can have no force
against the right of occupation in aborigines actually in
possession, — the presumption being that a country already inhabited when brought to our knowledge belongs
to the people who inhabit it.   And in the case of aborigines without a history, this presumptive title runs back
of the memory of man.   Calvo says, " Up to a certain
point, usucaption and prescription are even more neces-

sary between sovereign states than between individuals."[1]
And is there not also a certain right of usucaption and
prescription in the savage man, in the aboriginal tribe,
which "sovereign states" are bound to respect? The
starting point in all dealings with aborigines concerning
territory must be the recognition in them of some sort
of right to the territory upon which they are found. And
this *right* must be to the civilized man a mean of justice.

But this obvious principle is qualified by another,
which is sometimes pushed so far as quite to overlay the
primordial right of occupation. What *is* occupation?
No one would dispute that "a *state* in the lawful possession of a territory has an exclusive right of property
therein "[2] [*dominium eminens*] ; but can nomadic tribes
have an exclusive right of ownership and domain over
the vast territories they roam for pasturage and the
chase? Every right supposes a corresponding duty ;
and since the earth as a whole belongs to mankind as a
whole, and its products and resources are needed for the
sustentation and development of the human race, the
right of occupation in any portion of territory carries
with it the obligation to serviceable occupation. Hence
Calvo, in arguing the "legitimate and incontestable title"
of the United States to dominion over all the lands once
occupied by Indian tribes along the frontier of the original colonies, says, "The Indians were but ' half-sover-
eigns ' [*mi-souveraines*], and never in reality had more
than a bare right of occupation."[3] And Vattel is even
more positive: " The peoples of the vast countries of

---

[1] " L'usucapion et la prescription sont meme, jusqu'à un certain
point, plus nécessaire entre États souverains qu'entre particuliers."
Le Droit International, tome I., v. 173.

[2] Phillimore, *Comm. on International Law*, III., iv.

[3] *Le Droit International*, II. § 55.

North America wandered over them [*les parcouraient*] rather than inhabited them ; " and he lays down this principle : " Those who still adhere to this sort of idle life usurp more land than they would need with honest labor, and cannot complain if other nations, more laborious and too confined, come and occupy a part of it." [1] But even this sweeping principle reserves to wild tribes certain rights of possession ; they are not to be exterminated nor enslaved, but simply restricted to so much laud as " they are in a condition to inhabit and to cultivate." While insisting upon the right of colonists " to restrict savages to narrower limits," Vattel recommends conciliation rather than conquest. " One cannot but laud," he says, " the moderation of the English Puritans, who first established themselves in New England. Although provided with a charter from their sovereign, they purchased of the savages the land they wanted to occupy. This praiseworthy example was followed by William Penn, and the colony of Quakers which he conducted into Pennsylvania." [2]

The principle that the earth belongs to the human family for use and improvement was strongly put by Great Britain in her contest with Spain for the freedom of Nootka Sound (1790). Great Britain held that " the earth is the common inheritance of mankind, of which each individual and each nation has a right to appropriate a share, by occupation and cultivation." [3] Dr. Arnold pushed this doctrine to the extreme that only labor can create a right of property in the soil. " So much does the right of property go along with labor, that civilized nations have never scrupled to take possession of countries inhabited only by tribes of savages — countries

---

[1] Vattel, *Droit des Gens*, t. I. l. i. cvii. § 81.
[2] *Droit des Gens*, s. c. xviii. § 209.
[3] Wheaton, pt. II. 6. IV.

which have been hunted over — but never subdued or cultivated."[1] This doctrine was much canvassed in England, in the New Zealand question of thirty years ago.[2] It contains an element of substantial truth, and, in one aspect is humane — as proffering relief for over-crowded and starving populations. But it is also a doc-trine especially liable to abuse. It should be applied with caution and conciliation, and never pressed to the destruction of the right of aborigines to subsist, as best they may, upon the territory which they and their fathers, from time immemorial, have occupied. What is service-able occupation? What is the standard of cultivation, and who shall fix this and enforce it? If my neighbor suffers his land to become a nursery of weeds overrun-ning my premises, or a marsh distilling pestilence, I have just cause of complaint; but I have no right to insist that he shall use a subsoil plough and the best chemical fertilizers, in order to make his land most serviceable to the community, under pain of confiscation if he let it lie waste. Agrarianism and Communism would seize upon all private estates under the plea of making these more serviceable to mankind; yet such estates may be of the highest benefit as a means of culture and taste, and the basis of a cultivated class that lifts society and the state to a higher level of civilization.

---

[1] Dr. Arnold seems to have borrowed his doctrine from Cicero. "Sunt autem privata nulla natura; sed aut veteri occupatione, ut qui quondam in vacua venerunt; aut victoria, ut qui bello potiti sunt; aut lege, pactione, conditione, sorte; ex quo fit, ut ager Arpinas Arpinatum dictatur, Tusculanus, Tusculanorum; similisque est pri-vatarum possessionum descriptio: ex quo, quia suum cujusque fit, eorum, quae natura fuerant communia, quod cuique obtigit, id quis-que teneat; eo si qui sibi plus appetet, violabit jus humanae socie-tatis." *De Officiis*, lib. i. cap. 7.

[2] *The New Zealand Question and the Rights of Aborigines*, by L. A. Chamerovzow.

8

We must take heed not to enforce against aborigines a doctrine that might subvert the foundations of thrift and order in the best civilized states. My right to live and to improve the earth after my own fashion does not convey the right to oust or exterminate my neighbor, nor to compel him to get his living after my fashion, however superior this may be to his own. It may be the law of nature that savage tribes must become civilized or die out; but has a Christian nation the prerogative of enforcing or accelerating this law, by fire and sword?

It may aid in the adjustment of the two principles now stated, if we keep in mind that rude and even nomadic tribes do often have some notion of territorial limits and of public law, and also that they are amenable to other influences than force and fear. The desert of Arabia Petræa, for example, is parceled out among different tribes by lines, which, though marked by no natural features, are as sharply defined as the boundaries between any civilized nations. Arrived at Akaba on my journey northward from Mount Sinai to Petra, I must there change camels and escort, for I had come within the domain of the renowned Sheikh Husein. I found him seated in the midst of his men of war armed with their matchlocks, knives, and spears. He, however, refused to furnish us an escort to Petra, on the ground that the adjacent tribes were at war. As our party was large and well armed we offered to take the risk, if he would give us a guide. Drawing himself up to his full height, he answered, " You are now in my territory, under my protection. If I permit you to go into danger and one of you is robbed or killed, your consul at Cairo will send word to your country; and by and by, after one, two, three years, the big ships will come to Egypt, to Constantinople, and the Sultan and the Khedive will send soldiers to seize me, *and*" — here he drew his hand rapidly across his neck to signify that he would lose his head! Never was I so impressed with the omnipresence and majesty of that public law that holds even the Bedouins under its sway, and makes its presence felt in the silence of the desert. Mohammed Ali had taught that lesson.

But the roving tribes of the wilderness, the savages of Africa and of the Pacific, are susceptible to other approaches than by force and fear. We have but to remember that they are men, and we shall find them open to kindness, to vanity, to cupidity, and also to justice. The Indians, who were capable of making a treaty with the United States for reserved land, might have been induced to concede the privilege of scientific exploration, and that any mines found in their territory might be worked, on condition of paying a percentage to their tribes. In that case, the gold-hunting in the Black Hills, instead of being resented by them as a usurpation and a robbery, would have been welcomed as a source of wealth without toil. These are men of like passions with ourselves; and it is worth trying whether their right of occupation cannot be reconciled with the world's right of discovery and advancement. There may still be circumstances in which the two principles must come to strife; but it is the duty of Christian nations, first of all, to deal with non-Christian peoples as men having human rights, and, most of all, to show that they mean to be, and seek to be, just. In the manner advised by the King of the Belgians they should advance civilization through concord with native chiefs, and just and disinterested arbitration.

II. COMMERCE. Wheaton wrote thirty years ago, "The injustice and mischief of admitting that nations have a right to use force, for the express purpose of retarding the civilization and diminishing the prosperity of their inoffensive neighbors, are too revolting to allow such a right to be inserted in the international code." [1] But is it not time to ask whether nations have a right to use force for the purpose of *advancing* the civilization and enhancing the prosperity of less favored peoples? Is commerce, as the van-guard of our Christian civilization, to be quartered upon reluctant peoples by the rifle and the gunboat? We may well ask ourselves whether a civilization that puts on the horrid front of war, and goes on its mission bristling with cannon, is after all so much better than barbarism in the sum total of human happiness, as to justify an armed crusade to carry its commerce and arts through the world? — Whether humanity would be much the gainer if the whole world should be civilized up to the point where each nation should exhaust its resources and inventions upon improving and multiplying agents for the destruction of human life, and in every land every youth should be taken from the plow, the shop, the school, and trained to the art of war. Should it not shame Christian nations to make their first impression upon ruder peoples through superior powers of destruction, and by a commerce that sends fire and slaughter to prepare the way for opium and rum?

There is a right of commerce. The same principle that warrants mankind in reclaiming the earth for their needs, entitles them to share in the products of different climates and soils as means of comfort and enjoyment. But this right, like that of colonial settlement, should be asserted in the spirit of peace and good-will, and for the broad interests of humanity. The commerce of the Christian world with non-Christian peoples, looking beyond present economical advantages, should stimulate

---

[1] Wheaton, *Elements of International Law*, pt. II. c. 1.

such peoples to a higher development of their natural
resources, and a higher improvement in the arts of life.
Hence any traffic that would tend to corrupt and destroy
inferior peoples should be discountenanced by the law of
nations, at least to the extent that no person engaging
in such traffic should have the protection of his government in any conflict or difficulty arising out of the traffic.
Such a measure was proposed in 1858 concerning the
opium trade, by the plenipotentiary of the United States
to China. In a letter to Lord Elgin, Mr. W. B. Reed
suggested that the two governments should unite "in
urging upon the Chinese authorities the active and thorough suppression of the trade by seizure and confiscation, with assurances that no assistance, direct or indi-
rect, shall be given to parties, English or American, seeking to evade or resist the process." [1] By the laws of war
certain articles are liable to be seized and confiscated as
contraband of war. It is time that the law of nations
should brand certain kinds of traffic as contraband of
peace, contraband of civilization, and outlawed from the
protection of public law. If the accidental introduction
of contagious diseases by civilized man among the aborigines of the Pacific is deplored as a scandal to Christendom, if the traffic in human flesh is declared piracy by
the law of nations,[2] then surely any traffic in immoral-
ities, to the destruction of a weaker people, should be put
under the ban of Christendom.

How to open commerce with barbarous tribes is sometimes a difficult problem ; and there is need on this point
of concert among Christian nations, lest ill-advised action
on the part of one should prejudice the interests of all.
As a rule it might be said that this should be left to the

---

[1] *British Opium Policy*, by F. S. Turner, p. 92.

[2] In 1820 the Congress of the United States declared the slave-
trade to be piracy, to be punished with death.

private enterprise of trade. But it has happened, and will happen again, that injudicious or unscrupulous traders will bring on a collision with tribes ignorant of the customs of trade, by awakening the prejudices or fears of the people, or the jealousy of their rulers. A trader is robbed or murdered, his government steps in to avenge the wrong, and a cruel war ends in a treaty of commerce under which the vanquished are restive until the opportunity comes for their revenge. When at last the opium traffic was forced upon China, the Emperor Tao Kwang said, " Gainseeking and corrupt men will for profit and sensuality defeat my wishes; but nothing will induce me to derive a revenue from the vice and misery of my people."[1] Though there are no mails nor telegraphs, the suspicion has gone abroad among non-Christian peoples that the advent of Christian commerce means encroachment, usurpation, fraud, wrong — perhaps, by and by, armed dominion and extirpation. I would not impugn the duty of a government to look after the safety and lives of its subjects in all parts of the world — to hold the very hair of the head sacred from injury or insult. But in these times of incessant emigration and locomotion, if Christian governments would not be in incessant war with the ruder tribes of men, they should pause to inquire into the right and wrong of their own subjects before they threaten and strike their assailants. As human nature is, offenses must come ; and I would not pretend that it is possible wholly to dispense with force and terror in dealing with barbarous tribes. Yet the sad lesson of Ashantee and Dahomey may be a commentary upon the old policy of putting force first, and commerce and justice afterwards. Patience might sometimes win a surer conquest than precipitate action. I cannot forget that not many years ago one needed a passport for

---

[1] *British Opium Policy*, by F. S. Turner, p. 120.

every petty state of Europe ; that luggage was searched at every frontier ; that on entering Tuscany, Rome, Naples, one had to secrete his Bible and the " Times ; " that English political works were seized at the Russian custom-house ; that republican pamphlets or newspapers made the traveler liable. to arrest in Austria as a suspicious person ; that even now the innocent through traveler from Berlin to Paris or London is roused at midnight, and compelled to go into a pen under guard, while his hand-bag is examined, lest he should turn pedler in Belgium ; and that we cannot get out of this hospitable city of Bremen without being examined at the *douane* as if our purpose were to smuggle free goods to foreign parts ; and remembering these blights on our own intercourse, we should have forbearance with our weaker brethren of Ashantee and Dahomey, whose methods of challenging the persons and goods of foreigners are rougher than ours, but are part of the same system. The tariff stretched along the Atlantic coast to keep out the goods of England, France, and Germany may be as preposterous, and in the view of political economy as barbarous, as the hawser stretched across the Niger ; but it is not proposed to force the tariff by gunboats and ironclads. Let not Christian powers do to the weak what they would not dare attempt with the strong.

Once more, with respect to commerce, when this is opened in any new quarter of the globe it should be for the common behoof of mankind. That priority of discovery, or actual colonization, should secure to a nation certain commercial privileges by way of recompense for its outlay and risks, lies in the very reason of things. To deny this would be to take away one great stimulus to geographical discovery and commercial enterprise. But such special privilege, like copyright or patent-right, should be for a limited period, by way of reimbursement for toil and skill laid out; it should never be suffered to grow to a permanent monopoly. This is the age of the solidarity of nations; and though the nation, like the individual, must care first for self in order to be capable of caring for mankind, yet each nation should look upon the prosperity of every other with a favor next to its own. A good example of this international comity in commerce was given by the United States in their treaty with China in 1845. Having secured certain extraordinary concessions beyond those made to England, — such as the erection of hospitals, chapels, and cemeteries at the five ports, and permission to ships of war to visit any part of the coasts of China, — the United States stipulated that the same privileges should be extended to all nations. In this spirit should the pioneers of commerce prepare the way for the unification of humanity.[1]

III. HUMANITY. The law of nations has long ago settled the right of governments, severally or collectively, to interfere in the affairs of other peoples, "where the general interests of humanity are infringed by the excesses of a barbarous and despotic government."[2] The

---

[1] The ablest writers regard the system of international law as open to amendment, especially so far as it is based upon customs now antiquated. In this view Dr. Bluntschli has sought to formulate all recognized usages and principles in his able work, *Das Moderne Völkerrecht der civilisirten Staaten als Rechtsbuch dargestellt.* Professor Sheldon Amos believes the advance in the law of nations will be in "the influence of well-ascertained ethical principles and formal convention" as compared with customary usages. See his edition of Manning's *Commentaries on the Law of Nations* (p. 85). In this useful work the question is well put, How far "what *shall be* the practice of states" shall be dependent upon "what *has been* the practice of states" under the usages of "a less civilized period." The same powers that keep the law of the past are competent to *make* the law of the future. This they should not leave to precedent nor to accident.

[2] Wheaton, pt. II. c. 1.

eight contracting Powers to the treaty of Paris in 1814 agreed to take measures for the suppression of the slave-trade, as " a scourge which has so long desolated Africa, degraded Europe, and afflicted humanity." By the treaty of London, July 6, 1827, France, Great Britain, and Russia interfered in the affairs of Greece, as much in the interest of humanity as of the repose of Europe.[1] The pirate is treated as *hostis humani generis.*

The principle here is plain ; inhumanity tends to bar-barize the human race and so make the world unfit for the abode of man ; and the ties of brotherhood in the hu-man family oblige the strong to care for the weak, the free for the oppressed, all for each, and each for all. But this principle should not be pressed to the extreme of armed interference except in the last resort, when the wrongs inflicted on the helpless outrage humanity, and protest and remonstrance have been used in vain. That the outrages committed by the Turks in Bulgaria in May, 1876, call for such intervention on the part of Christian powers, the spontaneous outburst of public sentiment throughout Christendom, the accord of press, politicians, and people clearly shows. After every abatement is made for the rumors and exaggerations of war, and every allowance for the excesses of a panic, of religious hatred, and of an irregular soldiery, the report of the American consul-general at Constantinople is a tale of horrors that summons the Christian powers to deal resolutely with Turkey, in the name of outraged humanity and of public law. Mr. Eugene Schuyler is a gentleman of large experience in affairs, of mature judg-ment, of a candid and resolute spirit. He knows both Slavic and Oriental tongues and the habits of Slavic and Oriental peoples. Neither he nor his nation has the re-motest possible interest in the political affairs of Turkey.

---

[1] Wheaton, pt. II. c. 1.

Purely in the interest of truth and humanity he has traversed the desolated region of Bulgaria, and his report to the American minister is the result of careful personal investigation. I allow myself to quote just enough of the horrible story to make clear the summons of international duty. The first extract relates to the town of Panagurishta (Otluk-kui).

" Four hundred buildings, including the bazaar and the largest and best houses, were burned. Both churches were completely destroyed, and almost leveled to the ground. In one an old man was violated on the altar and afterwards burned alive. Two of the schools were burned, the third — looking like a private house — escaped. From the numerous statements made to me, hardly a woman in the town escaped violation and brutal treatment. The ruffians attacked children of eight and old women of eighty, sparing neither age nor sex.

"Old men had their eyes torn out and their limbs cut off, and were there left to die, unless some more charitably-disposed man gave them the final thrust. Pregnant women were ripped open and the unborn babes carried triumphantly on the points of bayonets and sabres, while little children were made to bear the dripping heads of their comrades. This scene of rapine, lust, and murder was continued for three days, when the survivors were made to bury the bodies of the dead. The perpetrators of these atrocities were chiefly regular troops commanded by Hafiz Pacha.

" While pillage reigned supreme at Kopriahtitsa and lust at Panagurishta, at Batak the Turks seemed to have no stronger passion than the thirst for blood. This village surrendered without firing a shot, after a promise of safety, to the Bashi-Bazouks, under the command of Ahmed Aga of Burutina, a chief of the rural police. Despite his promise, the few arms once surrendered, Ahmed Aga ordered the destruction of the village and the indiscriminate slaughter of the inhabitants, about a hundred young girls being reserved to satisfy the lust of the conqueror before they, too, should be killed. I saw their bones, some with the flesh still clinging to them, on the hollow on the hillside, where the dogs were gnawing them. Not a house is now standing in the midst of this lovely valley. The saw-mills — for the town had a large trade in timber and sawn boards — which lined the rapid little river are all burned, and of the 8,000 inhabitants not 2,000 are known to survive. Fully 6,000 persons, a very large proportion of them women and children, perished here, and their bones whiten the ruins or their putrid bodies infect the air. The sight of Batak is enough to verify all that has been said about the acts of the Turks in repressing the Bulgarian insurrection. And yet I saw it three months after the massacre. On every side were human bones, skulls, ribs, heads of girls still adorned with braids of long hair, and even complete skeletons still encased in clothing. Here was a house the floor of which was white with the ashes and charred bones of thirty persons burned alive there. Here was the spot where the village notable, Trandafil, was spitted on a pike and then roasted, and where he is now buried; there was a foul hole full of decomposing bodies ; here a mill-dam filled with swollen corpses ; here the school-house where two hundred women and children, who had taken refuge there, were burned alive, and here the church and churchyard where fully a thousand half-decayed forms were still to be seen, filling the inclosure in a heap several feet high, arms, feet, and heads protruding from the stones which had vainly been thrown there to hide them, and poisoning all the air."

Unfortunately for the interests of humanity, the same treaty of Paris that admitted Turkey to the concert of European public law stipulated, in its ninth article, that the *Firman* of reforms and obligations then issued by the Porte " cannot, in any case, give to the said [contracting] Powers the right to interfere, either collectively or separately, in the relations of his majesty the Sultan with his subjects, nor in the internal administration of his empire." But surely Turkey, who has broken all her pledges, could not be allowed the benefit of this provision to cover such atrocities. Back of the relation of individuals to a particular nation lies their relation to the human family, and when this is outraged, mankind have a common interest and a common right in demanding redress. No plea of "domestic relations" can avail against an interference to shield humanity from outrage. Even though the offending Power have no status in the family of nations, its victims belong to the family of man, and as such have a claim to intervention.

The case of Bulgaria should be made exemplary; whether by compelling Turkey to renounce her dominion, or to restore the desolated district, recompense the survivors, and punish the perpetrators of the outrages, would be for the Powers to determine. What concerns . this association is that whatever is done in the premises should be done not through the prejudice of race or religion, nor through the mere impulse of humanity as a sporadic feeling, but upon principles of law that shall be at once a precedent and a restraint. We must not dictate to Turkey what we would not also dictate to Spain, in the event of a political or religious persecution, or of outrages in Cuba; what we would not dictate to the United States, to England, to Russia, in the event of their violating humanity in feebler tribes. Public law must be law to the Powers that *give* it, as well as to the peoples on whom they impose it.

IV. PUBLIC PEACE AND ORDER. The right of interference "where the interests and safety of other powers are immediately affected by the internal transactions of a particular state,"[1] has perhaps been much more insisted upon, and much oftener practiced, than any other form of intervention. The interference of the Great Powers in Naples in 1820, in Spain in 1822, in Greece in 1827, in Belgium in 1830, was justified upon the ground of public peace and order. The preamble to

[1] Wheaton, pt. II. c. 1.

the treaty of France, Great Britain, and Russia for intervention in Greece sets forth that the Powers are "penetrated with the necessity of putting an end to the sanguinary contest, which, by delivering up the Greek provinces and the isles of the Archipelago to all the disorders of anarchy, produces daily fresh impediments to the commerce of the European states and gives occasion to piracies, which not only expose the subjects of the high contracting parties to considerable losses, but, besides, render necessary burdensome measures of protection and repression." There can be no question of the right, nay, the obligation of Christian nations to do all in their power to preserve the peace of the world. Neither can it be questioned that as self-preservation is the first instinct of the individual, so the right of self-preservation is the first law of nations. But the danger that threatens a nation must be direct and imminent to justify its interference in the affairs of a neighbor, and the endeavor to preserve the public peace and order should never be to the prejudice of liberty or right. It is within recent history that both these pleas have been used by arbitrary governments as a pretext for suppressing neighboring revolutions that were grounded in justice. The now exploded doctrine of "the balance of power" was liable to the same perversion. But the usage of Christian powers in Europe as to intervention for public order may serve as a guide to their duty in this direction toward non-Christian peoples.

It has been fitly said that "justice is the common concern of mankind." Much rather is it their supreme duty; and Christian nations, that themselves profess to be governed by justice, are under obligation to realize the noble saying of Savigny concerning the law of nations, that "its first and unavoidable vocation is to make the idea of right supreme and controlling [*herrschend zu machen*] in the visible world."[1] A notable example was given in the union of British and American squadrons for the police of the coast of Africa against the slave trade. To the United States belongs the honor of first effectually suppressing piracy in the Mediterranean. The time is ripe for a concerted movement in advance; for a union of Christian powers to make impossible such outbreaks of violence, rapine, and cruelty as in recent years have brought savagery into direct conflict with civilization. The horrors of Syria and Bulgaria, the bloody massacres of China and Africa, should be forestalled by the certainty of swift and decisive retribution. By their own example of arbitration, Christian powers can gain the right of control over the sanguinary passions of non-Christian peoples. Happy will it be when armaments shall serve only for the police of the world, and the one use of war shall be as a menace for restraining war!

V. RELIGION. The law and usage of Christian nations concerning intervention upon religious grounds, I do not scruple to say, call for a thorough revision to meet the conditions of the nineteenth century. In the Middle Ages the present condition of the Christian peoples of Turkey would have roused all Europe to a crusade for the expulsion of Mohammedan rule. Three centuries ago, the atrocities in Bulgaria, exceeding even those in Bohemia, would have brought Gustavus Adolphus like a whirlwind of retribution from the north. Two centuries ago Cromwell and the Great Elector would have made persecution quail by the threat of their swords. Not only is the time for such intervention gone by, but the interests both of society and of religion should forbid its return. Such intervention implies not only that the state makes religion its concern, but also makes itself the champion of some specific faith or form.

[1] *System des Römischen Rechts*, b. I. cap. ii. p. 9, 25.

Four centuries ago it was civilization itself that, under the banner of the cross, on the plains of Hungary, contested with the Turks the fate of Europe. There was then no state of Europe that was not in and of the church. The very existence of civilized society was identified with the maintenance of the Christian faith. To-day, in the nations of Europe foremost in the learning and arts of modern civilization, it is openly proclaimed in the name of science that the Christian faith is an antiquated superstition, and the church a hindrance to enlightened progress.

When, at the Reformation, Christianity itself was divided into hostile camps, church interests were still so closely bound up with the state that the civil powers almost of necessity took sides in the conflict of faiths. But these are the days of mutual toleration, of parity of confessions, of religious freedom and the rights of conscience. How is it then longer possible for a state to intervene for any particular form or faith in religion, without going back upon those very principles that have brought the state and religion to their present position of intelligent freedom ? Just now there is a cry for intervention on behalf of the oppressed Christians in Turkey. One sympathizes with the feeling that prompts that cry, — but we are after the law and philosophy of such intervention. Analyze the cry, and what does it mean ? Let us suppose that English evangelicals and German pietists join in the demand that Turkey shall cease to molest her Christian subjects. Might not Turkey reply, " You are the very parties who in your own countries invoke the civil power against the Jesuits. Now these Christians are to Turkey what you conceive the ultramontanes to be to England and Germany — an element of danger to the state." Sir Robert Phillimore gives an apt quotation from Bolingbroke, *à propos* of the queen's mediation for French Protestants in 1764. "He saw that if Queen Anne demanded too much of France for Protestants, France might retort with demands for Irish Roman Catholics."[1] Happily the day has gone by when either country would have much to fear from the recriminations of the other; but the keen-sighted Bolingbroke perceived that religious intervention could only be justified on the principle of reciprocal equality of practice. Are, then, those who demand intervention in Turkey on behalf of Christians, *as such,* prepared to meet the logical and equitable consequences of this demand? Are the Protestants of England and Germany willing that their governments should interfere to exact from Turkey the same freedom and protection for Jesuits and ultramontane propagandists which they desire for Protestant missionaries and their disciples? Are Spain and Austria ready to insist upon the same rights for Protestant and Greek Christians that they would demand for Roman Catholics? Is Russia prepared to become the champion of Roman Catholics and Protestants in Turkey? Unless all Christian powers are prepared to act in concert in demanding religious equality in Turkey without regard to faith, then intervention would resolve itself into each foreign government becoming the champion of a particular sect, and thus transferring to Turkey the religious rivalries of Christendom. Protestant missionaries in Turkey do not hesitate to say they have a better assurance of religious liberty under the Turkish government, bad as it is, than they could hope for under certain forms of Christian rule that might follow in its stead.

Again, in demanding of non-Christian peoples freedom and protection for Christians, as such, are Christian nations ready to allow Turks and Chinese, who may come to reside among them, absolute immunity in all the customs

---

[1] Bolingbroke's *Letters,* iv. 121, 171, 172, 459.

and practices sanctioned by their religions, however abhorrent to the manners and morals of Christian communities? If not, then upon what ground can the intervention of governments in matters of religion be advocated, save that each government should constitute itself the champion of some specific form of faith, thus arming faiths anew for conflict in Christendom, and making Christianity a scandal among non-Christian peoples?

In the present stage of the religious question the following principles alone seem tenable.

1. Any government may by treaty insist that its own subjects residing among another people shall have the free exercise of their religious faith and worship; being ready on its own part to guarantee the same right to subjects of the other party to the treaty.

2. Any power or powers may interfere in behalf of religion in any state by which said intervention is invoked. Sir James Mackintosh says, "Whatever a nation may lawfully defend for itself, it may defend for another people, if called upon to interpose." Hence, if a people attacked on account of their religion invoke foreign aid, it is in the discretion of the power thus invoked to grant such aid. But by parity of reasoning, no power should interfere in another country in a matter wherein it would not suffer itself to be interfered with. A nation should always be ready to give as much as it asks, and no nation should take what it would not give.

3. The Christian powers have the right to unite in demanding of all peoples the absolute freedom of religion. This, as a right of conscience, is one of the prime rights of humanity, and in insisting upon this there is no savor of zeal for any particular form of worship or of faith. The powers have a right to interfere for religious freedom as a naked human right; but to give justice and efficacy to such intervention, they must themselves furnish an irre-

9

proachable example of impartiality in religion. Any single nation may make itself the champion of universal religious freedom; and the more enlightened nations are under the same obligation to forbid tyranny over conscience as to forbid the slave-trade.

4. If religious persecution arises among any people, it is not only the right but the duty of Christian nations to interfere for its immediate suppression; but this *purely and solely upon grounds of humanity*, and with no reference whatever to the creed or worship that is assailed by violence. Christian nations should be as forward to rescue a Mohammedan, a Buddhist, a fetish-worshiper from outrage and torture, as the disciple of any form of the Christian faith.

5. Aside from these principles, *there is no right, and can be no law of intervention in the affairs of another people, on behalf of any class of religionists nor of any faith or worship as such.*

I speak here only of intervention by *governments*, which must hold themselves aloof from any partisanship in faiths. But there remains the potency of public sentiment — that moral intervention which is more efficacious than the force of arms. The sword of Cromwell is broken; the magic of his name is gone; but Milton's mighty invocation, "Avenge, O Lord, thy slaughtered saints!" still rings the knell of persecution. The words of an English statesman out of Parliament may be more quoted and more feared than the policy of ministers, the acts of Parliament, or the movements of fleets.

It remains only to sum up, in few words, the principles that should govern the whole intercourse of Christian with non-Christian peoples.

1. That intercourse should not be left to accident or caprice, but conducted upon the well-defined basis of law.

2. It should be based upon the recognition of all peoples as members of the human family, and entitled to the treatment and the benefits that belong to men as men.

3. It should recognize and express the obligation of higher and more favored peoples to protect the weak and elevate the low.

4. From first to last it should be pervaded by the spirit of justice and make justice its rule and end. No nation should ever do to a weak and inferior people what it would not dare suggest to a strong and equal people. It is a hundred years since Dr. Johnson wrote, " There is reason to expect that as the world is more enlightened, policy and morality will at last be reconciled, and that nations will learn not to do what they would not suffer." [1] Judged by that standard what progress has the world made in enlightenment since Johnson's day? We may not forget that Christian nations are responsible to mankind and to posterity for the impression they give to non-Christian peoples of Christianity and civilization. It is in the hope that something may be done to elevate the intercourse between these ever-approaching sections of the human family, that I respectfully request the association to appoint a commission to suggest rules and measures toward that end. That such a commission might issue in an international Parliament to proclaim the laws of civilized intercourse, the good auspices at Brussels, and other signs of the times, give reason to expect.

---

[1] " Thoughts on Transactions relating to the Falkland Islands.' *Works*, vol. xii. pp. 123, 124.

V.

CONCERNING TREATIES AS MATTER OF THE LAW OF NATIONS.

(Prepared for the " Association for the Reform and Codification of the Law of Nations," at its Conference in Antwerp, August, 1877.)

AMONG the sources of the law of nations some writers assign to treaties the highest value, others the lowest. Grotius, in his enumeration, puts treaties after usages, and last in the series, as matter of international law, — *ipsa natura, leges divinæ mores, et pacta,* — though this may represent the order of time and of thought, and not the gradation of value. Heffter, one of the most scientific and exact expounders of the law of nations, allows to treaties no obligation beyond the directly contracting parties, and, even in their widest agreement in fundamentals, no application beyond the attestation of a common accord in the consciousness and conception of right. " Ausserdem ist freilich jeder internationale Vertrag nur für die daran Betheiligten verbindlich, und selbst eine Vielheit von Verträgen, die denselben Grundsatz proklamiren oder zur Grundlage haben, aber unter verschiedenen Mächten geschlossen sind, kann an und für sich Anderen oder gegen Andere kein Recht zur Anwendung desselben Grundsatzes gewähren, sondern nur zur Beglaubigung eines damit einverstandenen allgemeinen Rechtsbewusstseins dienen." [1]

Much to the same effect is Bluntschli's position, that

[1] *Das Europäische Völkerrecht der Gegenwart.* Einleitung, § 9.

treaties do not in the first instance establish a rule of law, but only recognize and sanction a course of action according to legal principles which derive from other sources their binding force and authority.[1] Many other writers, among whom may be mentioned Manning and Phillimore, rate treaties chiefly " as *evidence* of the *customary* law of nations," and not as an independent and authoritative source of international law. Wheaton says, however, " an almost perpetual succession of treaties, establishing a particular rule, will go very far towards proving what the law of nations is on a disputed point."

Calvo, on the other hand, would raise treaties from the position of attesting witnesses to the matter of international law, to that of original and incontestable sources of the law itself. He looks upon treaties as not only enunciating or confirming rules and principles already recognized in practice, but as often introducing within the domain of international law the fruitful germ of new ideas, and thus preparing the way for the higher development of the comity of nations. " Le droit international a sa source principale dans les traités par lesquels les États fixent et déterminent leurs relations aussi bien en temps de guerre qu'en temps de paix. De même que la loi juridique est en général la manifestation du droit, les traités conclus entre les nations sont la manifestation la plus efficace et la plus légitime du droit international. . . . Quelquefois les traités affirment les principes du droit de gens généralement reconnus, ou établissent des règles particulières entre les contractants ; d'autres fois encore ils tranchent des questions douteuses ou apportent dans les relations internationales le germ fécond de nouvelles idées. Dans tous les cas, et quelle que soit la na-

---

[1] *Das moderne Völkerrecht der civilisirten Staaten*, b. i. § 12. Manning, *Comm. on the Law of Nations*, chap. iii. Phillimore, *Comm. upon International Law*, part I. chap. 6.

ture ou la portée de leurs stipulations, les traités sont incontestablement la source la plus importante et la plus irrécusable du droit international."[1]

Kent likewise says of treaties, "By positive engagements of this kind, a new class of rights and duties is created, which forms the conventional law of nations, and constitutes the most diffusive, and generally, the most important, branch of public jurisprudence."[2]

This seeming divergence of authorities upon the value of treaties as matter of the law of nations is owing largely to the fact that different treaties, and sometimes portions of the same treaty, are characterized by quite different features — the one sort conventional and stipulatory, the other ethical and declaratory. Now, the conventional in a treaty may be in its very nature local and limited, — like stipulations concerning territory or commerce ; but the ethical concerns public right and the welfare of mankind. Hence though the conventional can be adduced simply as evidence of usage in the law of nations, the ethical may express a principle of universal obligation and of humanizing progress. Keeping in view this distinction, we shall be able rightly to estimate the proportionate value of the matter of treaties to the law of nations, and shall find reasons for concurring in the opinion of one of our colleagues (Professor Sheldon Amos), that the ethical in treaties must eventually overbalance the prescriptive authority of custom. " Though the customary usages of states in their mutual intercourse must always be held to afford evidence of implied assent, and continue to be a main basis of the structure of the law of nations, yet there are several circumstances in modern society which seem to indicate that the region of their influence will become increasingly restricted as com-

---

[1] Calvo, *Droit International,* i. § 19.

[2] *Commentaries on International Law,* chap. 2.

pared with that of well ascertained ethical principles and formal convention."[1]

Indeed the main hope of the codification and reform of the law of nations lies in this assurance. If, as Heffter has so nicely expressed it, international law betokens and measures the common legal consciousness — that is, the consciousness of a common obligation to right — among the nations, then must we base the permanence of the law of nations upon its adaptation to the advance of human society in morals and civilization. This adaptation must be shown in practical rules which are accepted as just and useful, and in ethical principles which are felt to be right; and it can be most fitly manifested through formal conventions which are enforced by the universal sense of moral obligation. International law should represent the solidarity of nations in interests, which are material and temporal, and in responsibilities, which are human and moral.

However distant this ideal may seem, every sound discriminating statement of the essential matter of international law is a step towards its realization. What, then, at the present stage of political society, is the proper estimate of treaties as matter of the law of nations?

I. No treaty can be of perpetual obligation in and of itself. A treaty *quoad* treaty is of a friable texture; however durable in substance may be the several items that are cast in this particular mould. The instability of human nature forbids the hope that any treaty will continue to be held sacred merely because the original contracting parties regarded it as just and wise. The *morale* of a nation or a government in its corporate capacity is apt to be below the average of its better citizens; and history, unhappily, has made us too familiar with breaches

---

[1] Note to Manning's *Commentaries*, chap. 2.

of faith between high contracting powers. But aside from this, the circumstances of nations so change with time that it is sometimes impossible or morally inexpedient for one or other of the parties to a treaty to fulfill obligations entered into by foregoing generations. Quite often, too, a treaty embodies concessions or pledges extorted by war, or conditions and expedients of temporary service, which cannot be permanently wise and good. Hence it would be absurd to put all treaties upon record as integral parts of the law of nations, and of like force and value in determining international rights and obligations.

II. No treaty is in *form* obligatory upon any but the states which have subscribed it as parties to the covenant. In this respect a treaty between states resembles a contract between private individuals. But though the formal authority of a treaty is thus restricted by the nature of the instrument, its contents may furnish important matter for the public law of nations. A treaty between two or more Powers may, for the first time, formulate certain principles, — as for instance concerning extradition, arbitration, naturalization, allegiance, the amelioration of war, the rights and duties of neutrals, — which principles, upon being enunciated, commend themselves to the moral consciousness of mankind, and claim universal recognition. Thus the inner spirit of a treaty may awake a sense of obligation far beyond the limits of its formal authority. True, this wider obligation is due to the principles and not to the treaty ; yet the principles gain a certain prominence and weight by virtue of the treaty ; and when several of the more enlightened governments embody the same ethical principles in successive treaties, then such treaties serve not only to attest the usage of nations, but give to the principles a certain sanction as matter of international law. " Auch in den

Verträgen, welche zunächst nur unter *einzelnen Staaten* abgeschlossen worden sind, sind daher manche Bestimmungen zu finden, welche *ihrem Wesen nach Rechtsgesetze* und keineswegs blosse Vertragsartikel sind, welche die nothwendige Rechtsordnung, nicht die Convenienz der contrahirenden Staaten dartstellen." [1]

Sometimes when a principle or rule is introduced into a treaty for the first time, the parties to the treaty avow that this is intended as a precedent, to be thereafter incorporated into the law of nations. In such a case other Powers feel bound in their own interest to take notice of the declaration. Thus, in the treaty of Washington of 1871, the governments of the United States and of Great Britain laid down three rules by which " a neutral government is bound." At the same time they agreed to bring these rules to the notice of other maritime Powers, and to invite their assent to the same.

III. No treaty can be valid as matter of international law which contains stipulations contrary to the natural rights of man, or to the just rights and integral welfare of states not parties to the treaty ; or which would form the contracting parties into an alliance against the lawful existence and well-being of other states. Phillimore lays down the rule that " no treaty between two or more nations can affect the general principles of international law prejudicially to the interest of other nations not parties to such covenant." [2] This rule, however, in its broad terms, could hardly be maintained ; since it would create a perpetual barrier to the amendment of the law of nations. There are " general principles of international law " which have become antiquated by the progress of society, but which it might still be for " the interest " of particular nations to maintain. Or it might be

---

[1] Bluntschli, *Das moderne Völkerrecht.* Einleitung, p. 5.

[2] *Commentaries*, part I. chap. 6.

for the "interest" of certain nations to adhere to usages proscribed by modern civilization — such as the slave-trade and privateering — at which the law of nations once connived. Hence the mere fact that a treaty would "affect prejudicially" some customary material "interest of other nations not parties to the covenant," cannot make such treaty void in international law. The treaty may be the required medium for introducing a wholesome reform into the law of nations.

But it is quite otherwise when a treaty would infringe upon the essential rights of man, or the lawful existence and just liberties of states which are not parties to the covenant. No covenant of powers or numbers can make injustice valid.

It is conceivable that states might be justified in combining by treaty to coerce, subdue, and even politically to annihilate, a people so addicted to foray, pillage, piracy, the slave-trade, as to be an incorrigible pest to human society. Where it is clear beyond dispute that the pestiferous tribe or state can neither be curbed nor reformed, and its evil courses can no longer be endured, then a convention of states for the destruction of this public malefactor would violate no principle of the law of nations, and no natural right nor proper interest of mankind. But a convention of states to force upon a state, not a party to the covenant, laws and usages of their own, or some immoral or hurtful traffic, or to partition among themselves the territory and population of a foreign state because its institutions and usages were not congenial to their own — such a convention, though signed by all the Powers save its victim, could contribute nothing to the matter of international law, but, on the contrary, would be *ipso facto* void before that common consciousness of right from which the law of nations derives its highest sanction. No treaty could be valid that should have for its purpose the suppression of the natural rights of man, — such as personal liberty, the possession of property, the inviolability of home, freedom of conscience, — or that should form a league against the normal existence of an inoffensive state. No treaty could be valid in international law that should have for its object the propagation of any form of religious faith to the destruction or injury of others, as of Protestant against Catholic, Catholic against Protestant, either or both against Jewish, Mohammedan, or Pagan. The so-called " Holy Alliance " of 1815, in so far as it brought Catholic Austria, Orthodox Russia, and Protestant Prussia, to vow together that the precepts of their common Christianity should be the sole guide of their political action at home and abroad, was an advance in the international spirit of justice and fraternity. But inasmuch as the allied Powers declared the precepts of their " holy religion " to be " the sole means of consolidating human institutions and of remedying their imperfections," the treaty was dogmatically exclusive, and might be made fanatically hostile toward non-Christian peoples ; and hence can have no place nor authority as matter of the law of nations. Leaving each nation to its own internal code of morals and its own sources of right, — Moses, Confucius, Christ, Mohammed, — the law of nations admits to the benefits of its code all who are willing to abide by the rule of right as developed in the common consciousness of mankind.

IV. A treaty containing secret clauses which nullify its open professions can have no authority in the law of nations. Cases may arise — as during the Thirty Years' War in Germany — in which, for their own preservation or for some common cause, states can rightfully form a secret alliance, offensive and defensive. But when a treaty, defining the relations or intentions of the contracting Powers toward other Powers or to the general welfare, is openly promulgated to inspire public confidence, and said treaty is found afterwards to contain secret clauses which contravene its open declarations, such treaty, being of the nature of a fraudulent contract, is *ipso facto* void.

The negative view of treaties as matter of the law of nations being exhausted in the four preceding propositions, a few words will suffice to set forth their positive value.

I. Whatever stipulations in a treaty tend to facilitate the peaceful intercourse of nations, upon the assured basis of their coördinate and correlative rights, are of permanent account in the law of nations. Of this character are arrangements for the interchange of ambassadors and consuls ; for reciprocal trade ; for the mutual enjoyment and protection of the commerce of the seas.

II. All treaty stipulations for the common protection of human society against vice or crime, for the advancement of knowledge and the furtherance of mutual goodwill, belong to the law of nations. Such are treaties for the extradition of criminals other than political offenders ; international patent and copyright laws; rules of expatriation, naturalization, and the like.

III. Treaties made in the interest of humanity, and having in view the solidarity of nations in the higher civilization, are of the greatest value and promise to the law of nations. Of this sort are stipulations for suppressing piracy and the slave-trade ; for restricting the occasions of war and mitigating its severities ; for respecting the obligations of humanity in the movements of armies and upon the field of battle ; and above all, for substituting arbitration and the moral reason for the verdict of the sword.

Whatever may be the origin of treaties such as these,

how insignificant or how imposing soever the number and rank of their signataries, their subject-matter is the very stuff the law of nations is made of ; and the treaty that contains such elements and seals such promises carries within itself the authority of the moral consciousness of mankind, demanding universal assent to its principles and aims.

But the most essential point concerning treaties as matter of the law of nations is that the sanctity of the treaty shall be inviolable except by methods provided in the treaty itself or by the *consensus gentium*, for amending or abrogating the terms of the convention. Unless this point shall be assured, the making of treaties must degenerate to a solemn farce, and the law of nations to a name to conjure by in the game of diplomacy. The law of nations as a working power is strictly coextensive with the sense of honor or good faith among the nations. Burke, in his philippic against the East India Company for its breach of faith with Hyder Ali, denounced the men " who either would sign no convention, or whom no treaty and no signature could bind," as " the determined enemies of human intercourse itself."[1] And surely the reciprocal intercourse of governments and peoples would be impossible, should it come to be understood that treaties can be broken with impunity, at the will of either of the contracting powers, either with or without notice to the others. Yet there are recent indications that the civilized world is unconsciously drifting toward such a wreck of international faith. Now it is this faith " which holds the moral elements of the world together," and hence the utmost vigilance must be used against whatever tends to weaken or disparage it. The question whether the intercourse of nations shall be ruled by law or by force is simply the question between faith and mis-

[1] Speech on the Nabob of Arcot's debts.

trust. Honor and faith mean law; suspicion and fear mean force.

The comity of this association forbids the criticism of particular acts of nations which have entered into the concert of international law, nor would such criticism be pertinent to the object of this paper. But a calm statement of. the present phases of treaty obligations is indispensable to a legal estimate of the treaties themselves. One notable example will suffice to illustrate the state of the question.

The treaty of Paris of 1856, with the declaration annexed to it, was hailed as a permanent settlement not only of the Eastern Question, but of the outstanding accounts of the civilized world upon all questions involved in the conduct of war. By abolishing privateering, defining blockade, and establishing the immunity of all goods not contraband of war, the declaration sought " to settle once for all a uniform doctrine " of maritime law, and in lieu of heterogeneous and contested usages, " to introduce in this respect fixed principles into international relations." The gain to commerce and humanity from these rules was immense; and the fact that in addition to the seven Powers which signed the declaration, about forty states have given in their adherence to its principles, would seem to make that declaration a final authority in international law. The rules of the declaration are still respected, both by belligerents and by neutrals; yet the treaty of Paris is already regarded in some quarters as an antiquated document, having no vital force ! Besides the broadly human principles of the declaration, the treaty itself marked a new era in the law of nations, by incorporating an express provision for mediation as a guarantee against a renewal of war upon the so-called " Eastern Question."

" Art. 8. S'il survenait, entre la Sublime-Porte et

l'une ou plusieurs des autres puissances signataires, un dissentiment qui menaçât le maintien de leurs relations, la Sublime-Porte et chacune de ces puissances, avant de recourir à l'emploi de la force, mettront les autres parties contractantes en mesure de prévenir cette extrémité par leur action médiatrice." Cognate to this was the provision of art. 29 concerning intervention in Servia. " Aucune intervention armée ne pourra avoir lieu en Servie sans un accord préalable entre les hautes puissances contractantes." By these provisions mediation, hitherto but an occasional expedient under emergencies, was exalted to a definitive place of obligation and authority in the law of nations. Unfortunately, however, for the permanent force of the treaty of Paris in international law, the treaty itself contained two provisions that were almost sure to work its disruption.

In the first place, Turkey, which as yet had given small proof of either disposition or ability to conform to the law of nations as observed in western Europe, was admitted to an equal *status* in the concert of Europe, and the most emphatic pledges were given by the other six parties to the treaty " to respect the independence and the territorial integrity of the Ottoman Empire." " Leurs Majestés s'engagent, chacune de son côté, à respecter l'indépendance et l'intégrité territoriale de l'empire Ottoman, garantissent en commun la stricte observation de cet engagement, et considéreront, en conséquence, tout acte de nature à y porter atteinte comme une question d'intérêt général." (Art. 7.)

Not content with this sweeping obligation to cherish and defend the youngest member of the European concert, the Powers seem to have made Turkey the pet of their confidence. Though the firman of the Sultan promising to his subjects civil and administrative reforms, without distinction of race or religion, was the

ground upon which Turkey was admitted to the concert
of Europe, yet the Powers disclaimed any right of mixing themselves in affairs between the Sultan and his
subjects, and pledged themselves that, in the event of
any threatening disturbance in the principalities of the
Ottoman empire, there should be no armed intervention
without a previous agreement among the Powers, and
then only at the instance of the Sublime Porte itself.
"Il est bien entendu qu'elle ne saurait, en aucun cas,
donner le droit aux dites puissances de s'immiscer soit
collectivement, soit séparément, dans les rapports de Sa
Majesté le sultan avec ses sujets, ni dans l'administration
intérieure de son empire." (Art. 9.) " Si le repos intérieur des Principautés se trouvait menacé ou compromis,
la Sublime-Porte s'entendra avec les autres puissances
contractantes surs les mesures.à prendre pour maintenir
ou rétablir l'ordre légal.   Une intervention armée ne
pourra avoir lieu sans un accord préalable entre ces puissances." (Art. 27.)   One might have foreseen that such
wholesale guarantees to an untried order of things would
tend to precipitate the catastrophe which has now rendered them null.   But our concern is not with the un-
wisdom of certain stipulations of the treaty of Paris, but
with the preservation of that public faith upon which all
treaties must depend.

A second suicidal element in the treaty of Paris was
the neutralization of the Black Sea, which restrained
Russia and Turkey from converting its shores into a
naval arsenal.   The eleventh and thirteenth articles of
the treaty were especially humiliating to Russia, and
were dictated more by the exasperations of recent war
than by the necessities of lasting peace.   It might have
been foreseen that upon regaining the consciousness of
strength, Russia would refuse to be hampered by such
conditions.   Accordingly, in 1870, the Russian court

notified the Powers that " His imperial majesty cannot any longer hold himself bound by the stipulations of the treaty of 30th March, 1856, as far as they restrict his sovereign rights in the Black Sea." Here again our concern is not with the stipulation itself, but with the manner in which it was repudiated, as this affects the public faith. So keenly was this felt that when the signatary Powers to the treaty of Paris agreed at London in January, 1871, to condone the act of Russia, they put forth the solemn and earnest declaration that "it is an essential principle of the law of nations that no Power can release itself from the engagements of a treaty, nor modify any of its stipulations, save with the assent of the contracting parties, by means of an amicable understanding." It is at this point that we must make a resolute stand, if faith between nations is to be maintained, and treaties and laws are to have any value above the paper on which they are written. It may sometimes be allowed to sovereigns or judges in individual states to set aside a local law as obsolete, though it has not been repealed. But no such discretion can be conceded to any one of the signers of a treaty, since a treaty is a contract the parties to which must be held together by mutual faith and mutual respect.

To maintain this faith the first resource is the moral sentiment of just men. The sense of justice is becoming more and more potent in civilized communities, and in none could it be disregarded with impunity. But this sentiment, which is already a latent bond of union among civilized peoples, requires to be developed and unified in some intelligent and practical plan of action, for establishing the law of nations upon the common ground of right, and maintaining it by the inviolableness of public faith. The present perplexity of the public mind in respect to treaties and their obligations is opportune for some concerted movement in behalf of international faith. The treaty of Paris illustrates both the negative and the positive value of treaties to the law of nations ; it embodies the conventional and the ethical, the transitory and the permanent; it points out mistakes to be avoided and obligations to be fulfilled. The conservation of the Ottoman empire, the neutralization of the Black Sea, the pacification of the Provinces, were all contingent upon circumstances that could not be foreseen nor controlled ; and hence a treaty guaranteeing these things could not be of permanent force *quoad* treaty. On the other hand, this treaty contains principles of such wisdom and justice, and its declaration gives rules of such obvious utility, that the essence of the treaty will be incorporated with the law of nations, whatever may become of the form of this particular covenant. Moreover, the treaty anticipates the difficulties or failures that might occur in carrying out its stipulations, and provides for remedying these by mediation and the concert of the Powers — a principle of the highest moment to the peace of the world and the moral advance of nations. Yet this treaty has suffered a sudden and somewhat ignominious collapse. The signataries hardly seem to know whether or not it still exists ; if they would invoke it on some points, they would ignore it on others. Some accuse one party, some another, of having violated the clauses touching mediation and intervention ; some hold that the provision for mediation was practically met by the conference at Constantinople, others that it was violated by a preliminary conference from which one of the signataries was excluded. In this hopeless confusion, that which should most concern us is the collapse of international faith, without which, as we have seen, international law is but a figment. In a few months the great Powers of Europe will be summoned to form a new treaty of peace, supplanting or supplementing the treaty of Paris. But we want no more of specific treaties if they are so easily to go the way of that. What the law of nations does require is *a broad international compact of accepted principles, with adequate guarantees of international faith.*

Is this notion visionary? On the contrary it is directly practical, and might soon be realized if men would set resolutely about it. True, we can hardly look to governments to take the initiative in such a self-abnegating reform. Yet governments are quick to feel the pulse of public sentiment, and sooner or later they must give formal and authoritative expression to the spirit of the age. Notwithstanding the din of warlike preparation, the governments of Europe are heartily averse to war. The sentiments of all statesmen are expressed in these words of a distinguished general : " Happy will be the time when states shall no longer be in a position which requires them to expend the greater part of their income in protecting their existence; but when parties and peoples shall have convinced themselves that even a successful campaign costs more than it brings, since it can be no gain to purchase material good with the lives of men." That happy time will come when states shall have learned to look upon each other with mutual confidence instead of presumptive suspicion ; and this again will be when treaties which pledge their signataries to mediation or to concert of moral action shall be held inviolable, and the attempt to set aside a treaty by any other than the rational and moral methods therein described shall be followed by a declaration of war on the part of the other signataries against the offender. In other words, a rational and moral adjudication of international disputes being prescribed by a compact of the Powers, let war be reserved as the penalty for a breach of international faith. Thus honor, confidence, and peace, would grow to be the normal condition of things, and every government would gladly reduce its armament. Hence the consummation aimed at through a lasting compact of good faith, so far from being a restriction upon governments, would greatly augment their internal strength and authority. The effort after public faith in the law of nations should begin in confidence in individual governments — faith in their good intentions; and it should be conducted, not in the spirit of adverse criticism upon governments, but with cordial trust in these real bulwarks of the social order of the world.

The direct and obvious steps toward a permanent international faith are these four.

1. Since so many permanent ethical points of union among nations are to be found in treaties to which all leading Powers from time to time have given their assent, these points, omitting whatever is local and conventional, should be codified, and formulated scientifically, with a view to being laid before the governments for specific recognition. If it were in the power of this association to employ a trained jurist to devote his whole time to this preparatory work, the office would be worthy of the beneficence of a Peabody and the capacity of a John Stuart Mill. The materials for such a codification are already at hand in the valuable collections of treaties and other diplomatic documents in the English, French, and German languages.

2. Since, with the single exception of Russia, all the Powers now acting in the Concert of Nations have a parliamentary form of government, candidates for a seat in any parliament should be required to pledge themselves to consult and coöperate with the governments of other countries, in guaranteeing the mutual faith of nations, and the moral order of human society. The sense of justice, the desire of peace, and the interests of trade and

finance, are strong enough in all civilized peoples to secure this legitimate action of the parliamentary powers.
Wisdom and courage patiently applied to this line of direction will surely tell. The constitutional makers of
law in each nation will be employed to secure the sanction of law for all nations in their common interests.
The dangers of popular vehemence and of official usurpation are alike guarded against at each step of this calm
and logical procedure. The people of each country simply demand that their rulers shall be in earnest in establishing the relations of the country with all others upon
the firm basis of justice and peace. The President of the
United States has openly committed himself to such a
pacific policy.

3. A commission composed of deputies from each of
the governments shall elaborate and approve the *projet*
of a convention, to be ratified by the several Powers.
Upon the approval of its labors the commission shall expire, and there shall be nothing of the nature of a permanent tribunal above the several governments, but on
the request of any three of the signataries, the governments shall send deputies to a new commission for the
revision or expansion of the covenant, — any changes in
the same to be determined in a certain fixed and equable
ratio. This avoids the error of Kant, James Mill and
others, in attempting to constitute a permanent congress
or tribunal. It respects throughout the individuality of
each nation, and seeks to rule by faith rather than by
forms.

4. If a party to the treaty, refusing the prescribed
methods of complaint and consultation for its amendment, shall openly and defiantly violate the covenant,
said government shall be declared without the pale of nations, and subject to the penalty of war.

When faith is thus made more noble than force, the

law of nations shall have fulfilled its function — of choosing the good in each nation, that by combining the good from all, it may overwhelm the evil that lingers in any. No scheme of international law could provide effectually against misunderstanding, caprice, jealousy, rivalry, ambition, and the occasional outbreak of war. Such evils will always be incident to human organizations ; but it is believed that the scheme here presented would reduce the risk to a minimum. The point of weakness in most plans for securing the observance of the law of nations is that they propose an impracticable tribunal, with no power to enforce its decisions. But this scheme leaves the sovereignty of each nation intact ; provides how a deliberative convention of the Powers shall be summoned upon an emergency ; and recognizing that persistent violence can be repressed only by force, it reserves the military power as a police for punishing any infraction of the public peace, any violation of the public faith. In the nature of the case the scheme is tentative and imperfect ; but if it shall serve as a help or a hint to others who are studying the same problem, the writer will be more than recompensed.

VI.

ON INTERNATIONAL COPYRIGHT.

(Prepared for the Conference of the "Association for the Reform and Codification of the Law of Nations," held at Antwerp, August 28, 1877.)

THE chief moment of the question of an international law of copyright lies in the reciprocal relations of the book trade in Germany, Great Britain, and the United States, as established by law, custom, or courtesy. This section of the report will be devoted exclusively to those countries ; and will comprise : —

I. The law of copyright in each country for the protection of its native authors.

II. The laws or conventions of each country concerning foreign authors, as to reprint or original publication.

III. A digest of the principles and rules of copyright common to the three countries.

IV. Suggestions for concerted legislation for bringing the law of copyright in the three countries into accord, for the rights of authors and the interests of literature.

I. The protection of native authors.

A. GERMANY. The law of copyright in Germany has been greatly simplified by the acts of the Imperial Parliament codifying the independent laws and the mutual conventions of the several German states on copyright, as these stood prior to 1871. The constitution of the German empire (art. IV. § 6) provides for the protection of intellectual property by the empire, through appropriate legislation. This protection is assured equally to

.

authors in all parts of Germany, by the copyright law of
the North German Union of June 11, 1870. This law,
which covers literary works, artistic designs, musical and
dramatic compositions, is now incorporated into the statute book of the empire, and has the same force in Hesse,
Baden, Würtemberg, Bavaria, and Elsass-Lothringen, as
in the states of the former North German Union. The
Act of Parliament of January 11, 1876, having more
special reference to works of art, photographs, patterns
and models, completes the legislation of the German empire for the protection of original intellectual productions
within its bounds. The principal points established by
this legislation are the following : —

(1.) The original work of an author, artist, or com-
poser, is entitled to legal protection, and this upon the
ground that it is an original or independent product of
intellectual labor. It has been much disputed among
German jurists whether the right of an author in his
work is of the nature of an *Eigenthum ;* that is, a personal, exclusive, and indefeasible right in the substance
of the thing itself, — or is simply a *Vermögensrecht,* —
which may be created or at least determined by law, in
which the personality of the author is a less vital element
than the mere legal notion of property. An intellectual
Eigenthum inheres in one, a material *Vermögen* belongs
to him. However, the distinction is more one of words
than of fact. Singularly enough the phraseology of the
German constitution recognizes the author's right in the
creations of his intellect as an *Eigenthum,* while the Acts
of Parliament for the protection of this right treat it
rather as a *Vermögen.* Among the prerogatives of the
imperial government the constitution specifies (art. IV.
§ 6), " *der Schutz des geistigen Eigenthums* " — the protection of intellectual *Eigenthum.* But the Act of June
11, 1870 is entitled, " Gesetz betreffend das *Urheberrecht*

an Schriftwerken," etc.; and this term *Urheberrecht* —
the right of the creator, originator, author — is substituted for *Eigenthum* through the entire act. The same
is true of the Act of Parliament of January 11, 1876.
The substitution of this "right of the producer" for the
self-existent intellectual proprietorship recognized by the
constitution, was apparently made for a purpose; and in
an action for violation of copyright, no doubt the courts
would follow the phraseology of the laws rather than that
of the constitution.

In either case, however, it is clearly recognized that
the author has a right of property in his work as his own
intellectual labor. The property does not lie merely in
the material form in which his work appears, but in the
thought and labor which that form embodies. The first
article of the law of June 11, 1870, declares that the right
to multiply a manuscript by mechanical means belongs
exclusively to the author of the same. And the law provides also, in principle, that the right of the author passes
over to his heirs, but may be transferred to others by
contract or other disposition.

(2.) Any and every mechanical reproduction of a
work, in whole or in part, — even by writing in lieu of
printing, — without consent of the author, is forbidden.
The author alone has the right to give his work to the
public, and by the same right can withhold, alter, control it.

(3.) Under certain limitations as to time, notification,
etc., the author of an original work, or the translator of
a work from a dead language into a living tongue, is
protected against the publication of a translation of his
work, in the same manner as if this were a reprint of the
work itself.

(4.) The protection of the author against the reprinting of his work without his consent is guaranteed during

his lifetime and for thirty years after his death. The prohibition of the publication of translations holds good for five years after the first appearance of the original work, or of a translation sanctioned by the author himself.

These principles, covering the right of property in intellectual productions, the protection of that right against infringement, and the duration of copyright, fairly represent the German law, so far as this concerns native authors. The details must be looked for in the Acts of Parliament already cited.[1]

B. GREAT BRITAIN.

(1.) The Act of Parliament of July 1, 1842, expressly declares " that all copyright shall be deemed personal property, and shall be transmissible by bequest, or, in case of intestacy, shall be subject to the same law of distribution as other personal property, and in Scotland shall be deemed to be personal and movable estate." (5 and 6 Vict. c. 45, § 25.) Here the fact of property in the original creations of intellect is fully recognized, and the legal denomination of such property is distinctly fixed. The English law of copyright is uniform throughout the " British Dominions," which term includes " all parts of the United Kingdom of Great Britain and Ireland, the islands of Jersey and Guernsey, all parts of the East and West Indies, and all the colonies, settlements, and possessions of the crown which now are or hereafter may be acquired."

(2.) The law of Great Britain, like that of Germany,

---

[1] See O. Dambach, *Die Gesetzgebung des norddeutschen Bundes, betreffend das Urheberrecht an Schriftwerken, Abbildungen,* etc. 1871.

W. Endemann, *Das Gesetz betreffend das Urheberrecht an Schriftwerken,* etc. 1871.

R. Klostermann, *Das Urheberrecht an Schrift-und Kunstwerken,* etc. 1876.

makes the copyright cover every part or division of a work equally with the work as a whole; and treats the multiplication in any form for circulation of copies of any work, in whole or in part, without the consent of the holder of the copyright, as an infringement of said right.

(3.) The English law requires that "the proprietorship in the copyright of books, and assignments thereof, and in dramatic and musical pieces, whether in manuscript or otherwise, and licenses affecting such copyright, shall be registered in an official book kept for this purpose at the hall of the stationers' company."

(4.) The English law provides that the copyright in a book shall endure for a period of not less than forty-two years; that is to say, for the natural life of the author and for a further time of seven years from the date of his death; "provided always, that if the said term of seven years shall expire before the end of forty-two years from the first publication of such book, the copyright shall in that case endure for such period of forty-two years."

(5.) The English law has a peculiar provision for compulsory publication. The statutes do not place copyright upon abstract grounds of personal and indefeasible right in the author. Before the statute of Queen Anne it was held at common law that an author had a right of property in his works in perpetuity; but the statutes relating to copyright were enacted avowedly with a view " to afford greater encouragement to the production of literary works of lasting benefit to the world." (See 5 and 6 Vict. c. 45, § 1, and the titles of preceding acts cited therein.) Hence the statutes of copyright, while ostensibly conferring upon the author a privilege by way of a motive to labor for the public benefit, practically curtailed a right by virtue of which he had been master of his own time, talents, and productions.

In this view of securing to the world the benefit of intellectual labor, the law of 1842 enacts " that it shall be lawful for the judicial committee of her majesty's privy council, on complaint made to them that the proprietor of the copyright in any book, after the death of its author, has refused to republish or to allow the republication of the same, and that by reason of such refusal such book may be withheld from the public, to grant a license to such complainant to publish such book, in such manner and subject to such conditions as they may think fit, and that it shall be lawful for such complainant to publish such book according to such license." (5 and 6 Vict. c. 45, § 5.) This provision is obviously liable to abuse. If, for example, an author had published a book which his heirs were willing to let die as unworthy of his name or injurious to his reputation or the reputation of others, or to the public morals, or because of a change in the author's views and beliefs, — as from the Protestant to the Roman Catholic faith and *vice versa,* — then some huckstering publisher, trading upon the supposed popularity of the book, might obtain a license to violate the most sacred feelings of a family, and the presumable wishes of the deceased author himself. The very excellence of the purpose of this provision calls for uncommon care in its application.

(6.) The English law guards rigorously against the importation into the British dominions of foreign reprints, not authorized by the holder of the copyright, of any work first published under copyright in any part of the British dominions.

These several specifications contain what is most important to the purpose of this report, in the English law of copyright in behalf of native authors.

C. THE UNITED STATES. The provisions of the law of copyright in the United States may be concisely stated as follows : —

(1.) The constitution of the United States declares (art. I. sec. 8, § 8) that the "Congress shall have power to promote the progress of science and useful arts, by securing, for limited times, to authors and inventors the exclusive right to their respective writings and discoveries." Here the English notion of benefit to mankind is avowedly put forward as a motive for securing the rights of authors. Before the Revolution, an American author in either of the colonies would have had his rights under the common law as regulated and limited by the statutes of Parliament.

Under the confederation particular states enacted laws of copyright. Connecticut and Virginia by preamble declared that "it is perfectly agreeable to the principles of natural justice and equity that every author should be secured in receiving the profits that may arise from the sale of his works;" and Massachusetts went so far as to say that such security to authors of the fruits of their study and industry "is one of the natural rights of all men, there being no property more peculiarly a man's own than that which is produced by the labor of his mind."

The law of the United States, as approved July 8, 1870, under the revision of the statutes, does not define the nature of the right secured to authors, other than that it makes copyright an assignable property, and holds a manuscript to be inviolable. It secures to the author, his executors, administrators, or assigns, the sole liberty of printing, reprinting, publishing his works.

(2.) The copyright is valid for the term of twenty-eight years, with the privilege of renewal for the further term of fourteen years. These two terms are together equal to the English minimum of forty-two years.

II. Laws or conventions concerning foreign authors, as to reprinting or original publication.

A. GERMANY.

(1.) Before the constitution of the German empire, separate states of Germany had entered into conventions with foreign states for the reciprocal protection of the rights of authors. Such a convention was concluded between Prussia and Great Britain May 13, 1846, and between Prussia and France August 2, 1862; several of the minor states of Germany shared in the engagements of these treaties. The general principle of these conventions is that of exact reciprocity. For example: an English author shall be admitted to the same protection in Germany which the laws secure to a German author, it being stipulated that a German author shall in turn receive in England the same protection with a British subject. The single qualification is, that the foreign author shall not enjoy a longer term of copyright than is accorded to him in his native country. Thus the copyright of an English book would be respected in Germany for the term of seven years after the death of the author, as fixed by English law, and not for thirty years after his decease, as fixed by German law.

(2.) Since the constitution of the empire, the guarantee of copyright to foreigners has been lifted out of the sphere of literary conventions into that of parliamentary legislation. The conventions of the German states with France were dissolved by the war of 1870, but by the treaty of peace of May 10, 1871 (art. 11), and the supplementary convention of December 11, 1871 (art. 18), an international copyright was arranged between the German empire and France upon the basis of the former conventions.

The statute of June 11, 1870 closes with the general provision (§ 61) that the works of a foreign author shall be under the protection of this law of copyright if issued by a publisher who has his business establishment within the bounds of the German empire. This article, while it secures to the foreign author a reasonable protection, makes the profits of the manufacture and publication of his works inure to the benefit of German industry. The protection guaranteed to foreign authors through German publishers is absolute and universal, without respect to treaties of reciprocity.

B. GREAT BRITAIN.

(1.) During the present reign the Parliament of Great Britain has ratified conventions with several countries for an international copyright (e. g. with Prussia in 1848, and with France in 1852) ; and by a declaration of principles in the form of an act, by which the way is opened for similar conventions with all existing states.

The Act of July 31, 1838 (1 and 2 Vict. c. 59), entitled " An act for securing to authors, in certain cases, the benefit of international copyright," secured "protection within her majesty's dominions to the authors of books first published in foreign countries, and their assigns, in cases where protection shall be afforded in such foreign countries to the authors of books first published in her majesty's dominions, and their assigns." The term for such copyright was to be fixed by an order in council, but must not exceed the term for which British authors are secured by law. This act was repealed by the Act of May 10, 1844 (7 and 8 Vict. c. 12), and the authorization of copyright to works first published in foreign countries was renewed, with a more extended application to works of art, musical and dramatical compositions, etc. By this act it was provided, " That no such order in council shall have any effect unless it shall be therein stated, as the ground for issuing the same, that due protection has been secured by the foreign power so named in such order in council, for the benefit of parties interested in works first published in the dominions of her majesty similar to those compromised in such order."

The Act of May 28, 1852 (15 Vict. c. 12), " to enable her majesty to carry into effect a convention with France on the subject of copyright," protects the foreign author for a term of five years against unauthorized translations.

This legislation of Great Britain fixes the principle that wherever a convention of literary reciprocity exists between Great Britain and a foreign power, the subject of such power, or the author who first publishes his works within the dominion of such power, shall enjoy in Great Britain the privilege of copyright " for a period equal to the term of copyright which authors, inventors, designers, engravers, and makers of the like works respectively first published in the United Kingdom are by law entitled to."

(2.) Aside from conventions and legislation, the decision of the Court of Appeal in the case of Low v. Routledge appears to settle the point, that an alien friend can avail himself of the British law of copyright, by taking up his residence in any part of the British dominions for a brief period covering the actual date of the publication of his work either there or in any other part of the British dominions ; and by complying with certain formalities as to registration, etc. The legislative and judicial action of Great Britain for the past forty years has greatly favored international copyright.

C. THE UNITED STATES.

(1.) The law of copyright in the United States protects the author equally if he is a citizen of the United States, or simply " resident therein." Hence any person of foreign birth, without being naturalized, may obtain a copyright for his works in the United States, in the same way and upon the same terms with a native author, provided he is resident in the country.

(2.) The United States have no provision, either by convention or by law, for securing copyright to an alien who is non-resident.

(3.) By the courtesy of leading American publishers toward each other, in the best interest of the book-trade, and through their spontaneous sense of what is just and honorable toward authors, any foreign author of repute is enabled to make in advance exclusive arrangements with an American publisher, by which he receives the same royalty that he would receive if he were a citizen of the United States. Some English authors have even felt that this law of courtesy yielded them a larger return than they should have had under an international law of copyright.

III. Principles and rules of copyright common to the three countries now under review.

(1.) Germany, Great Britain, and the United States agree in according to the author a *right of property* in his works, which, for a specified term, is exclusive and inviolable.

(2.) In each of these countries this right endures for not less than thirty years, — this being the term fixed in Germany for the continuance of the copyright in a book after the death of the author, — an event which might occur in the very year of publication. In Great Britain the copyright in a book can in no case become void within a period of less than forty-two years; in the United States it may be extended to that period, by renewal.

(3.) In Germany and in Great Britain very fair provisions exist for securing a copyright to alien authors : in the United States such provisions exist by law for aliens resident in the country ; for others they exist only by the honor and courtesy of American publishers.

IV. Suggestions for bringing into accord the laws of copyright in Germany, Great Britain, and the United States for the mutual advantage of alien authors.

Since in each of these countries the principle of copyright is established by legislation and by judicial deci-

11

sions, it would be superfluous here to argue the right of property in intellectual labor. There is indeed a school of political economists who oppose copyright as a form of monopoly, prejudicial to the interests of society as a whole. An American writer of this school goes so far as to say, " the word *property* is only applicable to material substances ; " though he contradicts this materialistic notion of property when he adds, " a person's ideas or thoughts are his intellectual property only so long as they remain unuttered and unknown to others." But the property which he calls " intellectual " does not lie in the intellect, which is the creative power, but in the concrete product of intellectual power and activity — *embodied thought.* Hence the right of property in intellectual products cannot be extinguished by the self-same act which creates the property ; namely, the clothing such products with an outward form, whether the ideas be embodied in a book or in a machine of iron.

Dr. Noah Webster has defined this right with his accustomed clearness. " The labor of inventing, making, or producing anything constitutes one of the highest and most indefeasible titles to property. No right or title to a thing can be so perfect as that which is created by a man's own labor and invention. The exclusive right of a man to his literary productions, and to the use of them for his own profit, is entire and perfect, since the faculties employed and labor bestowed are entirely and perfectly his own." There is no analogy whatever between copyright and a protective tariff. Free trade, while it enables the consumer to choose in the markets of the world the cheapest or the best, at the same time secures to the producer a return for his labor in proportion to the extent of the market. Hence free trade stimulates production by opening to the producer the widest possible area for the sale of his products, and enabling him by large sales at small profits to realize more than by the limited sales under the factitious prices of a protective tariff. Thus the community is benefited with a corresponding benefit to the producer. Moreover, under the freest laws of trade trade-marks are respected and protected by law. But free trade in books would interdict production; since the abolition of copyright would take away that powerful incentive to production which is given in the prospect of a fair return for the outlay of time and labor. However cheaply the manufacturer of material products may put his goods upon the market, he still reserves to himself a margin of profit; and then the freer the sales the better he is remunerated. If, through excess of competition or of production, the selling price falls below the cost, he stops manufacturing and waits for better times. But if copyright is denied, the mind, which is the true manufacturer, receives no return. The publisher, or rival publishers, may increase their receipts by wide, cheap sales in an open market. But there remains no pecuniary incentive to authorship, and by and by the whole community must suffer through the wrong done to authors. This method of multiplying cheap books will end in few books being made.

To abolish copyright would be to deny to the highest and most beneficial form of labor, the labor of the brain, that which is conceded as a natural right to the commonest labor of the hand, — a share in the profits of its own time and toil. But the principle of copyright, founded in natural justice, is not likely to be set aside by the cry of monopoly. And besides, the sense of justice is in civilized communities too far advanced to permit a man to be deprived of any natural right simply because he is a foreigner. The laws, conventions, and legal decisions cited above show that in neither of the three countries under consideration is there any prejudice against remu-

nerating an author of foreign birth; since in one form or
another an alien friend resident in Germany, Great Britain, or the United States, can secure for his works first
published within the country the same protection of
copyright which is accorded to a native author. Hence
a formal declaration of international copyright between
these three countries is reduced to a question of expediency. The chief hindrances to such an arrangement
have arisen in the United States; and, setting aside the
limited school of political economists above referred to,
the objections raised to an international copyright are in
part selfish, in part sentimental. For many years there
has existed in the United States an " International Copyright Association," representing the most eminent names
in American literature; and it is believed that American
authors, with the cosmopolitan spirit that should mark
the guild of letters, almost without exception desire that
the works of foreign authors should enjoy in the United
States the same privileges and protection which are accorded to their own. Partly by the instrumentality of
this association, and partly through other agencies, the
subject of international copyright has been five times introduced into the Congress of the United States in the
last forty years, though without any practical result.
For some time past the association has suspended its
activity, and its secretary writes in a tone of discourage-
ment: " The present phase of the subject in this country is, as it was always, and will be: authors in favor of
the law; publishers (almost universally) opposed to it;
the public indifferent." So far as publishers are concerned this statement appears too sweeping. The comprehensive article by Mr. C. E. Appleton, in the " Fortnightly Review " for February, 1877, on " American
Efforts after International Copyright " gives several in-
stances of the activity of leading publishers in the United

States in behalf of such a measure. The leading opponents of international copyright, as Mr. Appleton clearly shows, are : —

(1.) The smaller publishers and the booksellers who are not publishers. These fancy that an international copyright would play into the hands of a few leading firms having special facilities of communication with the foreign market, and would secure to them a monopoly in the works of foreign authors. The case of such objectors is not made out. But if it were, the plea is one of self-interest based upon injustice. Why should the reading public support the bookseller by cheating the author ? As the general public would not, for the sake of cheapness, knowingly encourage an importer in defrauding the revenue, neither would they knowingly encourage a publisher in defrauding an author. They require simply to understand the case in order to right it.

(2.) But here comes in the second class of objectors, who argue that an international copyright would restrict the diffusion of knowledge, and so far prejudice the well-being of mankind. But this objection, if of any force, lies equally against all copyright, and not merely against the extension of copyright to foreign authors. Now, it has been shown above that to abolish copyright would be to restrict production, and consequently to deprive society of many of the best fruits of mental labor. In every other sort of manufacture the cost of production is covered in the price of the article. The producer, so to speak, is represented in and recompensed by, the thing produced. But in the book, as material, it is the publisher and not the author who is so represented and recompensed. The author's right calls for a separate and distinct recognition. No man who would not steal a book from the shelves of a library or a publisher would knowingly rob the author of the product of his labor.

The small percentage allowed to authors the reading public would not grudge in the cost of books.

Moreover, a publisher whose editions were covered by copyright would have an inducement to extend his sales by various and cheap editions, so that in the end the diffusion of knowledge and the facility of acquiring knowledge would be greatly increased by the proper nurture of authorship. And in no event can philanthropy to the general be rooted in injustice to the individual. Here, as before, to understand the case is to right it. Where governments would lead in such an enlightened step, public sentiment would assuredly follow.

Since Germany, Great Britain, and the United States are so far agreed in the fundamental principles of copyright, a very simple act by the Parliament of each country, declaring that *all rights of property in original works secured by law to its own citizens shall be in like manner secured to the citizens of every other country the laws of which secure reciprocal rights to alien authors*, would substantially settle the whole question. Indeed, since Germany and Great Britain are virtually upon this ground, such an act by the Congress of the United States would determine a copyright in common between these Powers. There is reason to believe that a judicious presentation of the case would secure the recommendation of such a measure to Congress by the President in his annual message. The settlement of the question by such a declarative act of the several governments, upon the sole condition of reciprocity, would be fair and final. Yet, in order to conciliate jealous and rival interests, it might be found expedient at the first to concede the point established in German law, and contended for by some American publishers, that as a condition of copyright to a foreign author his book must be printed in the country granting such copyright. Also, as a means of encouraging competition and thereby promoting cheapness, and extent of circulation, it might be open to any one to reprint a foreign work, upon binding himself to pay the author ten per cent. upon the retail price of all copies of such reprint that shall be sold. The duration of copyright to foreigners should be fixed at the same time for all countries. But the details of the law could be soon adjusted, if there were a concerted movement to press the law itself. To give expression to the ripened feeling on this subject, this association might appropriately memorialize the several governments to appoint each an equal number of members of a joint commission to determine and report a reciprocal law of international copyright, said law to take effect directly upon being enacted by each of the consulting Powers.

VII.

THE RIGHT OF WAR INDEMNITY.

(Remarks at the Conference of the "Association for the Reform and Codification of the Law of Nations," held at Frankfort on the Main, August 20th, 1878.)

THE author proposed the following Resolution : — Resolved, *That a committee be appointed to report at the next annual conference upon the question, By what right, and under what conditions, may an aggressive Power claim a war indemnity in the event of conquest?* And he sustained this resolution by the following considerations.

The cost of modern warfare has given rise to enormous exactions by the conquering Power, under the name of *Indemnity.* In justification of these exactions it is alleged, (1) That the right of the conqueror to subsist his army from territory actually conquered, implies the right to reimburse himself for all the expenses of the war, by levying a contribution from the nation which has surrendered to his arms ; (2) That by crippling the resources of the vanquished nation, and causing it to feel as severely as possible the costs and penalties of war, the conqueror secures a guarantee of peace which is better than the pledges of a treaty.

These pleas have more foundation in usage than in principle or right. They make no account of the causes or the motives of war; no discrimination between just and unjust wars, — wars of justifiable invasion or of necessary defense, and wars of sheer conquest and spoliation. But mere usage can no longer be held to justify in war any act or procedure which is tainted with injustice. In this all authorities agree. The proverb that war silences law is reversed, and law now rules war, and aims to suppress it. Says Heffter: " The property of a nation at war lying within the territory of the enemy, by the old law of nations, was subjected like other booty to the right of appropriation by seizure. But this position the modern law of nations *cannot* allow." Modern states indeed attempt to reach the same end under the names " reprisal " and " confiscation ; " but Heffter does not hesitate to say that "this so-called confiscation in fact shields common robbery." [1] As to pecuniary exactions by an invading power within the territory of the enemy, Bluntschli says : [2] " In earlier warfare, the exaction of contributions in money was wont to be justified by the consideration that by paying such a contribution cities and communities were redeemed from the fear of pillage or disturbance. But the laws of civilized warfare no longer recognize a right of loot or of wanton disturbance. Hence there exists no warrant for a ransom from such a right . . . The sense of justice in the Europe of to-day can no longer be reconciled with such remains of an old barbarian mode of warfare."

Now, is not the modern claim of war indemnity a heritage from the old barbarian right of conquest and spoliation ? Where, at least, in the law of nations, shall we find a justification of the *indiscriminate* levying of indemnity by a conqueror, in face of the humane and honorable restrictions imposed upon war in recent times ?

---

[1] Dr. August Wilhelm Heffter, *Das Europäische Völkerrecht der Gegenwart,* b. ii. § 140.

[2] Dr. J. C. Bluntschli, *Das moderne Völkerrecht der civilisirten Staaten,* b. viii. § 654.

The practice alone cannot justify the act. And the principle of indemnity being allowed, as a penalty for wantonly aggressive war and a restraint upon the lust of conquest, what shall hinder the prospect of an indemnification to be reckoned by *milliards*, from acting as an incentive to war? There is danger that the materialism of the times will devise a substitute for wars of spoliation under cover of indemnity, and that war shall become a commercial speculation on the part of greater states to maintain their armies at the cost of their weaker neighbors. This mercenary use of war was pushed to an extreme by Napoleon. Conquest opened the door to cupidity, and cupidity incited to further conquest. The exactions of Napoleon from the several states of Italy, from the Netherlands, from Würtemberg, Baden, Swabia, Franconia, Bavaria, Saxony, Prussia, Austria, Portugal, — exactions in the name of the French republic and of his own sovereignty, — in the twelve years from 1796 to 1808, reached to many milliards of francs. These "indemnities" read in history like the ransoms extorted by a chief of banditti. "Dearly," says Calvo, "has France expiated these abusive exactions " (first by the indemnity of seven hundred million francs in 1815, and next by five milliards in 1871). "One can understand how up to a certain point a victorious power may claim to indemnify itself from a vanquished foe for the expenses which the war has brought, at least when that Power did not provoke the war. But it is quite another thing to put forth demands out of all proportion to any reasonable calculation : demands fitted rather to ruin the country upon which they are imposed, and to prolong the evils of war after the actual cessation of hostilities. Is there not here a place for a moderating and conciliatory intervention ? Why should not such a liquidation of accounts be submitted to a disinterested, equitable, impartial arbitration?"[1]

The conditions of indemnity are not determined by clear, precise, equitable rules of international law. The committee which I propose may be able to suggest some feasible solution of a question which, in its newer aspects, is either ignored by writers on the law of nations, or is treated with too much of political partisanship. My resolution is limited to a single point — the right of an *aggressive* Power to indemnity in the event of conquest. This point will be made clear by a recent example. In 1870, France declared war against Prussia, and the war involved the whole of Germany. Germany being victorious, exacted from France an enormous indemnity. But though the form and amount of the indemnity caused much discussion, I am not aware that a single French publicist protested against the claim of indemnity, it being conceded that the French emperor had declared the war.

In 1877, Russia made war on Turkey. Whatever the offenses of Turkey, she had given no special provocation to Russia as an individual power. Yet Russia having conquered Turkey was allowed by the Congress of Berlin to recompense herself with a large accession of territory in Asia, including a coveted port which Russia had not captured, and whose inhabitants protested against her sovereignty. Russia has demanded also an enormous indemnity in money, sufficient to cripple the resources of Turkey for fifty years to come. This demand was shoved aside by the congress, but may hereafter be made a pretext for war.

One sees at a glance an important difference between

[1] M. Charles Calvo. *Le Droit Internationale.* T. ii. liv. 6, § 910. Calvo gives important statistics of indemnity as tempting the greed of conquerors.

the cases of Germany and Russia. If an aggressive
Power is allowed to indemnify itself equally with a
Power which had repelled and conquered its invader,
then indemnity, instead of being a restraint upon war,
may be an incentive to war. Such an anomaly cannot
fairly represent the law of nations. If it does, then the
law calls loudly for reform.

As a further argument for such a committee as I propose, I would suggest the following theses : —

1. Wars of mere conquest, ambition, or revenge, are no
longer sanctioned by the law of nations.

2. Aggressive war can be justified only in the following cases : —

(*a*.) To recover territory seized and appropriated by
an enemy.

(*b*.) To suppress the turbulence of a neighbor who is
constantly disturbing the peace of the frontier, and whom
no treaty can bind.

(*c*.) To deliver an oppressed people or race invoking
succor, and having a just claim for such intervention.

3. It shall not be permitted to convert a justifiable
war of invasion or intervention into such a war of conquest as would be forbidden *ab initio* by the law of nations, nor, under cover of indemnity, to reap the fruits of
unlawful spoliation.

4. To guard against cruel and crushing exactions, and
the cupidity of conquest, whenever the indemnity assessed
by the conqueror is deemed excessive by the conquered
party, said indemnity should be submitted to the arbitration of three neutral and impartial powers, whose award
shall be final.

Indemnity as now exacted is extortion by force. It
is a claim derived from conquest. But, as Halleck has
pointed out, " conquest expresses, not a *right*, but a *fact*,
from which rights are derived. The rights of conquest

are derived from *force* alone. They begin with possession, and end with the loss of possession."[1] Rights so capricious in their origin are especially liable to abuse in their application. Now, it is an important office of the law of nations to mitigate the evils of war, to restrain its excesses, and to reduce the occasions for recourse to arms. If the levying of indemnity by an aggressive power has in it any element of injustice or unreason, the exposure of this must lead to its abolition. The sentiment of justice among civilized nations is quick to rally around any authority which is competent to assert the right; and events are sometimes quick to ratify a principle of right or a measure of reform. Of this the Congress of Berlin is a notable example. It has been a standing objection to schemes of arbitration that they propose an impracticable tribunal with no power to enforce its decisions. In my paper "Concerning Treaties," submitted to this association at Antwerp, I showed that to obviate this objection, "treaties which pledge their signataries to mediation or to concert of moral action should be held inviolable; and the attempt to set aside such a treaty by any other than the rational and moral methods therein prescribed should be followed by a threat of war on the part of the other signataries against the offender." Thus arbitration would be backed by power.

Now the Paris treaty of 1856 provides for mediation and advises arbitration; and the London Convention of 1871 declared that " it is an essential principle of the law of nations that no power can release itself from the engagements of a treaty, nor modify any of its stipulations, save with the assent of the contracting parties, by means of an amicable understanding." The treaty of San Stefano would have annulled the treaty of Paris without the assent of the contracting parties; but the British govern-

[1] Halleck's *International Law*, chap. xxxiii. § 23.

ment refused to take part in a congress upon the Eastern Question except upon the basis of the treaty of 1856, and showed a determination to maintain the faith of treaties by force of arms. This tested my doctrine of "arbitration backed by power." To that act we owe it that the Congress of Berlin was convened " *conformably to* the stipulations of the treaty of Paris ; " and that treaty, and the treaty of London of March 13, 1871, " are maintained in all such of their provisions as are not abrogated or modified by the treaty of Berlin." Thus the great Powers of Europe are solemnly pledged to the continuity of the law of nations, and to the duty of an amicable consultation under any and every treaty which is their joint work, and requires their joint sanction to modify its stipulations. The Congress of Berlin began with this great triumph of international law, and ended with this great hope for future peace by arbitration. In like manner we may look to see the question of indemnity, and other vexed questions arising out of war, and indeed the question of war itself, determined before a high tribunal of the Powers, whose sword is sheathed at its side.

VIII.

SHALL ENGLAND SIDE WITH RUSSIA.

(A letter to the "Committee of the Peace Society," London, December 22, 1876.)

HONORED AND DEAR FRIENDS, — As one of the "Friends" to whom your address of November 24, 1876, was kindly sent, I desire to express my cordial approval of that able and timely paper, and to pledge my personal devotion to its principles and aims. Every sentiment of the address, and even every word of its clear and forcible utterances, commends itself to my judgment and to my moral feelings. Were I an Englishman, I should lose no opportunity for echoing and enforcing the exhortation that "on no pretext ought this Christian nation again to enter into partnership for purposes of war with Mohammedan fanaticism;" that "never again should English blood and treasure be poured forth to uphold the most execrable system of government under the sun," — " to perpetuate and consolidate the Turkish dominion in Europe, and to rivet the yoke of Mohammedan oppression on the necks of the groaning millions of the Christian subjects of the Porte."

But were I an Englishman I should also go farther, and say what England most needs to utter, and Europe needs to hear. I should say, " As an Englishman I hate oppression, and above all, tyranny over conscience and thought. I hate this because it is oppression, and therefore hate it under every name and form — Mohammedan or Christian, Turk, Servian, or Russian. I denounce

Turkey for her breach of faith, her intolerance and cruelty; and for the same reasons I denounce Russia also; and I refuse to be the ally of either in a war, which, whoever may triumph, can end only in prolonging the rule of bigotry and absolutism. Turkey and Russia were both signataries to the treaty of Paris of 1856; they both are treating its provisions with contempt and defiance; and therefore, in the interest of peace, honor, and humanity, England should exercise her prerogative for the rebuke and restraint of both." The statesman who should have the breadth and courage to take this position would draw around him the fusing elements of popular feeling, would shape these into one solid national sentiment, and lead a new and nobler departure for the cause of peace and humanity. It is because I recognize in your honored secretary the qualities for such a leadership, and in your own body the moral force to win such a position and hold it, that I venture to express my surprise and regret at finding in your address rebuke and condemnation for but *one* of the actual or intending belligerents in the East, and my hope that the Peace Society will yet seize this great opportunity for rising above the passing questions of English *policy*, and proclaiming the *principles* that England should assert and maintain for the peace and order of Europe.

If the position of England on the Eastern Question were merely a matter of English policy, of course I, as a stranger, would not presume to meddle with it. But I have no apology to offer for speaking on behalf of religious liberty at a crisis when this is outraged on one side and threatened on the other. I should be false to my own English ancestry if I did not put the rights of conscience above all other rights of the individual, and did not contend for these rights in others as if they were my own. Those rights so persistently outraged in Turkey

by Mohammedan fanaticism are now threatened with
the bigotry of the Greek Church and the intolerance of
the Russian ecclesiastical code, if Russia shall be allowed
to occupy Turkish territory or to direct the administration of Turkish provinces. If, for the cause of religious
liberty and the interests of peace and humanity, England, at all hazards, must free herself of complicity with
the perfidy and intolerance of the Turkish government,
how can she ally herself with the military antagonist of
Turkey, whose perfidy in respect of the treaty of Paris is
no less patent, and whose intolerance is no less stringent
and hardly less cruel? Or how can England give way
to Russian ascendency in Turkey without first demanding of Russia the same guarantees for religious liberty
which Russia professes to demand of the government of
the Porte?

The indignation and abhorrence so justly roused
against Turkey in England are due to two causes: the
perfidy of Turkey toward the Powers which had admitted her to the *concert* of Europe, and her intolerance
and inhumanity toward her Christian subjects. In view
of the Hatti' Humaïoun of February, 1856, in which the
Sublime Porte pledged to its Christian subjects certain
privileges and immunities, religious and political, the
congress of Paris, in March, 1856, admitted Turkey to
an equal *status* among the contracting Powers; at the
same time declaring [art. IX.] : " It is clearly understood
that it [the Hatti' Humaïoun] cannot, in any case, give
to the said Powers the right to interfere, either collectively or separately, in the relations of his majesty the
Sultan with his subjects, nor in the internal administration of his empire." One cannot but marvel now at the
easy confidence of the Powers in binding themselves by
such a clause. But Turkey cannot be allowed to screen
herself behind it, for she has deliberately and shamefully

12

violated her own pledges upon which this declaration
was based. The same may be said of the engagement of
the Powers [art. VII.], " to respect the independence
and the territorial integrity of the Ottoman empire."
By her own perfidy Turkey has forfeited all claim to the
joint protection pledged in that article. But does the violation of faith by Turkey warrant each and every of the
signing Powers in repudiating for *itself* the treaty of
Paris as null and void ? By no means. By article VII.
the Powers " guarantee *in common* the strict observance
of that engagement; and will, in consequence, consider any
act tending to its violation as a question of general interest." Article VIII. provides : " If there should arise between the Sublime Porte and one or more of the other
signing Powers any misunderstanding which might endan-
ger the maintenance of their relations, the Sublime Porte
and each of such Powers, before having recourse to the use
of force, shall afford the other contracting parties the opportunity of preventing such an extremity by means of
their mediation." And in the special treaty of 15th
April, 1856, between Great Britain, Austria, and France,
" the high contracting parties guarantee jointly and severally the independence and the integrity of the Ottoman
empire recorded in the treaty concluded at Paris on the
30th March, 1856. Any infraction of the stipulations of
the said treaty will be considered by the Powers signing
the present treaty as a *casus belli.*" Here every contingency is anticipated by provisions for joint action, for
consultation in common, or for mediation. Hence the
faithlessness of Turkey — so far from absolving the other
Powers severally from the obligations of the treaty of
Paris, or warranting any one of those Powers to threaten
Turkey with force, in the first instance — really summons those Powers to meet together under that treaty,
and to deal with Turkey for her breach of faith. There

were seven signataries to the treaty of Paris. If the perfidy of one could absolve the remaining six not only from obligations to the delinquent Power, but from engagements with each other solemnly entered into as a provision against any such delinquent, then why go through the farce of making a treaty ? What hope is there for the peace of Europe if a treaty having an express provision for mediation can be torn into shreds and thrown away at the will of either of the signataries, and then disowned by the rest ?

But Russia has violated the treaty of Paris no less flagrantly than has Turkey. Article XXVIII. of that treaty placed the rights and immunities of Servia "under the collective guarantee of the contracting Powers ; " and art. XXIX. declares that "no armed intervention can take place in Servia without previous agreement between the high contracting Powers." No doubt the grievances of Servia were great. In other circumstances these might have justified her in an act of revolution, — which, however, I suppose the Peace Society would hardly sanction. But though I believe in the right of armed resistance to oppression, I cannot see that Servia was called to that last and desperate resort. Servia, as a recognized principality, had her independent and national administration, as well as full liberty of worship, of legislation, of commerce, and of navigation. She was under the care of friendly and powerful guardians, to whom she could appeal to compel Turkey to fulfill the stipulations of the treaty of Paris. But Servia herself discarded that treaty ; and without being attacked by Turkey plunged into a war that has desolated her territory, brought misery to tens of thousands, and threatened the peace of Europe. Has then the Peace Society no word of censure for Servia as well as for Turkey ?

But was this the act of Servia alone ? It is notorious

that Russia poured supplies of men and material into Servia, organized her armies, and inspired her counsels ; and though all this was unofficial, Prince Bismarck has not hesitated to speak openly of " the sort of war that *Russia* carried on in Servia." Russia could have restrained Servia ; could have repressed hostilities, and have convened, upon equal terms, all her co-signataries to the treaty of Paris. But she chose to regard that treaty as practically annulled.

The course of Russia in Servia is the natural sequence of her own breach of faith in 1870. By art. XIII. of the treaty of Paris it was agreed that "the Black Sea being neutralized, his majesty the Emperor of all the Russias and his imperial majesty the Sultan engage not to establish or to maintain upon that coast any military-maritime arsenal." In 1870, taking advantage of the war between Germany and France and the general preoccupations of Europe, Prince Gortschakoff sent out the following note, under date of October 31st : " His imperial majesty cannot any longer hold himself bound by the stipulations of the treaty of 30th March, 1856 as far as they restrict his sovereign rights in the Black Sea." That was indeed an imperial way of disposing of a treaty ! Has Turkey committed any breach of faith more defiant ? The thing being done, the treaty of London of 13th March, 1871 was made to conform to it ; but for that act of Russia in 1870 there is but one word, and that word is *perfidy*. And now shall England, incensed at the perfidy of Turkey, condone the perfidy of Russia, and commit the dearest interests of religious liberty and the destiny of eastern Europe to a Power that no treaty nor convention can bind ? I love to think of England as caring for honor. There never can be peace in Europe until honor is held sacred between the nations. Your address closes with an eloquent appeal " that the Powers

of the civilized world should devise, and by mutual agreement establish, some settled form of international jurisdiction." But the basis of such agreement must be *honor*.
Now the treaty of Paris did contain a mutual agreement for "mediation." Is there then no rebuke for a
Power that has openly trampled on that agreement, and
violated the express provisions of the treaty where these
seemed against its own "sovereign rights?" Is perfidy
a crime only in a Mussulman? Never was it so important that England should speak out boldly for honor.
Let the friends of peace insist now upon this, and they
will soon have the peoples of Christendom on their side.

The other ground of indignation at Turkey is her fanatical intolerance, which has driven her to inhuman excesses against her subjects not of the Moslem faith. This
century has witnessed nothing more noble than the up-
rising of the English people in behalf of the oppressed
Christians of the East. These must be rescued from the
intolerance of their Turkish masters. But *intolerance*
is the thing to be guarded against, and in delivering the
lamb from the vulture we must not put it into the talons
of the eagle, though this be the nobler bird. How then
does Russia stand on this same count of intolerance and
inhumanity? I shall not go back to her intervention to
crush the liberties of Hungary, to her subjugation of Poland, to her proscription of Mohammedan tribes brought
under by conquest. It is alleged that the spirit of the
Russian government is more mild and liberal than formerly, and we have to do with the Russia of to-day. I
go back then but six years. In 1870 the Swiss Evangelical Alliance issued a "protest and appeal against the
fanatical outrages of Russian ecclesiastics in the East Sea
Provinces, in Poland, and in Lithuania, upon Protestants, Catholics, and Israelites." On June 23d of the
same year a deputation led by Monod, De Pressensé, and

others had audience of the emperor of Russia at Stutt-
gart, and laid before his majesty the grievances of his
Lutheran, Catholic, and Jewish subjects. His majesty
deplored the facts which the deputation stated, promised
to do what he could personally to relieve the sufferers,
but added that he could not interfere with the laws of
the empire or of the church. The following are specimens of these laws, not from the dark ages, but from the
Russian penal code of May, 1846.

" Whoever shall abandon the orthodox confession for
another Christian confession shall be handed over to the
ecclesiastical authority to be exhorted and enlightened,
and that he may be dealt with after the rules of the
church." What sort of dealing this would be may be
inferred from the next article. " Whoever shall solicit
another to secede from the orthodox to another Christian confession, shall be sentenced to loss of civil rights,
banishment to Tobolsk or Tomsk, or to corporal punishment and penal servitude for one or two years."

The poor Lutherans of Liefland were cajoled, by false
promises, into joining the Greek Church. Finding
themselves deceived, they attempted to return to their
old faith, but these penalties were visited upon them.
Wives who had not gone over with their husbands to
the Greek Church were threatened with divorce ; children were compelled with violence to be baptized and
confirmed. In 1871 the British Evangelical Alliance
issued a powerful appeal " on behalf of the Lutherans
of the Baltic provinces of Russia, and against their *persecution* by the Orthodox Greek Church of that empire."
I wish that appeal might go with your address into the
hands of every Englishman. On the 14th July, 1871, a
strong deputation of English, Americans, French, Swedes,
Swiss, Belgians, Germans (among the latter Professor
Tischendorf who had procured for the emperor the Sina-

itic Codex), sought an audience of the emperor of Russia, to renew the plea of the Evangelical Alliance for his persecuted subjects. Prince Gortschakoff threw dust in the eyes of this deputation, and the emperor declined to receive it because he could not yield to outward pressure in the internal administration of his empire, — precisely the reason that the Sultan gives for declining the intervention of foreign powers.

Affairs in Liefland were smoothed over, but the Draconian laws remain, and are by no means a dead letter. In April, 1872, a respectful application was made to the government at St. Petersburg for permission to circulate in Russian Armenia the Armenian version of the Bible, published at Constantinople, and freely circulated in Turkey. Copies sent to Russia had been confiscated at the custom-houses on the border ; and after twenty months' delay, the request that Russian Armenians, like the Turkish Armenians, should be allowed the Bible in their own tongue, was refused by the Russian government. Baffled in the request for Bibles, an Armenian teacher at Tiflis requested a visit from the missionaries who were laboring among his people at Constantinople. Two American missionaries going into Russian Armenia upon this sacred errand were expelled by the authorities. This was in February, 1873. In 1875 an agent of the Bible Society at Erivan, Russia, was put under arrest and banished from the country.

When Russia speaks of the " oppressed Christians " in Turkey, she means Christians of the Greek Church and of the Slavic race. What Russia thinks of the liberty of Roman Catholics, let Poland testify ; what sort of toleration she would grant to Protestant missionaries and converts, let Armenia witness. But religious freedom knows no distinction of creed or race. And the question for Europe, and especially for England, to consider is

whether the Greek Church in Turkey, notoriously ambitious to rule at Constantinople, shall be armed with
Russian battalions or a Russian police to enforce her bigotry against Jews, Moslems, Armenians, Catholics, and
Protestants.   Is it said the Greek Church can be reformed ?   Then *let her reform.*   But do not gird her
with the sword of Russia during the process of reformation.

It is not easy to penetrate the veil of Russian atrocities ; but here are specimens of what Russia has done
upon the soil of *Turkey,* warnings of what she would do
if she should be put in occupation of Turkish territory,
or into the administration of Turkish provinces.   In
April, 1870, one Medet, a native of Alexandropol, Russia,
went to Kars, in *Turkish* Armenia, to reside.   He there
attended an evangelical service, with which the Turkish
authorities did not interfere.   But as a Russian subject,
Medet was brought before the Russian consul, *flogged,*
imprisoned, and released only upon giving his oath that
he would never again go to the service.   In this very
year, 1876, another Russian of Alexandropol, who had
gone to Erzeroom, in Turkish Armenia, to take up his
abode, was *forced by the Russian consul to return* to
Russia because he had identified himself with the Protestant movement tolerated in Turkey !   American missionaries long resident in Turkey have openly testified
that " they have been mainly indebted to Russian influences for the persecutions that have attended their labors
for the last forty years."   One of these missionaries
writes me, " What are we to apprehend in the event of
Russian rule in Turkey but just that which now exists
over the Russian border ?   The point to be emphasized
is the vital importance of guarantees for religious freedom, in the English and American sense of the word,
whatever arrangements may be made, and *whoever* may

rule in any part of Turkey." I feel confident that every friend of peace and of religious liberty in England would respond to this appeal.

The danger is that Russia and Turkey will yet go to war. In that case Russia will find the conquest of Turkey no easy task; and Germany, which has not been forward in expressions of sympathy or measures of relief for the unhappy Bulgarians, will step in where England ought to stand as the arbiter of peace and of provinces.

It is agreed on all sides that England cannot now fight for Turkey. But can she side with Russia? What then becomes of that faith between nations upon which must rest our hope of arbitration in lieu of war? Shall the partner who in 1870 broke faith with the co-signataries of united Europe, and who, though pledged to mediation, has connived at war, now have the confidence and sanction of English honor? Shall England side with Russia? Where then is the hope of religious liberty, if Muscovite intolerance can have the confidence and support of English freedom? I cannot doubt that England will let the world know that she stands firm and true for the faith of treaties, for freedom of conscience, and the rights of man.

IX.

WHAT IS SCIENCE?

(From the *British Quarterly*, January, 1879.)

THE strife over science and religion would be greatly restricted by a rigorous and binding definition of the terms in dispute. Scientific theory and theological dogma would go on contending; but that which is true in science and that which is true in religion can never come in collision, and the demarcation of each would make their harmony apparent almost without discussion. To determine specific points in controversy between modern naturism and the Christian faith will be comparatively easy when the whole field of controversy shall have been circumscribed by· logical definitions. The definition of science and the definition of religion must form the exact limits by which every question .between them must be measured, and every line of argument must be tested and adjusted. But, first of all, a word should be given to the characteristics and functions of definition.

A definition should be framed with reference to the thing defined, and not to any use to which either the term or the definition may be applied in some wider statement or system of thought. It should include everything that is essential, and exclude everything that is not essential, to a conception of the thing defined. In other words, the thing should be defined as it is — *an und für sich* — "in itself, by itself, for its own sake." Archbishop Thomson has concisely stated the rules of defini-

tion. " A definition must recount the essential attributes
of the thing defined ; the definition must not contain the
name of the thing defined ; a definition must be precisely
adequate to the species defined ; a definition must not be
expressed in obscure or figurative or ambiguous language ;
a definition must not be negative where it can be affirm-
ative."[1] To these rules, so obvious in themselves, may
be added the following : (1.) A definition must not be
framed to fit a theory. Things must be defined as they
are, and generalization, or theory, must proceed from
things as logically defined. (2.) A definition must not
beg the question with regard to any dispute concerning
the thing defined. For example, a school of physicists,
nowadays, attempt to restrict the term science to knowledge founded upon observation and experience, to the
empirical in contrast with the intuitional and the speculative. Hence they refuse to philosophy or metaphysics a
place among the sciences. To meet this narrow position,
Avenarius, for instance, would limit the term philosophy
by the empirical character of its objects, the sole aim of
philosophy being to combine in one notion all the special
experimental sciences.[2] Of course, if science is knowledge gained by experience, and if philosophy has to do
only with facts of experience, then philosophy is a science
by the very terms of the definition. But as toward the
objection raised by some physicists against philosophy,
such a definition begs the question, and hence contributes
nothing to the reconciliation of science with philosophy.
If philosophy is truly entitled to be called a science, then
the supposed definition of science is too arbitrarily exclusive, and the definition of philosophy framed to meet it
is unphilosophically limited. So great a master of phi-

---

[1] *An Outline of the Laws of Thought*, § 57.

[2] *Vierteljahrsschrift für wissenschaftliche Philosophie.* R. Avenarius. Erstes Heft, pp. 1–14.

losophy and of English style as Coleridge speaks of
" Shakespeare's deep and accurate *science* in mental philosophy." Some German writers have attempted to draw
the distinction between *Philosophie* and *Wissenschaft* so
sharply as to exclude philosophy from the category of the
sciences ; but in the constitution of a German university
the philosophical faculty includes the physical or experimental sciences along with philology, history, and metaphysics. If physicists object to such a classification, their
objection is not to be overruled by a *petitio principii* in
the definition of philosophy. Any such device vitiates a
definition as the basis of an argument. (3.) A definition should not employ terms in a strained or unusual
meaning, nor should it coin new terms, where words in
common use would suffice for clearness and precision. If
an essayist defines the principal terms of his thesis by
some strange or forced meaning, he will be sure to mislead his readers, who will lose sight of his distinctions,
and carry along in their reading the customary meaning
of his words ; and he will also be in danger of misleading
himself, by unconsciously using his forced terms in their
old meaning, to the prejudice or perversion of his logic.
If, again, he coins new terms for old and familiar things,
for the sake of maintaining some novel proposition concerning them, he can at most make out but a technical
proof of this abnormal proposition — as with an algebraic
formula, in which all the terms should represent arbitrary
and unknown quantities. He cannot hope to establish
in the minds of his readers the conviction of an absolute
and universal truth.

　One who writes a philosophical or a scientific treatise
should frame his definitions upon the principles now indi-
cated, and must be held strictly to the meaning he has
himself assigned to the leading terms which he employs
in his discussion. To write without careful definitions

upon a subject in the treatment of which precision of language is of the very essence of truth is simply to play upon words, or rather upon the ignorance or credulity of the reader. An essay published in the interest of peace maintained that *honor* is a false, cruel, pagan principle of action ; that a Christian people should expunge honor from their code, and act only in view of what is just, true, and right. Now, had the essayist looked into his dictionary, he would have found that, according to the usage of the best writers, honor is defined to be " a nice sense of what is right, just, and true, with a course of life corresponding thereto ; " in short, honor is the sum and essence of all the virtues by which this writer would supplant it. Shenstone would have taught him that " true honor is to honesty what the court of chancery is to common law ; " Shakespeare, that in woman, honor is the equivalent of chastity ; and Wordsworth, —

> " Say, what is honor ? 'T is the finest sense
> Of justice which the human mind can frame."

There is indeed a conventional notion of honor which fashion has imposed, as, for instance, in the so-called " code of honor " which regulates the duel. Such honor has shown itself false, cruel, unchristian, and this code is fast being banished from civilized society. But to employ this perversion of honor for a tirade against honor as a principle of conduct is a fault in philosophy that necessitates a failure in rhetoric. Both would have been avoided by a careful definition of the thing to be discussed under the term honor.

How much of all controversy in philosophy and theology has been a mere war of words ! How many volumes of such controversy might have been spared, had the disputants respected logic and the dictionary ! Precision is of the first importance where the most vital interests of man are in dispute — his knowledge and his faith. Hence a clear definition of the terms *science* and *religion* — a definition framed strictly according to the rules already laid down — should be the starting-point of every comparison between them ; and however much the argument may be extended, the definition should hold it firmly as in the jaws of a vise. This care in defining the terms of the discussion is the more necessary because, in the controversy that has of late arisen between science and religion, these terms have been used with much vagueness, and some physicists have rushed into this controversy without even attempting to define the things about which they were contending. Dr. John W. Draper has written what he calls a " History of the Conflict between Religion and Science ; "[1] but in a volume of nearly four hundred pages there is no attempt at a precise statement of the things in conflict, nor of the grounds of the controversy. His conception of religion seems to be " a quiescent, immobile faith " (p. 364), as represented by the Roman Catholic Church ; his conception of science that " it relies on a practical interrogation of nature" (p. 33). On one page he tells us that " science is in its nature progressive ; but faith is in its nature unchangeable, stationary " (preface, p. vii.) ; on another, that " it is not given to religions to endure forever. They necessarily undergo transformation with the intellectual development of man " (p. 328). Faith, which on one page of Draper's history stands " quiescent and immobile," on another is subject to the same law of transformation and development with the intellect of man. The triumphs of science, he tells us, " are solid and enduring " (p. 365) ; but could anything be more fluctuating than have been the sciences of astronomy, geology, physiology, chemistry, heat, light, magnetism, though every new change of doctrine has

---

[1] One of the volumes of the *International Scientific Series.*

been put forth under the warrant of "a practical interrogation of nature"? A work written in such a vague slipshod style as this of Draper has no value for the phil-·osophical inquirer, and can only mystify the common reader. The author is guilty of that which he charges upon the teachers of religion, — assuming to speak with the authority of truth, he imposes upon the "blind faith" of the ignorant. Such a book shuns the test of definition, since, with any clear conception of either science or religion, it could never have been written.

Professor Ernst Haeckel has published what he styles the "History of Creation,"[1] with the avowed object of setting aside the religious conception of a personal Creator by the monistic conception of natural laws or forces as the cause of all things. Yet instead of defining with scientific precision such pregnant terms as "nature" and "religion," he seeks to put us off with puerile declamation. "Science, as an objective result of sensuous experience and of the striving of human reason after knowledge, has nothing to do with the subjective ideas of faith, which are preached by a single man as the direct inspirations or revelations of the Creator, and then believed in by the dependent multitude" (chap. xxiv.). As if there were no objective realities to faith, no knowledge as its ground-work, no religion apart from a professed revelation, no faith in any human soul except as this is imposed by some pretentious teacher, no religious thought or feeling in any great mind from Plato and Socrates to Leibnitz and Stuart Mill! Haeckel says again, with emphasis, "*Where faith commences, science ends.* Both these arts of the human mind must be strictly kept apart from each other. Faith has its origin in the poetic imagination; knowledge, on the other hand, originates in the reasoning intelligence of man" (chap. i.). As if it

[1] *Naturliche Schöpfungsgeschichte.* Von Ernst Haeckel. Jena.

were an "art of the poetic imagination" to accept the
report of a scientific explorer or investigator concerning
his discoveries upon simple faith in his testimony, with
no "sensuous experience" whatever! As if a faith
worthy to be brought into contrast with science did not,
at least, suppose itself to rest upon a basis of knowledge,
and bring its subject-matter to the test of "the reasoning
intelligence!" Borrowing a poetic figure from the faith
which he most contemns, Haeckel says, "Science has to
pluck the blessed fruits from the tree of knowledge, un-
concerned whether these conquests trench upon the poetical imaginings of faith or not" (chap. i.). But this,
forsooth, is no forbearance on the part of science, and
marks no such sharp discrimination between knowledge
and faith as the author has asserted in the formula,
"Where faith commences, science ends." So far is this
from being true, that at some point science *must* merge
its knowledge of details in a belief in laws, forces, principles. What science is there which does not summon
us to the exercise of faith, in order to its own comple-
tion? Not mathematics, which tasks "the poetic imagination" to conceive of lines, forms, figures, which have,
and can have, no corresponding realities. Not astronomy,
surely, for though this is perhaps of all sciences the best
attested by observation, yet the Copernican theory of the
earth's motion cannot be asserted as the absolute truth of
knowledge, but only as the highest attainable probability hitherto offered to faith. The theory accounts for so
many phenomena, it is confirmed by such a multitude of
observations, and reduces the unsolved difficulties to such
a minimum, that there remains no reasonable ground of
doubt that the earth revolves upon its own axis and
moves round the sun.

"Astronomy ventures itself upon the approval of mankind
through the practical realization of its theories of motion, though

it knows absolutely nothing concerning the first impulse of motion, and is utterly ignorant of the inner essence of the so-called
powers with which it works so boldly and successfully, and
which are only presented under happy mathematical images." [1]

Now these mathematical forms are but ideals of th
imagination — pure abstractions. We can build up a
universe upon them with as much confidence as we tread
upon the solid ground ; but we cannot see them, handle
them, nor make them in any way the " objects of sensuous experience." We do not arrive at these mathematical conceptions through " the interrogation of nature."
The most perfect instrument for the investigation of
physics is not itself physical, but a product of the imagination. And imagination from time to time devises new
terms and powers for the solution of problems in physics.
Kant laid down the proposition that " in each particular
natural science only so much of science proper could be
found as there was of mathematics to be found in it." [2]
To meet the more recent advances of science, Du Bois-
Reymond proposes to substitute for mathematics the mechanical force or action of atoms.[3] But here again we
are in the region of the ideal, since we know neither
" atom " nor " force." This simple and elementary term
force is as much misused and abused as any word in the
whole vocabulary of science. " We have, as yet, absolutely no proof whatever that force proper has objective
existence. In all probability there is no such *thing* as
force, any more than there is such a *thing* as sound, or
light, which are mere names for physical impressions pro-

[1] *Wahrheit und Wahrscheinlichkeit.* Von Wilhelm Förster, Professor und Director der Königlichen Sternwarte in Berlin. The true
place of probability in science and logic will be discussed in a subsequent article.

[2] *Vorrede zu den Metaphysischen Anfangs-gründen der Naturwissen-
schaft.*

[3] *Ueber die Grenzen der Naturerkennens.*

duced upon special nerves by the energy of undulatory motions of certain media." [1]   Gravitation, force, monad, ether, and the like, are not things that we know by sensuous experience, but names upon which we hang our faith.   So far from it being true that " where faith begins, science ends," there could no more be a science without faith than there could be extension without space.   Yet it is by such superficial, meaningless, untenable assertions, put forth with an air of scientific dogmatism, that Haeckel and Draper startle the timid and impose upon the credulous.

A much more respectable authority than these, Professor John Tyndall, recognizes " the immovable basis of the religious sentiment in the nature of man," and would have men of science regard the religions of the world as " the forms of a force, mischievous, if permitted to intrude on the region of *knowledge*, over which it holds no command; but capable of being guided to noble issues in the region of *emotion*, which is its proper and elevated sphere." [2]   It is now the fashion of a school of physicists in England to speak flippantly of religion as a matter of feeling without warrant of reason, of faith as fancy, and science alone as knowledge; and their use of the terms science and knowledge gives to this distinction an air of plausibility.   But is this exclusive, almost professional, appropriation of such words as science and knowledge warranted by etymology and usage?   There is wisdom and propriety in changing the terminology of science to meet the advancing conditions of knowledge.   Sciences may be subdivided, new classifications may be made, and a new nomenclature adopted to mark these distinctions.   It is the prerogative of men of science to make such divi-

[1] *The Unseen Universe.* By B. Stewart and P. G. Tait.   Third edition, § 97.
[2] Address before the British Association at Belfast, p. 60.

sions and classifications within the realm of science, and to promulgate these as the laws of their peculiar kingdom. Whether philosophy should be sharply discriminated from science, or at least the exact sciences should be kept distinct from philosophy, is a question of words which the masters of philosophy and of science are competent to determine. But *knowledge* is not a term that can be thus seized, tethered, and impounded within the pale of any school or sect. This is the common property of mankind, since in every human mind there is a something that answers to what we call knowledge, and in every language there is a word to denote that thing. The physicist might as well think to confine the atmosphere within the receiver of his air-pump, the chemist to compress the rivers into his retort, as to monopolize the term knowledge by the limitations of his particular science. To define science by knowledge is only to change the term without identifying the thing. Since *scio* means *to know* in the widest signification of the word, to say science is knowledge, and knowledge is science, is like knocking two billiard balls of equal size and color back and forth against each other, without ever driving either into the pocket: there is nothing gained or lost on either side. " Science is knowledge," is a toying with words which contributes nothing to preciseness of meaning, to the understanding of things. All men mean something when they talk of knowledge, and this common thought or element in the minds of men which differences knowledge from everything else must lie at the basis of our definition of the word. That single element is *the conviction of certainty.*

So long as one has the least doubt of a fact, he cannot be said to know it as a fact. What one guesses to be the truth, he does not know as true. What one estimates as having the highest degree of probability, he does not know to be real. What one imagines to be the solution of a phenomenon or a problem — for example, the atom in physics, the molecule in chemistry — he yet does not know to exist. Only when the mind has attained to the conviction of certainty can it properly be said to know. This conviction may be arrived at in very different ways. It may be a spontaneous state of the mind itself, which is not capable of being analyzed, and for which no logical reason can be assigned. It may be the result of a mathematical calculation or demonstration which leaves no room for doubt. Or it may be based solely upon the testimony of others. Thus we know at last the long-sought, much-disputed sources of the Nile and the Congo. We know from Livingstone, Cameron, and Stanley, that the continent of Africa can be crossed from coast to coast, and also to what extent Africa is inhabited. From the scientific reports of the voyage of the Challenger, we already know much of the form and character of the bed of the Atlantic. We are fast reducing the physical geography of the globe to certainty, but we do not yet know whether the North Pole is surrounded by an open sea or an impenetrable barrier of ice. The testimony of explorers is conflicting, and though Nares has pronounced the Pole inaccessible, new expeditions are organizing a final attack upon this hitherto unyielding mystery. Whatever knowledge explorers shall gain by observation and experience will become the common property of mankind through their testimony, which will be accepted as a sufficient basis of certainty. The difference between observation and testimony lies not in the *degree* of conviction, but in the *mode* by which it is attained. The conviction of certainty is perhaps more commonly derived from observation and experience, and some physicists would limit the term knowledge absolutely to that which is gained through the experience of

physical phenomena. But the nice distinction of Kant
is here of much importance. "Admitting that all our
knowledge begins *with* experience, it does not follow that
all knowledge likewise arises *out of* experience." [1]

*Knowledge is the assurance of certainty, without regard
to the way in which this assurance is attained.* This assurance may be premature, excessive, or even altogether
mistaken, having no warrant in fact, and no adequate
ground in reason. Nevertheless, as regards the conception of reality and the ground of action, this conviction
of certainty gives to him who possesses it the confidence
of *knowledge.* Where the conviction of certainty concerning a fact or truth is common to the mass of mankind, then such fact or truth becomes an article of universal knowledge.

Though we use the term *moral* certainty to denote the
highest degree of probability, yet, strictly speaking, certainty expresses a fact or truth established beyond question. "*Probability* and *certainty* are two states of mind,
and not two modes of the reality. The reality is one and
the same, but our knowledge of it may be probable or
certain. *Probability* has more or less of doubt, and admits of degrees. *Certainty* excludes doubt, and admits
neither of increase nor diminution." [2] But knowledge,
which begins in the conviction of certainty, may be increased or modified through familiarity with the object,
and in matters of detail without affecting the basis of
certainty. Suppose a Londoner has for years resided in
Berlin. Before going there he had the conviction of certainty of the existence of such a city, otherwise he would
not have gone. A residence of years has modified his
notions of Berlin in some things and enlarged them in
others ; but it has not strengthened by one iota his pre-

[1] *Kritik der reinen Vernuft.* — Einleitung, i.
[2] Fleming, *Vocabulary of Philosophy.*

vious conviction of the certainty that there is such a place. In matters of detail he may now know Berlin better than he knows the London of to-day, with its rapid changes. Indeed, after a few years he might not know London in such particulars; yet he could never lose his conviction of the certainty that London exists. The degrees of which knowledge admits without disturbing the fundamental conviction of certainty are neatly expressed in German by the terms *Kenntniss* and *Er-kenntniss*. *Kenntniss* is the simple, obvious knowledge of an object as such; *Er-kenntniss* is the discerning, discriminating, *qualifying* knowledge, in which the object, through characteristics and details, is distinguished from others, and fixed in the scale of knowledge in a position of its own. *Kenntniss* can be communicated as a matter of fact or of information; but *Er-kenntniss* is always the product of one's own mental activity. Hence they who would limit knowledge to that which the mind becomes assured of through the observation of nature would deprive knowledge itself of that higher assurance which comes of the criticism of facts, phenomena, impressions, in the crucible of thought.

"Though the phenomena of nature are all consistent with each other, we have to deal not only with these, but with the hypotheses which have been invented to systematize them; and it by no means follows that because one set of observers have labored with all sincerity to reduce to order one group of phenomena, the hypotheses which they have formed will be consistent with those by which a second set of observers have explained a different set of phenomena. Hence the operation of fusing two sciences into one generally involves much criticism of established methods, and the explosion of many pieces of fancied knowledge which may have been long held in scientific reputation." [1]

Science itself would be the chief loser if physicists

[1] *Nature*, vol. xv. p. 389. Article on Helmholtz.

should succeed in restricting the term knowledge to that
which is ascertained by observation of nature. However
extensive and minute may be the facts accumulated by
observation in any given department of nature, and however valuable the knowledge of such facts may be for
practical uses — as, for instance, the facts observed and
tabulated in meteorology — yet these serve only as materials towards a science, until they are colligated in principles or laws. But this colligation of facts is the distinctive aim of science ; till this is accomplished, the
observation of phenomena remains at the level of empiricism, and cannot claim the dignity of science. How
serious then would be the defect, how lamentable the
failure of science, if the principles and laws under which
its recorded observations are finally colligated could not
command that assurance of certainty which is the first
rudiment of knowledge. And of what avail would be
all the knowledges (*Kenntnisse*) derived from outward
phenomena, if these could not be compared, sifted, classi-
fied, and finally elevated into that higher appreciative
knowledge (*Er-kenntniss*) which is a possession of the
mind itself ?

This region of *Er-kenntniss* Mr. Herbert Spencer recognizes as the proper home of science. " Science is simply a higher development of common knowledge." But
development is more than observation or experiment,
more than the accumulation and classification of facts,
more than the sensible impressions received from external
nature. It is a product of the self-activity of the mind,
sifting, eliminating, combining the knowledges which are
conveyed to it by observation. Hence, as Herbert Spencer further says, " the sciences severally germinate out
of the experiences of daily life ; insensibly as they grow
they draw in remoter, more numerous, and more complex
experiences ; and among these they ascertain laws of de-

pendence like those which make up our knowledge of the most familiar objects."[1] Now these "laws of dependence" in spheres remote from physical inspection are intellectual conceptions, by which the mind seeks to classify and to account for phenomena brought to notice or suggested by experience. But Mr. Spencer does not hesitate to claim for these, when duly tested, the same conviction of certainty that comes of the testimony of the senses.

"As certainly as the perception of an object lying in our path warns us against stumbling over it, so certainly do these more complicated and subtle perceptions, which constitute science, warn us against stumbling over intervening obstacles in the pursuit of our distant ends. Thus, being one in origin and function, the simplest forms of cognition and the most complex must be dealt with alike."[2]

Now it were a great mistake to suppose that this higher knowledge, this complex conception, is the apex of a pyramid, to which one mounts by successive layers of solid facts. Quite commonly the conception is first formed as an image within the mind itself — it is a creation of the imagination in the higher regions of abstract thought, which is then tested by observation or by mathematical calculation, and thus the conception grows to the assurance of certainty; — the apex of the pyramid being at first the shapely scaffolding which imagination has framed to be filled up with materials gathered from the wide regions of observation, and which can only be brought into one orderly, harmonious, and enduring structure because the scaffolding is there. Indeed, as in the science of pure mathematics, the structure reared within the mind — which has no corresponding reality in the outward world of physics — may be more sure,

[1] *First Principles of a New System of Philosophy.* By Herbert Spencer. Part i. chap. 1.
[2] Ibid.

exact, and permanent than a pyramid of stone. If, as some suppose, the great pyramid was designed to furnish a standard of lineal measure and of the heavenly motions, not even this huge mass of stone, that has outlasted so many ages, dynasties, and peoples, can give a conviction of certainty to be compared with that ideal structure of mathematics by which it is shaped and built. In this case it is the pyramid which is the phenomenal appearance, the mental ideal which is the substantial reality.

In his anxiety to secure a scientific basis for philosophy, Avenarius makes the concession that " the objects which should form the contents of a science must be actually given by experience. Otherwise one has to do with merely phantom objects and a phantom science." [1] But in fact this is often reversed, and the physical appearance is the phantom, while the spiritual creation, though this may be purely a thing of the imagination, produces the impression and power of reality. One sees this, for example, in Shakespeare's " Hamlet," a spiritual creation so fine, so lofty, so subtile, that not even the classic representations of Booth, Irving, Salvini, or Ludwig, can give to it that effect of reality which the scholar feels as he reads the play meditatively in his library. No man of culture can read alone the ghost-scene, especially at " the witching time of night," and not feel a mysterious super-sensible power taking hold of his inmost being, shaking his science and his skepticism, and producing a momentary conviction of the reality of a spirit-world. But the attempt to realize that scene upon the stage scatters this momentary allegiance to a spirit-power, and makes him feel that the supernatural is a delusion. Here it is the physical apparition, the thing of observation, the ghost seen and heard, that is felt to be an unreality, an invention, a *Schein*, a sham. This is the sole point of

---

[1] *Vierteljahrsschrift für wissenschaftliche Philosophie*, vol. i. p. 6.

this illustration. It would be absurd to assert the ap
pearance of ghosts as an article of knowledge, or even to
rest the existence of disembodied spirits upon so slender
a basis as the felt presence of the supersensible which is
awakened by the creation of the dramatist, though the
native susceptibility of the mind to such conceptions *is*
an argument for some corresponding reality in the unseen universe. The witch of Endor may have been a
clever sorceress, the "weird sisters" of the heath expert
jugglers. With mirrors and chemicals we may be able
to reproduce their spectres ; yet after we have suborned
science to a masquerade, that she may tear off the mask
of sorcery, it still remains that we hear the voice of Sam-
uel and see the smile of Banquo behind the scenes. We
have dispelled the ocular illusion, but there remains a
suggestion of reality in that which is invisible. This experience, familiar to minds accustomed to introspection,
reverses the distinction which some physicists would
draw between images of the mind as phantoms, and
physical phenomena as realities. Sometimes the physical appearance may be scattered as a phantom, while the
mental image makes an abiding impression of reality —
the "airy nothing" takes on "a local habitation and a
name." To return, for a moment, to mathematics. This
field-marshal of the sciences, which prescribes to each
particular science its laws of organization and its grade
in the general system of knowledge, wields an impalpable wand of theory. Itself the most exact and certain of
all the sciences, and supplying to the physical sciences
forms, measures, quantities, equations, formulas ; yet
mathematics is not built upon the observation and induction of physical facts, but springs from that "spontaneity
of initiative" which is the creative faculty of the mind.
What is the differential and integral calculus but a
pure invention of this creative power for gauging the

physical universe and caging this within the immaterial but invincible barriers of abstract thought? An acknowledged master in the science of mathematics, the discoverer of the " Dialytic Method of Elimination,"[1] says of the algebraical forms called *quantics :* " These are not properly speaking geometrical forms, although capable of being embodied in them, but rather schemes of processes and of operations for forming, for calling into existence, as it were, algebraic quantities." Here is a most subtile abstraction. The algebraic " quantity " itself may be purely imaginary, but behind this is conjured up the *quantic,* the merest shadow of a shade, and this *quantic* is conceived of as capable of calling quantities into existence. Yet upon such unsubstantial forms as these the mind can rest in the assurance of certainty at every step ; with these it can weigh and measure the solid globe ; by these it can mount to the stars. To this abstract knowledge external nature *must* conform, " complementing and substantiating theory by visible and palpable experience." The mathematician, says Sylvester, " has to train and inure himself to a habit of internal and impersonal reflection and elaboration of abstract thought." But it is in this region of abstractions, and not in the outer physical world, that the mathematician finds his certainties ; and back of all his knowledges, and the most sure of all, lies his thought-power. For the one thing that every man knows with the conviction of absolute certainty (and possibly the only thing he does absolutely *know ?*) is *himself as knower.* If one does not know this, he cannot know anything ; and it may well be doubted whether one can know anything else with the same absolute certainty with which he knows that he *is.* No amount of negation can impair this certainty. Augustine has pointed out the self-contradiction of a universal skepticism, in that " he who

[1] Professor Sylvester, of the Johns Hopkins University, Baltimore.

doubts is *certain* that he doubts." And Thomas Aquinas, with diacritical nicety, has said, " He who denies that truth is, at the same time concedes that truth is ; since, if truth is not, it is true that truth is not." [1] Only by confidence in himself as knower can one know any object outside of himself. " The light by which we see in this world comes out from the soul of the observer. Nay, the powers of this busy brain are miraculous and illimitable. Therein are the rules and formulas by which the whole empire of matter is worked." [2] The Ego, which is *consciousness come to itself*, is the one fundamental fact of universal knowledge. What consciousness is and whence it arises, what the Ego is and how recognized and defined, are questions beyond the scope of the present article. We introduce the Ego here with reference simply to the definition of knowledge, and thus of science.

It might be, as Spinoza taught, that " the object of that idea which constitutes the human mind, is body — that is, a certain mode of extension existing in reality — and nothing else ; " [3] and that " the mind does not know itself except in so far as it perceives ideas of affections of the body " [4] (so finely did the great Dutch philosopher of the seventeenth century, by pure metaphysical abstraction, anticipate the Darwinian theory of the evolution of consciousness by cerebral excitation through the instrumentality of the sensorium). Or it might be, as Kant held, that the Ego (*Ich*) " cannot even be called a

---

[1] " Etiam qui negat veritatem esse, concedit veritatem esse ; si enim veritas non est, verum est veritatem non esse." — Thomas Aquinas, *Sum. Theol.*

[2] Ralph Waldo Emerson, *Success.*

[3] " Objectum ideæ humanam mentem constituentis, est corpus, sive certus extensionis modus, actu existens, et nihil aliud." — *Eth.* ii. prop. 13.

[4] " Mens se ipsam non cognoscit, nisi quatenus corporis affectionum ideas percipit." — *Eth.* ii. prop. 23.

conception, but is merely the consciousness which accompanies all conceptions — a simple representation which in itself is totally void of contents;" [1] or, as he otherwise puts it, the pure, original, unchangeable self-consciousness, that is the Ego, is simply a " transcendental apperception " which does not carry within itself the conception of a distinct substance, or self-substantiality. This " transcendental unity of self-consciousness," Hegel illustrates by an analogy from mathematics : —

" In geometry you are told to conceive the circumference of a circle as formed of an infinite number of infinitely small straight lines. In other words, characteristics which the understanding holds to be totally different, the straight line and the curve, are expressly declared to be identical. Another transcendent of the same kind is the self-consciousness, which is identical with itself, and infinite in itself, as distinguished from the ordinary consciousness which derives its character from finite materials. That unity of self-consciousness, however, Kant calls transcendental only ; and he meant thereby that the unity was only in our minds, and did not attach to the objects apart from our knowledge of them." [2]

Again ; in direct opposition to the view of Kant that the Ego represents pure apperception with no content of real conception, it might be, as Hegel maintains, that " in the Ego there is a variety of contents, derived both from within and from without, and according to the nature of these contents our state may be described as perception, or conception, or reminiscence. . . . *I* is the vacuum or receptacle for anything and everything ; for which everything is, and which stores up everything in itself." [3]

---

[1] " Von der Paralogismen der reinen Vernunft ; erstes Hauptstück des zweiten Buchs der transcendentalen Dialektik." ·

[2] *Encyclopädie den philosophischen Wissenschaften*, § 42. See the translation of Mr. Wallace, *The Logic of Hegel*, p. 75.

[3] Wallace, *The Logic of Hegel*, p. 40.

Or the Ego might be presented in the abstract concept of Lotze : —

" Selfhood, the substance of all personality, does not rest upon a contrast, completed or in process, of the Ego with a non-Ego, but consists in an immediate being-in-and-of-itself (*Fürsichsein*) which conversely forms the ground of the possibility of that contrast, at the point where itself emerges. Self-consciousness is the actualization of this being-in-and-of-itself through the medium of conception, and this also is in no way necessarily dependent upon the discrimination of the Ego from a substantial non-Ego set over against it." [1]

And still further ; the very opposite extreme of certain physiologists might be accepted, which represents the Ego to be nothing more than a succession of impressions upon the brain, or an on-going chain of sensations.

But whichever of these views, or whatever modification or combination of them be taken for true, they all are comprehended within the brief formula — THE EGO IS CONSCIOUSNESS COME TO ITSELF. If the Ego be an immediate, intuitive conception, emerging from that vague background which some writers call *sub*-consciousness, then in this self-recognition consciousness comes to itself, as one awaking from a swoon is said to come to himself. If the Ego is simply a feeling or sensation, or a chain of impressions, then, as the point at which the spark flashes makes visible the electricity engendered in a whole battery of Leyden jars, so the Ego is the point of manifestation at which the feeling or impression culminates in consciousness come to itself. And so of all intermediate stages in the definition of the Ego. It has been remarked of the child, that in the earlier manifestations of consciousness he speaks of himself in the third person — possibly in imitation of the mother and nurse, who always speak to him in the third person (What ails

[1] Hermann Lotze, *Mikrokosmus*, vol. iii. p. 575.

baby ? What will Charlie have ?) ; but of a sudden he *comes to himself*, and says *I* think, *I* feel. Consciousness has evolved itself as Ego.

The Germans have a neat expression for the clearing up of consciousness through the certainty of conviction. *Ich bin jetz mit mir im Reinen* — " At last I have cleared up myself to myself ; " like Milton's — " The mind through all her powers irradiate ; all mist from thence purge and disperse." But Jevons goes even further, and maintains that certainty can be predicted *only* of an actual present consciousness and of a correct logical infer ence ; that is, of certain states and acts of the Ego.

" We can never recur too often to the truth that our knowl- edge of the laws and future events of the external world is only probable. The mind itself is quite capable of possessing certain knowledge, and it is well to discriminate carefully between what we can and cannot know with certainty. In the first place, whatever feeling is actually present to the mind is certainly known to that mind. If I see blue sky, I may be quite sure that I do experience the sensation of blueness. Whatever I do feel, I do feel beyond all doubt. We are, indeed, very likely to confuse what we really feel with what we are inclined to associ- ate with it, or infer inductively from it ; but the whole of our consciousness, as far as it is the result of pure intuition and free from inference, is certain knowledge beyond all doubt." [1]

It is sufficient to our present purpose that the Ego is (1) a fact of absolute knowledge ; (2) a fact of univer- sal knowledge ; (3) not a fact of physical experience.

1. That the Ego is a fact of absolute knowledge re- quires no proof and indeed admits of none. There is nothing that a man asserts with such absolute certainty as the fact that he *is*, he *knows*, he *feels*, he *thinks*, he *wills*. And, indeed, if one should take it upon him to

---

[1] *Principles of Science.* By W. Stanley Jevons. Second edition, chap. xi. p. 235.

deny consciousness of the Ego, the more stoutly he should
deny himself the more vehemently would he invoke us
to believe in *him* and in *his* denials. " I who speak to
you am conscious that I have no consciousness of being
I ! "

2. That the *Ego* is a fact of *universal* knowledge —
that every other man has the consciousness of the Ego as
truly as I have, — is plain (*a*) from *language*. Every
language has some term or terms to represent *I* and *me*,
he and *him*. " Now language is the work of thought,
and hence all that is expressed in language must be universal." [1] (*b*) From the notion of *possession*. In every
human being there exists the notion that something belongs to *him* in distinction from all others. In asserting
the right of property, he asserts the consciousness of the
Ego. (*c*) From *history* and *tradition*. Among all peoples there exist in history or tradition names of heroes,
sages, poets, kings, that represent individuals, persons ;
and the history or tradition becomes nothing if stripped
of that conception. Indeed, so universal is the consciousness of the Ego, that mankind clothe even myths with
personality, to give them character or force. No amount
of historical criticism will ever destroy men's faith in the
personality of Homer, Romulus and Remus, King Arthur,
William Tell. Having resolved the man into a myth,
we at once make the myth a person, an Ego to the imagination. (*d*) The universal conviction of the Ego is
shown by *laws* and *penalties*. These are enacted because
in every case of crime or wrong the human mind directly
ascribes the act to a person as the wrong-doer ; and *he* in
distinction from all physical things and from all other
persons is to be held accountable, because he is a conscious Ego. If he is shown to be an idiot or insane, then
the criminality of his action is lost in the clouding of the
Ego as to the character of the act.

_____
[1] *Logic of Hegel*, p. 32.

3. The Ego is not a fact of physical experience. Though physical experiences may lead up to it, though the Ego may be the flash of electric light from the chain of sensations, yet it is not itself a sensation. The Ego is conscious of the physical experiences as *his* experiences. This is equally true whether the non-Ego is given in the same instant and in the same mode with the Ego, or the Ego is discriminated from the non-Ego by a process of reflective analysis, or the Ego becomes directly conscious of the non-Ego as distinct from itself.

We have seen that the one fact of knowledge which is absolute, fundamental, and universal, the knowledge which must attend all other knowledges, and without which there could be no other, — this consciousness of *the Ego as a knower*, — is not, either as to its nature or as to its origin, knowledge in the sense to which a recent school of physicists would limit that term. Hence the oppugnation between science and philosophy, or science and religion, if any there be, cannot lie in the distinction between knowledge and opinion or belief. Neither are the terms science — in the sense of exact science or of physical science — and knowledge strictly interchangeable.

We are now prepared for a nearer view of the contents of the term *science*. Knowledge is the conviction of certainty. The Ego is that — be it person, substance, mode, fact, condition, manifestation, result, or what not — THAT in which this conviction of certainty is given, felt, recorded. Sensations are not knowledge; these may be tentative, deceptive, even negative. Sensations are the *media* through which the Ego receives impressions of the outer world. The Ego being conscious of sensations, through these sensations is cognizant of external phenomena ; and by weighing, analyzing, comparing, combining these impressions and experiences, it attains to that conviction of

14

certainty which, in respect of the outer world or nature, is the scientific equivalent for fact or knowledge. Hence Whewell has laid down these aphorisms as preliminary to a definition of science.

" 1. *The* senses *place before us the* characters *of the book of nature ; but these convey no knowledge to us till we have discovered the alphabet by which they are to be read.*

" 2. *The* alphabet, *by means of which we interpret phenomena, consists of the* ideas *existing in our own minds ; for these give to the phenomena that coherence and significance which is not an object of sense.*

" 3. *The two processes by which science is constructed are the* explication of conceptions, *and the* colligation of facts.

" Knowledge requires us to possess both facts and ideas. Every step in our knowledge consists in applying the ideas and conceptions furnished by our minds to the facts which observation and experiment offer to us. When our conceptions are clear and distinct, when our facts are certain and sufficiently numerous, and when the conceptions, being suited to the nature of the facts, are applied to them so as to produce an exact and universal accordance, we attain knowledge of a precise and comprehensive kind, which we may term *science*." [1]

Such is the testimony of a master in physics to the office of the ideal in conception in bringing into scientific order that which lies in consciousness as matter of experience. Also, from the purely philosophical side, Hegel found the union of reflection with experience essential to the construction of a science. In the introduction to his " Encyclopædia of the Philosophical Sciences," Hegel defines philosophy as " a peculiar mode of thought — a

[1] *Novum Organon Renovatum*, pp. 5, 27. In selecting these aphorisms, we have changed the numerical order of Dr. Whewell, for the sake of convenience of arrangement.

mode through which thought becomes discriminating and comprehensive knowledge." In other words, philosophic thought is reflective and speculative thinking. In science this reflective and speculative thought is employed in investigating the facts of experience and in evolving the laws which these suggest.

" The principle of experience involves the infinitely weighty condition [1] that in order to take in a subject-matter and hold this for true, the man himself must be *in contact* with it : more precisely, he must find such subject-matter in union and combination with *the certainty of his own self.* He must himself be in contact with it, be it only by his outward senses, or rather with his deeper spirit — his essential self-consciousness." [2]

Hence Hegel would assert for speculative philosophy the maxim, *Nihil est in sensu quod non fuerit in intellectu* — the converse of sensationalism. This is true in the meaning that nothing outward can have reality for us till it is attested in consciousness and shaped in thought. Though we may not give existence to the outer world, nor even preconceive it as to its constituents, yet nothing can be known to us as existing in sense until we have somehow shaped it as reality in our minds. " No less than empiricism, philosophy only recognizes what is, having nothing to do with what merely ought to be, and what is thus confessed not to exist. . . . Empiricism labors under a delusion if it supposes that while analyzing the objects, it leaves them as they were : it really transforms the concrete into an abstract." [3] Thus science must use the materials and methods of philosophy in the very attempt to build up a barrier between itself and philosophy. We must see if we cannot help science to a

---

[1] *Bestimmung* = *determinatio, constitutio* — that which is fixed or defined in the nature of the subject ; hence, a requisite condition.

[2] Hegel, *Encyclopædia,* Einleitung, 57.

[3] *Encyclopædia,* p. 538. See Wallace, *Logic of Hegel,* p. 65.

better standing-place — to a truer knowledge of herself and her means of knowing. In mind alone can be had that conviction of certainty which is the assurance of knowledge; by mind, the objective facts of nature, as ascertained through the senses, must be tested and set in order; and the master-architect is the Ego.

Some of the most liberal and advanced thinkers in physical science have openly recognized the truth that although science must gather her materials from nature, she must lay her foundations, not in nature but in mind. This homage of science to mind was a striking feature of the fiftieth meeting of the German Association of Naturalists and Physicians, at Munich, in September, 1877. Professor Haeckel, who surpasses Huxley in facility of assumption and audacity of assertion, read a paper in which he assumed that evolution and the monistic philosophy are established in science, and asserted that " whoever to-day still asks for proofs of the theory of descent [*i. e.* the descent of man from the ape], proves by that only his own want of knowledge or reason." Haeckel even went so far as to argue that this doctrine of evolution should be taught in the common schools as a fixed branch of knowledge.[1] Haeckel, however, has but small influence in scientific circles in Germany; and the modesty of true science appeared in the subsequent addresses of Professor C. von Nägeli,[2] of Munich, and Professor R. Virchow,[3] of Berlin, which distinctly recognize the reflective action of mind in bringing within the category of knowledges the facts of nature observed by the senses. Says Nägeli: " The solution of the question, In what way

---

[1] *Die heutige Entwickelungslehre im Verhältnisse zur Gesammtwissenschaft.*

[2] *Ueber die Grenzen des Naturerkennens.*

[3] *Die Freiheit der Wissenschaft im modernen Staat.* All these addresses were well translated in *Nature*, Nos. 414–423.

and how far may I know and understand nature? is evidently determined by three different things, namely, by the answers to three questions : (1) The condition and capacity of the Ego ; (2) the condition and accessibility of nature ; and (3) the demands which we make of knowledge." He makes the correctness of knowledge depend not merely upon the correctness of the senses in observation, but equally upon the fidelity of that finer internal sense through the mediation of which the mind partakes in these observations of the bodily organs ; and " by conclusions from facts which were recognized by the senses we arrive at facts *equally certain*, which can no longer be perceived by the senses." Having defined the limitations of the senses and of the Ego, Nägeli comes to mathematics as the one certainty in the domain of knowledge — a science,

" perfectly clear to us because it is the product of our own mind. We can understand real things with certainty, as far as we find mathematical ideas, number, magnitude, and everything which mathematics deduces from these realized in them. Natural knowledge, therefore, consists in our applying mathematical methods to natural phenomena. To understand a natural event means nothing else, as it were, than to repeat it in thought, to reproduce it in our mind."

Here is the distinct admission of one of the most careful physicists that our knowledge of nature is not merely a sense perception, but an innerly-accordant conception (*die innere Vermittelung*) of the mind itself. In respect of outward nature, " we can know only the finite ; but we can know all the finite which comes within reach of our sensual perception." But on the other hand, as Nägeli teaches, " we know mental life only from our subjective experiences." He does not qualify the term knowledge in respect of these inner experiences, nor limit knowledge to the objective world of sense. " We *know* that we draw conclusions, that we remember, that we feel pleasure and pain." It is this conscious, this knowing Ego, which measures and compares the results of sense-perception, and thus brings nature within the purview of knowledge — the assurance of certainty.

Virchow, while adhering strongly to the objective side of science, recognizes the utility of that speculative method "which sets problems, and finds the tasks to which modern investigation is to be applied, and which anticipatively formulates a series of doctrines which are still to be proved, and the truth of which must yet be found, but which in the mean time may be taught with a certain amount of probability, in order to fill certain gaps in knowledge." In natural science, no less than in the church, Virchow finds the three phases which attach themselves to all systems of human knowledge — " *objective* and *subjective* knowledge, and the intermediate phase of *belief*.

Still more pronounced on this point is Professor Challis, F. R. S., of the University of Cambridge, who says : —

"Physical science, when complete, rests not on experiment alone, but on experiment combined with *reasoning*. . . . Empirical philosophy is only a step towards true and ultimate philosophy; and physical *science* is really *advanced* only so far as the physical laws discovered and formulated by means of experiment are shown by mathematical reasoning to be consequences of ulterior intelligible principles. The perfection of physical science consists in giving reasons for physical laws." [1]

Hence the mere observation of nature cannot monopolize the term knowledge, nor indeed claim to be. knowledge at all until certified by the scrutiny of the rational and judicial *Ego*. And this carries us back to the great founder of physics, who believed equally in metaphysics.

[1] *Journal of the Transactions of the Victoria Institute*, vol. xii. No. 45, pp. 2, 11.

Aristotle [1] made science well-nigh the equivalent of art (τέχνη), in which term he included both the methodical handling of facts and the theoretical development of principles and causes; or rather, with Aristotle, art was a stage intermediate between experience and the wisdom of true science.

"Experience is the knowledge of particulars, art is the knowledge of the universal. The artist is wiser than the mere experiencer; his knowledge stands nearer to wisdom, because he comprehends also the grounds or reasons of things, which the experiencer does not. The experiencer knows only the *What,* not the *Wherefore,* but the artist knows also the Wherefore and the Cause. . . . Wisdom is the science of certain, *i. e.* ascertained, causes and beginnings."

The union of experience with art in Aristotle's meaning constitutes science according to our modern idea — the knowledge of particulars upon a given subject acquired by experience, then generalized by the art-faculty of the mind into principles and laws. It remains for philosophy, the higher wisdom, to rise into the sphere of origin and cause. "All science," says Bluntschli, "is the work and acquisition of individual mental labor — of thought. The active spirit in the individual man seeks and arrives at truth by unfolding self-consciousness, by observing carefully outward circumstances and studying the processes of the mind itself." [2] This is in strict accordance with what Humboldt says in the introduction to his "Cosmos." "Science does not present itself to man until mind conquers matter in striving to subject the result of experimental investigation to rational combinations. Science is the labor of mind applied to nature; but the external world has no real existence for us beyond the

---

[1] *Metaphysics,* lib. i. c. 1.
[2] Bluntschli, *Politik als Wissenschaft,* lib. v. c. 6; *Lehre von modernen Staat,* vol. iii. p. 263.

image reflected within ourselves through the medium of the senses." Humboldt discriminates also between a merely empirical knowledge of external nature and true science, in which observation is under the constant scrutiny of reason.

" Empiricism originates in isolated views, which are subsequently grouped according to their analogy or dissimilarity. To direct observation succeeds, although long afterward, the wish to prosecute experiments, that is to say, to evoke phenomena under different determined conditions. The rational experimentalist does not proceed at hazard, but acts under the guidance of hypotheses founded on a half indistinct and more or less just intuition of the connection existing among natural objects or forces. That which has been conquered by observation, or by means of experiments, leads, by analysis and induction, to the discovery of empirical laws."

Science can be attained only " by subjecting isolated observations to the process of thought ; " and the " ' Cosmos ' is based upon a rational empiricism, that is to say, upon the results of the facts registered by science, and tested by the operations of the intellect."

This comprehensive view of Humboldt gives color to the saying of an eminent philosophical naturalist : " All true science of nature is philosophy, and all true philosophy is natural science." With more exactness it may be affirmed that science requires the unifying process of philosophy, and philosophy requires the scientific basis of experience ; and if any distinction be made between philosophy and science, it should lie in the relative proportions in which the two factors, speculation and experience, — which are common to both, — are combined in either. Zeller goes further, and finds the distinction of philosophical science from other sciences in this : that " every other science has in view the exploration of some one particular domain, whereas philosophy has its eye upon the totality of existences as a whole, strives to comprehend the particular in its relation to the whole and to the laws of the whole, and thus to establish the coherence of all knowledge." [1] But is it not true also of each science that it seeks to gather the facts that lie within its domain into one systematic whole, and then to articulate this unit of particular knowledge with that aggregate of knowledges which constitutes the universe? And is not philosophy rather the highest of sciences — *scientia scientiarum* — in that whereas *a* science concerns itself with investigating and unifying experiences, philosophy or *science* takes the sciences themselves as *data* for its generalizations? Science is not merely knowledge, but knowledges comprehended by the judging faculty, and set in orderly relation to laws or principles. The recorded observation of facts or experiences does not alone constitute a science. This furnishes material out of which " reflective and speculative thinking " may construct a science. Thus the patient, wide-spread, long-continued record of observations concerning the weather may indicate the laws of wind, rain, heat, storms, and the systemization of phenomena apparently so variable will by and by erect meteorology into a proper science. On the other hand, an abstract theory, however perfect in its parts and complete in the adjustment of those parts to a system, cannot alone constitute a science. Even in pure mathematics the a, b, c, x, y, and z of an algebraic formula, and the lines and angles of geometrical figures for the purposes of demonstration, are conceived of as objective realities. Though in nature there is no such thing as an absolutely straight line, nor two lines strictly parallel, nor a perfect square or circle ; yet reason does not build the vast and orderly system of the higher mathematics

---

[1] Dr. E. Zeller, *Die Philosophie der Griechen.* Vierte Auflage. Ein-. leitung, vol. i. pp. 6, 7.

upon abstract nonentities, but upon ideal entities which, for the time being, the mind clothes with reality. Yet an hypothesis, though springing from the imagination — like Kepler's notion of the harmony of the spheres — may lead to the discovery or detection of facts which will serve as links for binding facts, before unexplained, into the chain of laws. Hence it is that facts and laws, or the knowledge of phenomena and the systematic adjustment of phenomena in their relations to each other and to underlying causes, forces, or principles, must combine in order to constitute a science.

Science is the summation and colligation of all the knowledges pertaining to a given subject-matter, and the formulation of these in abstract general conceptions.

Under this category stand the physical sciences, metaphysics, logic, and *religion* itself.

X.

WHAT IS RELIGION?

(From the *British Quarterly*, October, 1879.)

In Professor Max Müller's "Lectures on the Science of Religion,"[1] the best part of the book is its title. This suggests that religion may be treated scientifically, after the same method of induction and classification which has been applied so successfully to the study of language, and which is in use in the physical sciences. Indeed, Müller would associate comparative theology with comparative philology not only in method, but also in material. He finds "the outward framework of the incipient religions of antiquity" in a few words — such as names of the Deity, and in certain spiritual and technical terms — which were substantially the same among all earlier peoples. "If we look at this simple manifestation of religion, we see at once why religion, during those early ages of which we are here speaking, may really and truly be called a sacred dialect of human speech ; how, at all events, early religion and early language are most intimately connected, religion depending entirely for its outward expression on the more or less adequate resources of language."[2] But while finding in words the key to religions, Müller furnishes no terms by which to define

---

[1] *Introduction to the Science of Religion.* Four Lectures delivered at the Royal Institution. By F. Max Müller, M. A.

[2] *Ibid.* p. 153.

or describe religion. His nearest approach to this is a formula which would cause physicists peremptorily to reject religion from the category of science. " As there is a faculty of speech, independent of all the historical forms of language, so there is a faculty of faith in man independent of all historical religions; . . . that faculty which, independent of, nay, *in spite of sense and reason* (!), enables man to apprehend the Infinite under different names and under varying disguises. . . . In German we can distinguish that third faculty by the name of *Vernunft*, as opposed to *Verstand*, reason, and *Sinne*, sense. In English I know no better name for it than the faculty of faith, though it will have to be guarded by careful definition, in order to confine it to those objects only which cannot be supplied either by the evidence of the senses or by the evidence of reason. No simply historical fact can ever fall under the cognizance of faith." [1]

The phrase we have italicized above would bar the claim of religion to a place among the sciences ; for though the physical sciences themselves employ faith as a prelude and guide to discovery, science could never admit an hypothetical belief in " spite of sense and reason." And, on the other hand, the Christian faith does rest throughout upon the " simply historical facts " that Jesus Christ was born of the Virgin Mary, was crucified under Pontius Pilate, was buried, and rose from the dead.

By the " science of religion " Müller intends what is better styled " comparative theology." Now, to theology, as the logical statement and systematic arrangement of the facts and doctrines within its province, the title of a science is commonly conceded ; and the comparison of different systems of religious belief and worship, by discovering resemblances in conceptions, in terms, and in

[1] *Introduction to the Science of Religion*, pp. 16, 17.

usages and forms, and by classifying these systematically under general principles, may create a science — say, if there be not a contradiction in the terms — the science of beliefs. Since the faculty of believing, equally with the faculty of knowing, is a native quality of the human mind, not only must this faculty itself fall within the categories of psychology, but the objects of belief must be capable of being reduced to some form of logical statement and classification. But theology and comparative theology are themselves but outward forms or expressions of the religious idea or sentiment. In religion we have to do with a conception, a feeling, a state of mind, which is common to mankind; and the essence of religion lies at the back of all forms of theology and of worship. What, then, is this universal phenomenon of the human spirit? — this which experience and history testify, through all migrations and mixtures of races, through all fluctuations of social and political institutions, through all systems of philosophy and theology, and through all developments of science and art, is the one transmigratory soul, forever inspiring human thought, forever influencing human life?

It is said of Comte that, towards the close of life, he openly confessed that " the human mind could not rest satisfied (*ne peut se passer*) without a belief in independent wills which interfere in the events of the world." Of this concession Comte's biographer says : " Never was there an avowal more fatal to the positive philosophy. If this be true, the human mind is necessarily *theologic*, and it would be as great a folly to contend against that necessity as against all other necessities, physical or organic." [1] This fatal concession of Comte, Littré imputes to the weakness induced by excess of work, " a

[1] *Auguste Comte et la Philosophie Positive.* Par E. Littré, p. 578. Troisième partie, chap. vi.

serious nervous disease," which caused the author of the
" Philosophie Positive " to relapse into the subjective
method and its theological tendencies. But the influences under which the great positivist admitted the universal necessity of a religious faith are of minor importance; what here concerns us is that the thing itself is
true; that the human mind is " *necessarily* theologic ; " [1]
that a something within us impels us to religion; that
metaphysical analysis lands us at last in the absolute ;
that the induction of physical facts and the unification
of the laws of the universe, through the correlation of
forces, leads us to the conception of a supreme cause or
power; and that the study of mankind under all conditions forces us to conclude with Spencer, that " religion,
everywhere present as a weft running through the warp
of human history, expresses some eternal fact." [2] That
fact is the aim of our inquiry.

Religious questions shift their ground, change their
form, vary in interest and importance, according to the
temper of the times, the schools of thought, the bent of
leaders in church or in state, in politics or in philosophy.
The theological, the ecclesiastical, the speculative, the
practical phases of religion are by turns predominant or
antagonistic. Many a dogma and theory has been exploded, many a form set aside, many a practice abandoned, in the endeavor after that union of knowledge
and freedom, of reason and will with faith, which is the
ideal of a philosophical religion. But while religious
questions have been thus relative and fluctuating, *the
question of religion* has suffered no abatement in its mo-

---

[1] The late Professor Trendelenburg, of Berlin, once said to the
writer, " I believe in logic as strongly as did Hegel, but I believe
also in *theo*-logic."

[2] Herbert Spencer's *First Principles*, p. 20, chap. i., " Religion
and Science."

ment to the individual man and to the well-being of mankind.

Whether with Lecky we regard religion as "modes of emotion," in distinction from theology, which consists of "intellectual propositions;"[1] or, with Kant, hold that "religion, subjectively considered, is the recognition of all our duties as divine commands;"[2] whether, with Comte, we "refer the obligations of duty, as well as all sentiments of devotion, to a concrete object, at once ideal and real — the human race conceived as one great being;"[3] or, with Herbert Spencer, we find the root of religion in "mystery of an inscrutable power in the universe;"[4] whether, with Mill, we rest in a dry formula of "the infinite nature of duty;"[5] or share with Schleiermacher "the immediate feeling of the dependence of man upon God;"[6] — under all modes of statement, of expression, and even of negation, behind all objects of adoration, personal and impersonal, humanity, nature, God, there lies the reality of religion — an inalienable, indestructible, irrepressible *something* in the constitution of man, testified to by the finer instincts of the soul, by its sense of duty, its aspirations after virtue, its yearnings toward the invisible, and confirmed by man's experiences of nature and by the course of human history. It is this something in man that we are seeking to analyze and define: What is Religion? This question is

---

[1] *Rationalism in Europe*, vol. i. p. 356.

[2] *Der philosophischen Religionslehre*, viertes Stück, erster Theil.

[3] *The Positive Philosophy of Auguste Comte*, p. 121. By John Stuart Mill. With Comte *le grand être* is always *l'humanité*.

[4] *First Principles*, chap. ii., "Ultimate Religious Ideas."

[5] John Stuart Mill, Essay on Comte.

[6] *Reden über die Religion*. In the same discourse Schleiermacher says, "Religion is neither a special mode of thought nor a special mode of deportment; it is neither knowledge nor action; it is *feeling*."

broader than any question of natural science or of theology ; broader than the question of adjusting theology with natural science ; broader than the stream of human history, with all the collective interests of society, government, letters, art ; broader than the measure of the earth and of the peoples that inhabit it ; more vital and imperative than any question of reform in church or in state, or of progress in knowledge and in society ; it is the question of every race and of every time, from the savage with his fetich to the Platonist with his ideas, and the positivist with his laws ; a question new to each man and binding upon every man — the question of his own being,[1] its origin, its relations, its obligations, its possibilities, its destiny : " What can I *know?* What *ought* I to do ?   What may I *hope?*"[2]

As in defining science we were careful to eliminate from the definition all theoretical prepossession — all that the Germans style *Tendenz* — so, in seeking to define religion, we should divest ourselves of every theological bias, and in the very spirit of science search for the primary facts in this phenomenon of human consciousness.   We should especially guard against a devout tendency to forestall

---

[1] John Stuart Mill says in his autobiography, " I was brought up from the first without any religious belief, in the ordinary acceptation of the term." Yet we find Mill feeling his way toward " an ideal conception of a perfect Being," as the guide of conscience ; we find him arguing " the beneficial effect " of a hope in God and in immortality, in that " it makes life and human nature a far greater thing to the feelings ; " and at last rendering a sublime homage to the character and teachings of Christ.   Then, with a pathetic weakness, which in a Bushman he would have smiled at as superstition, this great philosopher, after the death of his wife, records: " In order to feel her still near me, I bought a cottage as close as possible to the place where she is buried. . . . Her memory is to me a *religion.*"

[2] Kant, *Kritik der reinen Vernunft : *" Der Kanon der reinen Vernunft," zweiter Abschnitt.

the inquiry by assuming that this or that religion is the true religion ; and should accept only that as truth which gives the *reality of things.* In every sphere of investigation truth is the sole demand of an honest mind ; in physical science, the facts of nature and the true explication of her phenomena ; in the science of mind, the facts of consciousness, the laws of a true psychology, and also what logic may determine to be true in the region of ultimate ideas and of the absolute ; in the sphere of ethics, the true ground of virtue, the true science of rights, and the ultimate source of moral obligation ; in history, not only truth in the record of events, but the true philosophy of human society ; in theology, truth as seen in nature, felt in consciousness, or revealed by God. It is truth that Helmholtz is in quest of in his laboratory and Darwin in his cabinet ; it is truth that Lepsius would decipher from the hieroglyphics of Egypt, and Broca from the remains of prehistoric man ; it is truth that Sir William Hamilton and his critic Mill have sought with equal honesty in the study of the human intellect and of the unconditioned ; ·it is truth that Huxley seeks in the hints of biology and Spencer in ultimate ideas ; from Plato to Schleiermacher, his translator and expounder, truth has been the ideal in the world of thought ; from Aristotle to Humboldt, his royal successor in the priesthood of nature, truth has been the objective in the world of fact ; above all sects in Christianity, above all schools in theology, truth is confessed as the standard and authority. Truth is the pole of every explorer, around which he hopes to find an open sea, and either safe anchorage or a sure outlet into the infinite. And what if science at last shall discover that the star that must guide to that pole is religion, which there sits enthroned above all night, unchanged by all the revolutions of the world ? What then is this constant

15

fact of human experience ? In the name of truth we ask, *What is Religion?*

It should be easy to define a term which the Romanic and Teutonic peoples have alike appropriated from the Latin for the same thing; or to describe the thing itself, which exists almost universally in the experiences and usages of mankind. Yet the conception of religion varies according as the term is taken etymologically, popularly, or scientifically. Cicero has given the etymology of the word *religio* with a precision that has the air of authority.

" They who diligently and repeatedly review, and as it were rehearse again and again everything that pertains to the worship of the gods, are called religious, from *religendo* [going over again in' reading or in thought] ; as the elegant from *eligendo* [choosing with care, picking out] : the diligent from *diligendo* [attending carefully to what we value] ; the intelligent from *intelligendo* [understanding persons and things]. In all these words the derivation of meaning is analogous to the word religious." [1]

Lactantius,[2] however, derives *religio* from *religare*, to bind back or fast. This meaning is retained in the French *religieux*, which denotes a person who is bound by vows to a life of sanctity. Critics are pretty evenly divided between these two derivations. Under the first, religion is a voluntary act, either mental or outward, though inspired no doubt by a sense of obligation ; under the second, religion is the sense of obligation, which finds expression in pious feelings and in acts of devotion. In Cicero's meaning, religion corresponds nearly to the German *Andacht*,

---

[1] " Qui autem omnia, quæ ad cultum deorum pertinerent, diligenter retractarant et tanquam relegerent, sunt dicti religiosi ex *religendo*, ut elegantes ex *eligendo*, itemque ex *diligendo* diligentes, ex *intelligendo* intelligentes. Iis enim in verbis omnibus inest vis legendi eadem quæ in religioso." — *De Natura Deorum*, lib. ii. cap. 28.

[2] Lactant. iv. 28.

"the careful pondering of divine things," [1] which Kant so beautifully describes as "the tuning of the soul to a susceptibility to divinely given impressions." [2] But apart from his etymology of the word *religio*, Cicero uses the term in a gradation with "piety" and "sanctity," which requires for "religion" the sense of moral obligation.

" *Pietas* is a sincere loyal disposition toward those with whom one stands in near relations, — relatives, colleagues, superiors, and especially toward the gods as rulers and benefactors. *Sanctitas* is an irreproachable, faultless carriage towards the gods. But *religio* is the recognition of the obligation by which one feels himself bound." [3]

With the Greeks religion, though perhaps more assiduously practiced than among the Romans, was less rigidly defined. Their θρησκεία was religious worship and usages, rather than the essence of religion in spirit and motive; εὐσέβεια was the *pietas* of the Latins, reverence for parents, elders, superiors, authorities, gratitude toward benefactors, though Plato uses this term to describe a reverent devotion toward the gods, and bids us "exhort all men to piety, that we may avoid the evil and obtain the good." [4] Mommsen goes so far as to say that " the Roman designation of faith, *religio*, that is to say, *that which binds*, was in word and in idea alike foreign to the Hellenes." [5] Perhaps " that idealizing sense, which knew how to breathe a higher life even into inert stone," refused to be confined within the bonds of duty.

What religion was among the Greeks in respect of wor-

---

[1] See Andrew's Freund's *Lexicon*, art. " Religio."

[2] Kant, c. 353.

[3] Schömann, *De Natura Deorum*, lib. i. cap. 2, 3. See, also, Cicero's own definitions, lib. i. chap. 41 : " Est enim pietas *justitia adversum deos :* sanctitas autem est *scientia colendorum deorum.*"

[4] Symposium, 193.

[5] Mommsen's *History of Rome*, book i. chap. 2. Dickson's Translation.

ship, beliefs, rites, and customs, it is easy to learn from their poets and philosophers, their temples and statues. The presence and agency of the gods were universally recognized in nature and in human affairs: through the Amphictyons religious union became the basis of political confederation; behind the symbols of faith and the objects of worship lay an inner spiritual devotion to higher spiritual powers; above the circle of the gods was a supreme unifying principle, rule, or fate; man, as the head of the physical creation, was divinized, and the divinity was humanity idealized. The religion of the Greeks was anthropomorphic, even to reproducing the baser passions of men in the persons of the gods. But all this helps little toward a conception of religion in respect of ground or motive; and in the absence of an infallible hierarchy, a dogmatic revelation, and even of systematic treatises on theology, it is not possible to reduce to a simple definition the Greek conception of religion in itself. This is remarkable if one considers how early the Greek mind showed its bent toward synthesis and speculation; how the Greek poetry is pervaded with the presence of divinity, and Greek philosophy with the ethical sense; and with what a free and unclouded spirit the Greek religion contemplated the relations of the gods with men. Perhaps the very natural and human way in which the lives and doings of the gods were conceived of, and the childlike simplicity with which the gods were honored and served, rendered a definition of religion as difficult and as superfluous as a description of light and air. " The most godly man was he who cultivated in the most thorough manner his human powers, and the essential fulfillment of religious duty lay in this, that every man should do to the honor of the divinity what was most in harmony with his own nature." [1]

---

[1] Zeller, *Die Philosophie der Griechen*, erster Theil, vierte Auflage, Einleitung, p. 42.

Then there was the δαίμων, or tutelary deity, a connecting link between gods and men, which might be a celestial attraction toward the good or a fatalistic impulse toward the evil, in either case modifying that freedom of choice which gives to actions their moral quality. And yet, by faith in his attending genius, how gradually did Socrates struggle after the pure and just, the beautiful and good. No reader of the " Phædo " can fail to feel how deep and vital is the religious spirit that here endeavors to give a dialectic form to the conceptions of God, the soul, right, duty, immortality ; and yet the highest morality and the highest philosophy combined in the subject and the framer of this most perfect of the Platonic dialogues have failed to direct us to the origin and nature of the faith which it fundamentally implies. For the mythology of Greece there is a rich vocabulary ; for its religion, none.

Turning from the greatest sage of Greece to the older sage of China, we find in the dialogues or analects of Confucius a system of social and political ethics pervaded with the religious spirit, but which gives no distinct conception of the nature or the source of religion itself. Customs, ceremonies, proprieties, filial piety, the worship of the spirits of ancestors and of sages, as also of the spirits of the land and of places, these all are enjoined, though in a somewhat formal, perfunctory way, and with no express statement of the principle or the authority upon which their obligation rests. Virtue and righteousness in the outer life are prescribed with a sententious wisdom ; but the ultimate law of righteousness, whether in nature, in reason, or in God, is nowhere clearly enunciated.

Admirable, indeed, were some of the rules given by Confucius for the conduct of life. " To subdue one's self and return to propriety is perfect virtue ; " " Benevolence is to love *all* men ; " " We should be true to the principles of our nature, and the benevolent exercise of them to others;" "Let the will be set on the path of duty;" "Let every attainment in what is good be firmly grasped;" "Let relaxation and enjoyment be found in the polite arts;" "Let every man consider virtue as what devolves on himself. He may not yield the performance of it even to his teacher;" "The man who, when gain is set before him, thinks of righteousness; who, with danger before him, is prepared to give up his life; and who does not forget an old agreement, however far back it extends, such a man may be reckoned a *complete* man;" "Virtue is more to man than either water or fire. I have seen men die from treading on water and fire, but I have never seen a man die from treading the course of virtue." When, however, he was asked to define virtue, Confucius described it under certain manifestations, without pointing to its inward essence: "To be able to practice five things everywhere under heaven constitutes perfect virtue; to wit, gravity, generosity of soul, sincerity, earnestness, and kindness." Again, he seemed to resolve virtue back into obedience to knowledge.

"The ancients who wished to exemplify illustrious virtue throughout the empire, first ordered well their own states. Wishing to order well their states, they first regulated their families. Wishing to regulate their families, they first cultivated their persons. Wishing to cultivate their persons, they first rectified their hearts. Wishing to rectify their hearts, they first sought to be sincere in their thoughts. Wishing to be sincere in their thoughts, they first extended to the utmost their knowledge. Such extension of knowledge lay in the investigation of things."

It is a special honor of Confucius that he applied his teachings to the benefit of mankind at large, and had no esoteric doctrines: "The man of perfect virtue, wishing to be established himself, seeks also to establish others:

wishing to be enlarged himself, he seeks also to enlarge others." And it is certain that this remarkable sage did anticipate the "Golden Rule" of Christianity, at least upon its negative side: " What I do not wish men to do to me, I also wish not to do to men." A favorite disciple asked, " Is there not one word which may serve as a rule of practice for all one's life?" Confucius answered, " Is not *reciprocity* such a word? What you do not want done to yourself, do not do to others." When, however, we seek for the ultimate principles upon which Confucius founded such lofty precepts of morality, we find a certain vagueness and reserve quite in contrast with the clearness and force of the precepts themselves. Though after his death Confucius was worshiped by his disciples with divine honors, and though he remains to this day a chief object of religious homage to the Chinese nation, he never claimed divinity, and hardly assumed a divine commission and warrant for his teachings. Once, when his life was threatened, he said, " Was not the cause of truth lodged here in me? If Heaven had wished to let this cause of truth perish, then I should not have got such a relation to that cause. While Heaven does not let the cause of truth perish, what can the people of K'wang do to me?" Yet he spoke of himself with humility, as the compiler of the wisdom of the ancients, and not an originator of wisdom or the author of a system.

That all which Confucius said and did was prompted by a religious sentiment is the impression one receives from an impartial reading of his works. " Man," said he, " has received his nature from *Heaven*. Conduct in accordance with that nature constitutes what is right and true — is a pursuing of the proper path. . . . The path may not for an instant be left. . . . There is nothing more visible than what is secret, and nothing more manifest than what is minute, and therefore the superior man is watchful over his *aloneness.*" This seems to carry the distinction of right and wrong behind actions to the innermost thoughts and feelings, and to find in conscience "the eye of the mind" implanted by Heaven. It is held by some commentators on Confucius that he had no conception of a personal God, but used the term heaven impersonally, to denote the pantheistic principle in the universe; but Professor Legge,[1] whose careful translation and commentary we have followed in the foregoing citations, is of opinion that the term heaven is fitly explained by "the lofty one who is on high." There seems to be internal evidence of this in the saying of Confucius, "He who offends against Heaven has none to whom he can pray." The idea of offense, of prayer, and of such alienation by offense that prayer can no longer avail, implies the recognition of a personal being, and the term heaven is but a reverential veil for the name of God. Upon the whole we may gather from Confucius that religion is an inner sense of rightness or fitness implanted in man by his Creator, and which prompts to reverence toward God and the spirits of sages and of ancestors, to virtue in the conduct of life, and to justice and kindness toward others.

Pursuing our analysis of the religious idea to a still more remote antiquity, we pass from China to India, from the preceptive philosophy of Confucius to the mythological poetry of the Vedas.[2] In Greece were divinities and a worship, but neither sacred books' nor a hierarchy; in China sacred books of morality, and a hierarchy of

---

[1] *The Life and Teachings of Confucius.* By James Legge, D. D.

[2] Socrates died B. C. 399; Confucius died B. C. 478. The hymns of the Rig Veda are the most ancient remains of Indian literature. No authority in Sanskrit assigns to those a date more recent than B. C. 1000, while some scholars carry them back to a period between B. C. 2000 and 2400.

sages, but in the more ancient times, little of organized worship or of priestly functions; in India, however, as far back as we can trace her records, institutions, traditions, we find sacred writings, a sacred order,[1] and sacred observances, public and domestic: religion the very warp and woof of her literature and history. To a superficial view the religion of the Vedas might seem a mass of fables worthy of the childhood of the race, — the crude polytheism of primitive tribes. But in reality this was preëminently the religion of thought, — the spiritual nature of man tasking itself with speculations upon the origin of things, and using this visible material universe to personify the spiritual and unseen. Behind the multifarious array of gods and goddesses, and the sensuous, sometimes grossly material, conceptions under which these are presented, there is a subtle spiritual essence which is " the ONE," supreme, infinite, eternal, absolute.

" There was then neither non-entity nor entity; there was no atmosphere, nor the sky which is above. . . . Death was not then, nor immortality; there was no distinction of day or night. That One breathed calmly, self-supported; there was nothing different from It [that One] or above It." [2]

This abstract, self-sustained essence is afterwards described as Mind. " Desire first arose in It, which was the primal germ of mind; [and which] sages, searching with their intellect, discovered in their heart to be the bond which connects entity with non-entity."

All the attributes of this mysterious impersonal One are ascribed in different hymns to different divinities, which again are clothed with material forms, and are subject to the incidents and the passions of human life.

---

[1] It is uncertain how old is the origin of four castes, but the priestly office is of great antiquity.

[2] *Hymns of the Rig Veda*, x. 129. Translated by Muir. *Original Sanskrit Texts*, vol. v. p. 356.

Thus, " Purusha himself is this *whole* [universe], whatever has been, and whatever shall be. He is also the lord of immortality. . . . This universe was formerly *soul* only, in the form of Purusha."[1] Yet Purusha was born, and was immolated in sacrifice. Again, " This entire [universe] has been created by Brahma." And yet " Brahma the eternal, unchanging, and undecaying, was produced from the ether."[2] These discrepancies are perhaps best harmonized by the supposition that each divinity who is invested with supreme attributes is but another expression for that One who is himself unnamable ; or all the several divinities are but members of one soul, attributes or manifestations of the eternal, invisible essence. Whether the Vedic hymns mark an upward tendency of the religious feeling from naturism to theism, and from polytheism to monotheism, or whether their symbolism, like the adornments of a cathedral, used at first to body forth the supersensible, had come to supplant spiritual worship by a species of idolatry, can hardly be determined from the internal evidence of the books, or from contemporary monuments or traditions. Rather the subjective and the objective seem here to be combined, to a degree which transcends the union of the subtleties of the Schoolmen, with the sensuous worship of images in the Middle Ages. In the Vedic religion there is scope for every faculty of the human mind, — the dialectic, the speculative, the imaginative, the contemplative, the observative, — and these all struggle together to give expression to the theme which comprehends all thought, all being, all space, all duration.

> " There is no great and no small
> To the soul that maketh all :
> And where it cometh, all things are;
> And it cometh everywhere." [3]

---

[1] Muir, *Sanskrit Texts*, vol. i. pp. 9, 25.

[2] *Ibid.* vol. i. pp. 17, 115.   [3] R. W. Emerson.

Hardly a theory of physics, hardly a speculation of metaphysics, concerning the origin of things, — force, motion, heat, evolution, light, spirit, — but is anticipated in the Rig Veda. There nature is etherealized and spirit materialized. "The intellectual and the sensible, the ethical and the naturalistic, are there conjoined in the most inartificial and also inseparable way, as kernel and shell in the yet unripe fruit grow indissolubly together."[1] Nature and Soul are one. The powers of nature personified, and by turns invested with all the attributes of Deity, or the universal soul manifesting itself in the phenomena of nature, especially in light, — the dawn, the sun, the sky, — all-pervading, all-renewing, all-beneficent, these worshiped with hymns, prayers, oblations, represent the religion of India in the oldest and purest of the Vedas.

In reading these hymns of more than thirty centuries ago, one is puzzled by the frequent mixture in the same verse of seeming puerility with real profundity. Where we find such metaphysical acumen and such poetic sublimity as often occur in the Rig Veda, it is fair to presume that connected passages, which a literal translation makes meaningless or childish, had a higher meaning, which is veiled from us by some symbol or mystery of language. Yet this very commingling of metaphysical acumen and poetic fervor with a certain childish credulity, which characterizes the Rig Veda, is found also in the Hindoos of to-day. Indeed, as these qualities are combined rather than contrasted in those early hymns, do they not show how human nature, at all points, was open to the influence of religion, — the philosophic thought, the poetic fancy, equally with the childlike faith? And if at length materialism shall establish its

[1] O. Pfleiderer, *Die Religion, ihr Wesen und ihr Geschichte,* vol. ii. p. 82.

atomic theory of the universe, this vaunted outcome of *physical* science could but reaffirm an old *metaphysical* theory of the Indian mind, — the development of the universe from motion and heat, "impregnating powers and mighty forces, a self-supporting principle beneath, and energy aloft."[1] If physical science would make God "the sum of all the forces of the universe," the Vedic religion made of Nature "a metaphysical deity."

Recent researches in Babylon have brought to light evidences of a religion there remarkable for simplicity and purity, — teaching the unity of God and doctrines concerning sin, forgiveness, and the resurrection of the body, with singular analogies on some points to the Hebrew Scriptures.[2] But as there is still some controversy among Assyrian scholars concerning the proximate date of these memorials and their inscriptions, we simply bring them into notice here, and pass to a single additional example.

Older than the oldest of the Vedas, and with the possible exception just mentioned, the most ancient landmark between the prehistoric chaos and the recorded course of the world's history is the religion of Egypt, as read in her temples and monuments, and especially in the "Book of the Dead." If in the liturgy of Egypt, as in that of India, we find a mingling of the puerile and grotesque with the thoughtful and sublime, there is, on the whole, in the faith of Egypt more of mystery, and in her worship more of majesty. In Egypt, as in India, we find in the religious odes a frequent interblending of subjective and objective, of metaphysical conceptions rising to pure monotheism and nature-worship, taking upon them much sooner than in India the symbolic form of idolatry. At the same time we are left in suspense as to the order of

---

[1] *Rig Veda*, x. 129.
[2] Sayce's *Lectures on Babylonian Literature.*

manifestation, — whether polytheistic forms sprang from a monotheistic root,[1] or from the broad base of nature-worship religion rose like a pyramid tapering upwards to a single point. But the Egyptian — whether he worshiped the sun as god or as a manifestation of the Deity, whether he worshiped Osiris as the vivifying, fructifying potency in nature, or as a type of the ever-living, ever-progressing soul — did certainly conceive of a supreme divinity, self-originated, invisible, incorruptible, imperishable, the creator and lord of all. The worship was elaborate and imposing, and the priesthood almost absolute over domestic life, and even in affairs of state. "The Egyptians," said Herodotus, "are religious to excess, far beyond any other race of men." But that faith can hardly be called a superstition which projected itself beyond the world and time into the regions of spiritual life, and drew thence motives to the noblest conduct of this life, — to justice, honesty, temperance, chastity, truth, reverence, piety, kindness, and beneficence.

It seems a complete collapse to pass from the high plane of religious thought and worship in Egypt and in Ethiopia to the fetichism of inner Africa. Yet even in fetichism is found a belief in supernatural power, in fate and mystery, in the spirits of the dead, and in other spirits of good and evil ; and in all this the groundwork of a spiritual faith. In attributing to a doll the speech and passions of a human being, the child makes this thing of wax or wood a reflection of the personality which is just developing in its own consciousness ; it projects the spiritual beyond its inner self to be mated with some other spirit which it feels *must* be. And so, in the infancy of the race, man makes the stone, the block, the material thing that pleases him or does him harm, a spirit to be

[1] Bunsen held that "all polytheism is based on monotheism." *Egypt's Place in Universal History*, book v. part I. sec. 2, C.

conversed with, to be propitiated, or to be shunned. The spirit within him, felt though unseen, reaches forth after the spiritual without, which is felt though it cannot be seen.

Whether belief in a personal God is so general that it may be regarded as native, or at least normal to the human mind, it does not fall within our present scope to consider. Neither is this the place for a general review of comparative mythology. Our sole aim in analyzing the religions of different races and different periods has been to get at a conception of religion itself at once so fundamental and so comprehensive that, in defining this, we shall fix the place of the religious idea or sentiment in the system of philosophic thought, distinct from forms of worship and dogmas of theology. Thus far it is evident that religion is reverence or homage to an object external to the worshiper, which is looked upon as superior in nature, in character, or in power. That this object should be conceived of as a personal Being, or as one only God, is not essential; but religion does require an *object* of faith or worship, a something exterior to the man, which he looks upon with a sentiment of admiration, of loyalty, or of awe, which leads him to acts of homage. The virtue which proceeds solely from one's inward impulses, or from self-regulation, with no reference in thought or feeling to any external source or motive of obligation, is morality or goodness, but not piety or religion. But, on the one hand, the lowest form of fetichism, having an object of worship, is called a religion; and, on the other hand, usage allows the term religion to the homage to an ideal, such as nature or humanity in the abstract; since such an ideal as the commanding motive or power over the soul is to all intents personified or deified as the object of worship. This application of the term — perhaps a little overstrained — Mr. Mill has pointed out in the

case of Comte, and also of his own father. Speaking of
Comte's homage to collective humanity as the "*grand
être*," Mill says : " It may not be consonant to usage to
call this a religion ; but the term, so applied, has a meaning, and one which is not adequately expressed by any
other word. Candid persons of all creeds may be willing
to admit, that if a person has an ideal object, his attach-
ment and sense of duty towards which are able to control
and discipline all his other sentiments and propensities,
and prescribe to him a rule of life, that person has a religion." He then argues that, in the majesty of his idea
of humanity as the object of reverence and love, and in
his golden rule of denying self to live for others, — " *vivre
pour autrui*," — Comte " had realized the essential conditions of a religion." [1] And in describing his father's
character and opinions, Mr. Mill contends that many
whose belief is far short of deism may be " truly religious," since " they have that which constitutes the principal worth of all religions whatever, — an ideal conception of a perfect Being, to which they habitually refer as
the guide of their conscience." [2] This ideal, though existing purely in thought, is nevertheless projected before the
mind as a reality ; and the bare conception of such an
existence creates an obligation to conform to this as the
standard of life. Hence there enter into religion three
elements or conditions more or less pronounced — Nature,
Man, or God ; and the precedence of one or the other of
these elements, in the proportion in which they are combined, gives to different religions their distinguishing
characteristics. The first of these elements is Nature.
Now this term is so used by materialists as to exclude
from the categories of science every form of the religious

[1] *The Positive Philosophy of Auguste Comte.* By John Stuart Mill,
pp. 121-124. Also, *Westminster Review*, April, 1861.
[2] *Autobiography*, book 46.

idea; hence a strict definition of nature must precede and prepare our definition of religion.

Going back to the Greek conception of nature, we find τὸ φυσικόν sharply distinguished from τὸ ἠθικόν and τὸ λογικόν.

In his "Metaphysics" Aristotle gives a definition of φύσις, or nature, which separates it equally from the sphere of mathematical speculations and from that of spiritual powers.

" Physics are concerned with things that have a principle of motion in themselves; mathematics speculate on permanent but not transcendental and self-existent things ; and there is another science separate from these two, which treats of that which is immutable and transcendental, if indeed there exists such a substance, as we shall endeavor to show that there does. This transcendental and permanent substance, if it exists at all, must surely be the sphere of the divine, it must be the first and highest principle. Hence it follows that there are three kinds of speculative science, physics, mathematics, and theology." [1]

When he comes to speak of nature more specifically, in his lectures on physics, Aristotle gives this twofold definition : "Nature may be said in one way to be the simplest and most deep-lying substratum of matter in things possessing their own principle of motion and change; in another way it may be called the form and law of such things." [2]   And so Bacon, in the second book of the " Novum Organum, in the first aphorism, speaks of *forma* as *natura naturans*, and in the thirteenth aphorism as *ipsissima res*.

Passing over from the Greeks to the Latins, we find the equivalent of φύσις in *natura*, from *nascor*, which the German accurately renders by *geboren werden*, — not simply born or coming into being, but both origin and gene-

---

[1] *Metaphysics*, x. vii. 7.

[2] *Nat. Aux.* II. i. 8.   See Sir Alexander Grant's *Ethics of Aristotle*, Essay iv.

sis. Hence *natura* denotes not only result, but ongoing process, that orderly becoming which comprehends both that which is produced and also the producing agent. In the individual, nature denotes the constitution or the quality of a thing as produced; and when conceived of collectively or in continuity, nature is the order or course of things, as being and "about-to-be."

Curiously enough, Lucretius, in his poetical disquisition on "The Nature of Things," has omitted to give a strict definition of nature. Cicero, however, in discoursing of "the nature of the gods," gives these notions of the term : —

"Some think that nature is a certain irrational power, exciting in bodies the necessary motions; others, that it is an intelligent power, acting by order and method, designing some end in every cause, and always aiming at that end. . . . And some again, as Epicurus, apply the word nature to everything." [1]

Cicero himself personifies nature, using this as an equivalent for the gods, and speaking of nature as an artificer and an intelligence.

Nevertheless, in strict usage, nature stands in contrast to both spirit and art. Etymologically, as we have seen, the *natura* is generation, but in the double sense of that which is born and that which is in course of parturition, — the thing or event which is and is continually becoming; *Werden* and *Dasein* in perpetual flux and reflux. Hence nature comes to mean the constitution of the world and the universe and the course of things. In German philosophy the term *Natur* is chiefly used to denote the world of matter in contrast to the world of spirit or intelligence. How, then, do we form our conception of nature? In strict contemplation of philosophy, nature is that established constitution and course of

---

[1] Cicero, *De Deorum Natura*, ii. xxxii.

things the knowledge of which we gain by observation or
experience, and by induction; whereas that which we
know by intuition, or establish by logic, or which the imagination conceives, lies within another category. Observing certain phenomena in regular sequence, we learn
by experience to depend upon their relations, and to look
for their repetition ; and thus we ascertain, for example,
that it is the *nature* of fire to burn, and the *nature* of
water to expand with heat and to freeze with cold. Ex-
tending the range of such observations and inductions,
we find an established course or order of things in general, and this we term nature. But that which makes
the observation, records the experience, classifies the induction, call this what we may, — whether a spiritual entity or the functional activity of the brain, — though it
may have *a* nature of its own, is not included within that
nature of whose phenomena it thus takes cognizance.
From a higher plane of vision the observer might perhaps be comprehended within the scope of nature ; but
to him nature is confined within the periphery of *things*,
from which he, at least *quoad hoc*, is distinguished as
a person. Hence in worshiping nature, whether as a
whole or in detail, the worshiper sets before him, either
in visible form or as a conception, an *object* separate from
himself, to which he renders his homage and devout regard. In nature-worship, religion takes its hue from the
phases of physical phenomena as these are reflected in
the phases of the mind. Sometimes it is the propitiation
of terrible and hurtful elements ; again it is the worship
of sensuous beauty ; [1] and, with a more advanced culture,
it becomes the homage of reason to material laws, and of
the imagination to the divinity immanent in the universe
as a soul ; now its prevailing sentiment is an awe of phe-

---

[1] " The Homeric gods spoil no man's full enjoyment of the desires of his senses." — Curtius, *History of Greece*, bk. i. 64.

nomena which suggest mysterious and destructive forces;
and again, this feeling of reverence is modulated in art
and worship, to a delight in whatever ministers to taste,
beauty, love, as being either a divinity or some divine attribute or gift. In a word, the extremes of superstition
and naturalism meet in nature as the central object of
the religious idea. Religion is, then, either the worship
of objects and forces in the material world as themselves
divinities, or the symbols of divinities; or it is a rationalistic atheism, which makes nature, or the universe in
its totality, the only power above man; or again, it is a
sentimental, poetic personification of the grand and beautiful in the physical universe; or, it may be, a subtile
pantheism, which denies to its divinity personality and
independence, and holds the unconscious world-principle
bound within the visible universe, as the life-principle is
imprisoned within bodily forms. Thus nature-religion,
starting from fetichism, runs at last into sheer *neuter*ism,
the favorite form of modern pantheism — "modern" in
a certain freshness of assertion by recent schools of philosophy, but not modern as a theory of the universe,
since Pliny held that the world and the heaven, or universal ether, which embraces all things in its vast circumference, may be regarded as itself a deity, immense, eternal, never made, and never to perish; and the Stoics
declared that " God is the world, and the world is God;
God is all matter and all mind."

Where man is made the chief factor in the world-
scheme, the type of religion is *Humanism,* whether as
hero-worship or a divinized selfhood. To that spiritual
worship of the invisible and unknown God which the
Hellenic races shared with other branches of the Aryan
family, and to the individualizing of divine attributes
and powers as themselves separate and local divinities,
the Greeks added myths of heroes whom they first rever-

enced as nearer to the gods in gifts and powers, and afterwards worshiped with divine honors. These heroes personified successive acts and periods in the development of man above nature ;[1] and yet the deified humanity of the Greeks was still, in some sort, under bondage to nature through the doctrine of *fate*, or through that dread of mysterious and destructive forces which overhangs the religions of paganism.

By conquering this dread of nature, modern science has ministered to a yet bolder man-worship. A supreme selfhood, an intensified egoism, characterizes much of the rationalism of our time. Humanity and reason alone are divine, and worship is homage to human nature. "Ineffable," says Emerson, "is the union of man and God in every act of the soul. The simplest person who in his integrity worships God, becomes God." The highest theology of this school is man *divinized.*

Such are the results of an exaggeration either of nature or of man, as terms in the scheme of religion. But there is also a conception of God which relegates Him to the sphere of the past or the unknown, as an abstraction or a fate, not personally cognizant of human affairs, not providentially acting in them — a deism which postulates nothing concerning the Deity but the infinite and the absolute, and ends with making of God an infinite and absolute nothing. "God is a name for our ignorance." For God is nothing to a man as a conception unless He is conceived of as an objective, substantive reality, possessing personality, will, holiness, and authority ; and God is nothing to us as the cause of nature unless He is the author of nature in a sense which distinguishes Him from nature, and sets Him above nature as the intelligent and controlling cause of all things.

---

[1] Thus Heracles, Cadmus, the Argonauts, Danaus, etc. This point is well treated by Curtius, *History of Greece*, i. 2.

Yet this view may be so exaggerated upon the other side, that God becomes the *Deus ex machinâ;* and the miracle or the intervention is ever at hand to supply any defect of observation or of logic upon the facts of nature. And so, paradoxical as it may seem, religion may be falsified by introducing into it too much of God! It is through this tendency to use the name of God as a dogmatic formula, and to resort to the supernatural as an expedient for solving all mysteries in nature, that some theologians have brought religion into a seeming contradiction of science.

But our analysis has shown that under all forms of conception and representation the religious idea is constantly the same. *Religion is an inner sense of obligation in man to an external object of a nature different from his own, which is regarded as superior in nature, position, or power ; which obligation prompts to acts of reverence, devotion, or obedience, with a view to please or to placate its object.* Recalling our definition of science, we see how readily religion falls within these limits — the systematic summation of all the knowledges pertaining to a given subject-matter, and the formulating of these in abstract general conceptions. Physical science purports to concern itself exclusively with things ; but, in reality, science is not concerned directly with things, but with our *thoughts* of things. Professor Jevons has shown that "scientific method must begin and end with the laws of thought," and we cannot better conclude this reference of religion to the categories of science than by quoting the words with which Jevons concludes the second edition of his " Principles of Science."[1]

"Among the most unquestionable rules of scientific method is that first law that *whatever phenomenon is, is.* We must ignore

[1] *A Treatise on Logic and Scientific Method.* By W. Stanley Jevons. 1877.

no existence whatever ; we may variously interpret or explain its meaning and origin; but if a phenomenon does exist, it demands some kind of explanation. If, then, there is to be competition for scientific recognition, the world without us must yield to the undoubted existence of the spirit within. Our own hopes and wishes and determinations are the most undoubted phenomena within the sphere of consciousness. If men do act, feel, and live as if they were not merely the brief products of a casual conjunction of atoms, but the instruments of a far-searching purpose, are we to record all other phenomena and pass over these? We investigate the instincts of the ant and the bee and the beaver, and discover that they are led by an inscrutable agency to work towards a distant purpose. Let us be faithful to our scientific method, and investigate also those instincts of the human mind by which man is led to work as if the approval of a Higher Being were the aim of life."

XI.

CHRIST, THE CHURCH, AND THE CREED.

(A Letter to a Professor of Philology in Berlin, December 25, 1877.)

THE interest you so kindly expressed in what I said to you the other day, of the use of the "Apostles' Creed" in the churches of the United States, and the request of several German friends that I would bring this American usage into public notice here, prompt me to address to you, by your courtesy, the following statement of principles and usages concerning confessions of faith, especially among churches of the Congregational order, in America. Let me here explicitly disclaim any thought of entering into the discussion of the "Hossbach case," or of the differences that now agitate the Evangelical Church of Prussia. I know too well the warning of Solomon to him "that meddleth with strife belonging not to him!" At the same time, all Christian men, of whatever church or country, have a common interest in the preservation of Christian truth and Christian liberty; and at a moment when the foundations of all belief are assailed by materialism, and the exercise of all liberty is threatened by ultramontanism, he who seeks the unity of the Church in love, above its uniformity in dogma, is not a meddler but a mediator.

I. In treating of confessions of faith, we must not lose sight of the distinction between that simple confession which, according to the New Testament, is necessary to personal salvation, and the formal confessions which may be expedient for ecclesiastical organization. If we inquire what confession the Apostles made the condition of personal salvation, we find this always one and the same: "Believe on the Lord Jesus Christ, and thou shalt be saved." Upon that confession, Peter, acting in the full inspiration of the Holy Ghost, baptized three thousand on the day of Pentecost. On that confession, Philip baptized the eunuch of Ethiopia. On that confession Paul baptized the jailer of Philippi. Jesus himself declared that the substance of all faith was to believe on Him as the Son of God. This was the simple Christian confession upon which whoever should believe it from the heart should be baptized and received into the fellowship of the disciples of Christ. No apostle added anything to this as an article of saving faith. And what the Apostles forbore to do, no pope, priest, presbytery, council, consistory, or church may presume to do — to add anything to the one simple condition of salvation which Christ himself laid down. "As many as received Him, to them gave He power to become the sons of God, even to them that believe on his name." (John i. 12.) All who thus believe, — be they Catholic or Protestant, Churchmen or Quakers — are by Christ's own warrant members of "the body of Christ," are in and of "the communion of saints," which is the one holy and universal Church. No one of these, nor any number of these, can deny to any other such believer his title to fellowship in the communion of saints, and to "an inheritance among all them which are sanctified." Peter, speaking for all the disciples, said, "Thou art the Christ, the Son of the living God." And Jesus answered, "Upon this rock will I build my Church;" not upon Peter as a person; but taking his name as a symbol, Jesus changed from the masculine name Πέτρος to the feminine term πέτρα; thus clearly meaning, "Upon this confession *as a rock*, upon this firm

and unchanging confession of me as the Son of God, will
I build my Church." With Congregationalists this confession is fundamental to the conception of the Church
of Christ as one, as spiritual, as universal and perpetual ;
and this is the only confession which is absolute and exclusive for personal salvation.

But Congregationalists recognize the fact, that to give
expression to Christian faith, and to facilitate the communion of believers and the propagation of the gospel,
some visible ecclesiastical organization is requisite ; and
the unity and efficiency of such an organization demand
that its members shall be in substantial accord in matters
of doctrine, of regimen, and of practice. Hence it may
be expedient for such an organization — that is for a particular church — to adopt a formula of faith more in detail than the simple confession appointed by Christ and
required by the Apostles for baptism into the communion
of Christian believers. Where, as in England and in the
United States, there is perfect liberty of ecclesiastical organization under the state, Christians of like views and
tastes in regard to doctrine and worship will gravitate
toward one another, and various churches will arise having a substantial unity in faith under a diversity of forms.
The liberty conceded to particular churches of framing
their own confession and liturgy — as was done for instance by the Evangelical Church of Prussia — has been
found by experience to conserve purity of doctrine as well.
as peace of communion.

Such particular creeds have also their uses for the definition and explication of Christian doctrine ; but, at this
point, care should be taken that these are not substituted
for that simple faith in Christ which is the token of salvation, nor made damnatory against those who cannot
accept their phraseology in detail. Where the attitude
of the State toward the Church, or the habit of society,

does not favor the organization of separate churches, and especially where membership in the Church is compulsory by law or by custom, there should be the more liberty of dissent within the Church itself. "Him that is weak in the faith receive ye, but not to doubtful disputations." (Rom. xiv. 1.)

II. The place assigned to a creed in any particular church will be determined largely by the basis upon which that church itself is supposed to stand. If the Church stands upon dogmatic history and tradition as its foundation, then its creed may be taken for *organic;* but if the Church stands directly upon the New Testament as its organic law, then the creed can be only *functional.* The foundation of the Church spiritual and universal was laid by Christ himself, and none can add to that nor take away from it. "Other foundation can no man lay than that is laid, which is Jesus Christ." (1 Cor. iii. 11.) But particular churches, being the work of human organization, are not always built directly and solely upon this foundation. Protestant churches profess to be established upon the New Testament as their fundamental law; and Luther no doubt set the authority of the Bible above all creeds. But some churches in practice appeal more to dogmatic history than to the Bible as their standard of belief and rule of discipline. Now it is of great moment to our conception of the faith, whether we come at the Bible through a creed, or come at the creed through the Bible. The creed is valuable as formulating the teachings of the Bible in a scientific method; and great importance should be attached to the historical continuity of the faith through eighteen centuries. But a creed almost of necessity assumes the philosophic language of the age in which it is framed; and it is apt to give emphasis to controversial statements current at the time. Now in theology, as in other sciences, words change their mean-

ing with the progress of thought, and the relative moment of doctrines changes also with each succeeding age.
Hence to impose upon the Church a form of confession as
obligatory for all ages would be to make of the Church a
mere symbolic monument in the stream of Time, as antiquated for the purposes of a living Christian society as is
a Catholic cathedral for the uses of a Protestant congre-
gation. Where a church is built upon the New Testament, creeds may well serve as buttresses to the faith;
but it is a sorry spectacle when the Church stands as a
decaying shell, the creed projecting only in grotesque
gargoyles.

Thus to stereotype a creed in antiquated forms of verbal philosophy is to rob Christianity of that *flexibility of
adaptation* which distinguishes it from all other religions
as the religion for mankind, of all races and in all ages.
This was clearly seen by the Reformers in separating
themselves from the Romish Church, and seen more clearly still by John Robinson, the father of the Congregational polity, in separating himself from the Established
Church of England. This remarkable man, honored by
the University of Leyden for his learning, and revered
by his flock for his piety, was pastor of the band of Pilgrims which in the beginning of the seventeenth century
went over from England to Holland, and afterwards emi-
grated to America. The governor of Plymouth Colony
has left on record the parting words of Robinson to the
Pilgrims as they set sail from Leyden. " He charged us
before God to follow him no farther than he followed
Christ; and if God should reveal anything to us by any
other instrument of his, to be ready to receive it as ever
we were to receive any truth by his ministry; for he was
very confident the Lord had more truth and light yet to
break forth out of his holy Word. He took occasion also
to bewail the state of the reformed churches, which were

come to a period in religion, and would go no farther than the instruments of their reformation. The Lutherans could not go beyond what Luther saw; for, whatever part of God's word He had farther revealed to Calvin, they had rather die than embrace it ; and so too the Calvinists, — they stick where he left them. A misery much to be lamented ; for though they were precious shining lights in their times, yet God had not revealed his whole will to them ; and were they now alive, they would be as ready to receive further light as that they had received. For it is not possible the Christian world should come so lately out of such anti-Christian darkness, and that full perfection of knowledge should break forth at once."

What noble words are these ! " *Truth and Light ;* " this is science. "*More* Truth and Light; " this is progress. " The Lord will cause to break forth ;" this is faith. "Out of his holy Word ; " this is law and authority. By these tests we may determine what place should be assigned to any particular creed.

If we would preserve that political freedom and that freedom of science for which our age has struggled so earnestly, we must be no less jealous for Christian liberty, and not suffer an *effete* patristic philosophy to dogmatize in the Church, against the simple teachings of Christ and the conscientious faith of any who have received his word.

III. I come now, in conclusion, to speak of the so-called " Apostles' Creed." That this creed was composed *totidem verbis* by the Apostles, there is no evidence to satisfy the critical student of church history. Happily we are able to test the articles of this confession by the writings of the Apostles themselves. Though in the Aquileian Creed, as recorded by Rufinus, we find the articles of the descent into hell, — *descendit ad inferna,* — and the resurrection of the flesh, — *hujus carnis resurrectionem,* —

yet the former rests upon a single doubtful passage (1 Peter iii. 19), and the second, the literal rising of the *flesh*, has not a single text to support it in the New Testament.[1] We have the testimony of Rufinus himself that the clause " He descended into hell " came into the creed at a late period. "Sciendum sane est, quod in ecclesiæ Romanæ symbolo non habetur additum, Descendit ad inferna, sed neque in Orientis ecclesiis habetur hic sermo; vis tamen verbi eadem videtur esse in eo quod sepultus dicitur." (Rufin. Expos. Symboli, p. 22.)

The Episcopal Church in the United States, which in doctrine and worship corresponds to the Established Church of England, does not enforce upon its clergy the reading of this article in the public service of the Church. The Liturgy provides that " any churches may omit the words, He descended into hell, or may, instead of them, use the words, He went into the place of departed spirits, which are considered as words of the same meaning in the creed." Here is a wise example of refraining to enforce through a creed a dogma which finds such doubtful warrant in the writings of the Apostles.

The " Resurrection of the *flesh* " is nowhere taught by the Apostles. This article came into the creed as a protest against Origen's idealistic view of the resurrection; yet in the Nicene Creed we do not find this doctrine, but only the expectation of the resurrection of the *dead;* προσδοκῶμεν ἀνάστασιν νεκρῶν. The early Christian Fathers were quite as much given to metaphysical speculation as are the theologians of our time, and were no less liable to prejudice and error. They foisted into creeds their metaphysical definitions of doctrines, and these often framed

---

[1] In the German this article reads not "body," but "resurrection of the *flesh;* " and a party in the Prussian Church seek to make this gross literal notion of the rising of the *natural flesh*, in distinction from a bodily *form*, a test of soundness in the faith !

in the heat of controversy. Why then should we enforce
as the essential faith of the Church such *definitions*, no
longer tenable in the light of science, and never in the
least supported by the Scriptures?

In your letter to Superintendent Dr. Brückner you said
with much force that "doctrines *about* Christ have been
substituted for the doctrine *of* Christ;" and in like manner the so-called Apostles' Creed has been substituted for
the creed of the Apostles.

The New Testament does teach the resurrection as a
fundamental doctrine of the Christian system. But what
is the resurrection as taught by Christ and the Apostles?

The word ἀνάστασις (*resurrection*) occurs in the New
Testament as follows: in the Gospels 14 times, in the
Acts 11 times, in the Epistles 13 times, in the Revelation
twice. In several of these passages it is used simply of the
resurrection of Jesus as a fact and a simile. In Matthew
xxii. 31, Mark xii. 25, Luke xx. 35, it is the resurrection
of the *dead*, τῶν νεκρῶν; in Luke xiv. 14, the resurrection
of the *just*, τῶν δικαίων; in John v. 29 the resurrection of
life, ξωῆς and of *condemnation*, κρίσεως; and in John xi. 24,
25 simply the resurrection at the *last day*. There is not
one solitary case in the New Testament where the resurrection is spoken of as a resurrection of the *flesh*, σαρξ;
nor even of the *body*, σῶμα; and this notion is contrary
to the teachings of Paul. In his speech on Mars' Hill,
and in his defenses of himself at Jerusalem (Acts xvii.
32, xxiii. 6, xxiv. 15, 21), Paul speaks expressly of the
resurrection of the *dead*. And in his great argument for
the resurrection, 1 Cor. xv., Paul speaks four times of the
resurrection of the *dead*, but not once of the resurrection
of the *flesh*. This indeed he virtually denies. He supposes some one to ask, "How are the dead raised up?
and with what body do they come?" And he answers
triumphantly, "It is sown a natural body, it is raised a

spiritual body." This spiritual body, though it shall possess individuality and shall give assurance of personal identity, shall not be the same mortal flesh that was sown, for "flesh and blood cannot inherit the kingdom of God."

The English version of the Apostles' Creed, "I believe in the resurrection of the *Body*," is better than the German reading of the resurrection of the *flesh ;* but it would be far better to adopt the grand, inspiring phrase of the Nicene Creed, "I look for the Resurrection of the dead, and the Life of the world to come." If our preaching had more of Paul's largeness of thought and breadth of charity, I am confident it would attract to the Church men of intelligence and science, who are now repelled by the narrowness of dogmatic speculation and the anti-quated phraseology of a creed. "The letter killeth, but the Spirit giveth life ;" and "where the Spirit of the Lord is, there is liberty." My training as a Congrega-tionalist has taught me to honor the great lights of the Church in every age; to accept truth from whatever source it may come; but to acknowledge no authority for Christian doctrine but the New Testament. Hence in seeking comfort concerning the dear departed, and hope for myself in view of death, I do not pin my faith upon any theory of the resurrection as put forth by Ire-næus, Justin, Tertullian, in the period of Apologetics, but go back to the promise of Jesus and the grand argument of Paul. How the dead are raised up I know not, any more than I know how grass grows, or how God exists. What is that "spiritual body" of which Paul speaks, I can no more conceive than I can conceive how my spirit and body now act as one. But we may rationally be-lieve upon evidence that which we cannot fully explain. This we do constantly in the facts of science, of history, and of daily life. And feeling as sure that Jesus rose

from the dead as that he was crucified and buried, I rest
upon his own declaration as my all sufficient hope : " This
is the will of Him that sent me, that every one which
seeth the Son, and believeth on Him, may have everlasting life ; and I will raise him up at the last day." (John
vi. 40.)

XII.

LUCRETIUS OR PAUL.

MATERIALISM AND THEISM TESTED BY THE NATURE AND THE NEEDS OF MAN.

(An Address delivered in the American Chapel, Berlin, on Thanksgiving Day, November 25, 1875.)

THE favor with which you have received two Thanksgiving addresses seemed to bring me under obligation to accept your invitation for a third, in the hope that this might at least serve for the utterance of such sentiments of gratitude, fellowship, and devotion, as to-day are common to us all. With your hearts quickened by the anticipations of the coming year, you might naturally expect that the grateful memories of a hundred years would find vent to-day in an outburst of patriotic joy. But everything in its season. That debt of gratitude is so great, so high, so deep, that I shall not presume to discount it in advance. Let it come with its whole weight to the heart of the whole nation, in the year and the day that Time has marked as one of the most bright and blessed in its calendar.[1]

[1] In commemoration of the first century of the existence of the United States as a nation, I propose to give a course of lectures upon the following topics: —

I. The Grounds and Motives of the American Revolution.

II. The Doctrines of the Declaration of Independence.

III. The Adoption of the Constitution, — Washington as Head of the Nation.

As in the days of chivalry, he who would be enrolled a knight spent the hours preceding his investiture in acts of devotion in the chapel, so if we would be found worthy to bear aloft the shield of liberty decked with the garlands of the century, we should give ourselves the rather now to studies and acts of devotion, which shall lead us to the source of all gratitude, the theme of all praise.

To Americans no sentiment is more normal or more patriotic than the recognition of God in their history. The words with which Washington opened his first address to the first Congress assembled under the Constitution have but gained in emphasis with succeeding years. " No people," said he, " can be bound to acknowledge and adore the Invisible Hand which conducts the affairs of men more than the people of the United States. Every step by which they have advanced to the character of an independent nation seems to have been attended with some token of providential agency ; " and he who had won the independence of the nation, had shaped its Constitution, and was now to order its administration, called upon Congress and the people to join with him, not in patriotic exultation, but in " pious gratitude."

Two years ago I spoke of the reasons we have for National Thanksgiving, as Americans residing in a foreign country ; last year, of the Heroic Age of America and our grateful pride in our fathers. The matter of these addresses was objective — critical and historical ; but underneath them both was the religious assumption that from whatever point we view our country we are called

These lectures will be given in *Sachse's Kunstsalon*, Tauben-Strasse 34, on Monday and Friday evenings, commencing Monday, February 21st, 1876. [These lectures were subsequently printed.]

to gratitude, and that this gratitude has at once its source and its end in the loving care of a living Father.

Let me now attempt to lead you up to this highest view of thanksgiving, a view in which rest all reasons of thanksgiving for ourselves and our country, and which is equally present and imperative at home and abroad, — God here, God there, God then and now and always, — the living Father with his loving care.

But is God here, there, everywhere? Is He anywhere? or is He nowhere? Around this question of a personal God the battle rages most fiercely in the world of modern thought, and if we look to the clouds, as in the battle of the Huns, we there see the ghosts of ancient philosophy still fighting over the same field. A personal God, Creator, Governor, Redeemer, Father, or, matter, force, motion, evolution, and final extinction, — this was the issue in the last generation in the sphere of metaphysics, renewed in our time in the sphere of physics, — in one word, theism or materialism, the issue which must determine whether thanksgiving is a reasonable virtue or a foolish superstition.

I need make no apology for handling such a question before an audience having more than an average of thinkers, and more than an average of training in the facts of science and the laws of thought, and especially before minds whose course of study brings them in contact with materialism, either tacitly assumed or plausibly presented almost as a synonym of science. But in propounding this theme, I do not propose to make a scientific disquisition, nor to enter the field of modern controversy; but taking the materialistic and theistic schemes of the universe as stated by the foremost advocates of each in ancient times, to test them severally in their adaptation to man, as an explication both of himself and of that order of things with which he is inseparably con-

nected. This test is strictly scientific. Science would
not accept as a definition of a thing or a creature a statement that failed to include or account for some of its
most distinguishing properties; nor would science record
as a law a formula that did not fairly cover all the characteristic and undeviating phenomena of the subject-matter. Now, man is a creature of a certain characteristic
and undeviating constitution as to its essential elements
and their normal manifestation; he is capable of observation, understanding, reason, imagination, emotion, affection, volition, moral judgment, as truly and universally
as he is capable of growth, speech, nutrition, and locomotion. Also, the order of things with which he stands
connected — call it nature, the cosmos, the universe —
addresses itself not only to his bodily senses, but to each
and all of these capacities or faculties that go to make up
the man. The scenes and sounds that impress his organs
of sight and hearing address themselves also to his imagination and taste; excite within him joy, fear, hope, memory, love; move him to action, or lull him to repose.
What an unscientific absurdity, then, is a scheme of the
universe which would define its origin, its nature, and its
workings simply through its impression upon the physical senses of man, or as known to his observation, and
should leave quite out of account the rich and manifold
aptitudes of the universe to the nature of man as a being
of thought and imagination, of emotion and desire, of
affection and will? How shallow the pretense to science,
in a definition of the universe, that should ignore all its
relations to the nobler and better part of man.

It is to this test of the universe as related to man and
man as related to the universe, that I propose to submit
the schemes of materialism and theism. In the statement of these schemes I shall take for each its foremost
representative, Lucretius and Paul; each in his kind the

highest type of man. I take these because, while they can be contemplated apart from the prejudices and passions of contemporary disputants, they are also fairly balanced, and are unsurpassed by any of the whole race of philosophers, be they scientists or sciolists, of to-day. Lucretius and Paul were alike in the rare combination in equal measure of the logical and the imaginative faculties; strong-armed for blows of argument, strong-winged for flights of poetry. They were alike in the love of truth, in the desire to free mankind from superstition and error, and in courage to avow their opinions and obey their convictions. They were alike in seeking the foundation of things, and from this to grasp the infinite, and with thought and fancy to girdle the universe. Nearly contemporary, — Lucretius having died barely fifty years before Paul was born, — they both grew up amid the culture of the Roman empire in its most brilliant and classic age. That Lucretius enjoyed this culture, his poem furnishes intrinsic evidence in its mastery at once of Greek philosophy and of Latin verse, which last, indeed, he perfected, as did Shakespeare the English and Goethe the German.

Paul, too, had the best culture of his time: first, at Antioch, then a foremost seat of learning; next at Jerusalem, in the famous school of Gamaliel, where were taught not only the history and laws of Judaism, but philosophy, science, literature from every quarter, especially from the East."[1] That Paul was a man of intellectual rank is evident, not only from the thought and style of his writings, but from his being intrusted at an

[1] In the higher schools of Palestine were taught law, ethics, history, grammar, languages (Coptic, Aramaic, Persian, Median, Latin, Greek), mathematics, astronomy, botany, zoölogy, etc. See a full account of these schools in the *Literary Remains of Emanuel Deutsch*, pp. 21–25, and 140.

early age with high responsibilities by the leaders of his
nation ; by his familiarity with Greek philosophy and
Greek authors, as shown for instance at Athens and Lystra ; and by his " disputing in the school of one Tyran-
nus ; "[1] and that he was of a scholarly habit appears
from his message to Timothy, " The cloak that I left at
Troas bring with thee, and the books — but especially
the parchments,"[2] which he had written or needed for
writing. He could ill afford to lose an outer garment,
but, like a German professor, he cared more for books,
and especially his own writings, than for clothes!

Of Lucretius it must be said that he not only wrought
out the doctrine of materialism with a completeness of
statement and profuseness of illustration not attained by
any of his predecessors, but also made his system of the
universe so comprehensive that modern materialists have
added absolutely nothing to his conception, but have
simply confirmed at certain points, by observation and
experiment, what he had reasoned out from his speculative postulates.[3]

---

[1] Acts xix. 9.　　　　　　　　　　[2] 2 Tim. iv. 33.

[3] Too little is known of the life of Lucretius to enable us to judge
how far he subjected his philosophical theories to experimental tests.
His poem exhibits a perfect acquaintance with the discoveries and
opinions of the Greek philosophers, and a minute observance of Nature as to her more patent phenomena. But of experimental observation, — what the Friar of Messina styled

　　　　　　　　" Observation
　Which with *experimental seal* doth warrant
　The tenor of my book," —

Lucretius seems to have had little or none. The lack of facility
for this makes his system the more wonderful, as a structure of vast
and logical consistency, a metaphysical creation to so many parts of
which physical observation has now put its " experimental seal."
Thus, as to the properties of vacuum Lucretius argues not from experiments in an artificial void, but abstractly, from the nature of
void — " sua quod natura petit." — L. ii. 237.

Did Galileo demonstrate that in a vacuum all bodies fall through equal spaces in equal times? Lucretius had already said that "whenever bodies fall through water and thin air, they must quicken their descents in proportion to their weights, because the body of water and subtle nature of air cannot retard everything in equal degree, but more readily give way, overpowered by the heavier; on the other hand, empty void cannot offer resistance to anything in any direction at any time, but must, as its nature craves, continually give way; and for this reason all things must be moved and borne along with equal velocity though of unequal weights through the unresisting void."[1] Has modern astronomy, by the most rigorous test of calculation and of instruments, settled upon the nebular hypothesis as the most plausible explanation of the formation of the masses of the planets, their rotation, their rings and satellites, and also of the asteroids and comets? Lucretius had anticipated this in his conception of minute, innumerable atoms in perpetual motion through the realms of space.[2] Do modern physicists boast the discovery that in nature there is no annihilation, but a perpetual conservation of energy, a correlation of force, and transmutation of form? Lucre-

---

[1] " Omnia qua propter debent per inane quietum
Æque ponderibus non æquis concita ferri."
De Rerum Natura, l. ii. 230–240.

For the convenience of readers who may not be able to consult Lucretius in the original, in quoting his poem, I have followed throughout (as upon the whole the best) the neat, terse, and accurate prose translation of Mr. Munro, Fellow of Trinity College, Cambridge, third edition. There is also a good French prose translation by Ernest Lavigne, avec une Étude sur la Physique de Lucrèce, par Frédéric André. Among the many editions of the original, that of Lachman is to be commended.

[2] L. i. 988–1052. " All things are ever going on in ceaseless motion . . . hence many forms must arise." Helmholtz suggests a vortex motion in an incompressible, frictionless liquid.

tius had already said, "Nature does not annihilate
things;"—"a thing never returns to nothing, but all
things after disruption go back into the first bodies of
matter. None of the things, therefore, which seem to be
lost is utterly lost, since nature replenishes one thing out
of another, and does not suffer anything to be begotten
before she has been recruited by the death of some
other."[1] And again he speaks of latent forces in things,
and of "an imperishable residuum into which all things
can be dissolved at their last hour, that there may be a
supply of matter for the reproduction of things."[2] Has
Darwin coined the phrases "struggle for existence,"
"natural selection," "survival of the fittest," to account
for species and varieties? Again Lucretius is beforehand in saying, "Not by design did the first-beginnings
of things station themselves each in its right place,
guided by keen intelligence; nor did they bargain, sooth
to say, what motions each should assume; but because
many in number, and shifting about in many ways
throughout the universe, they are driven and tormented
by blows during infinite time past, after trying motions
and unions of every kind, at length they fall into arrangements such as those out of which this our sum of
things has been formed."[3]

Above all, the fundamental conception of Lucretius
that the atom is the unit of structure in all bodies is in
part confirmed by Dalton's discovery of the law of multiple proportions,[4] and by other recent discoveries in

---

[1] "Huc accedit uti quicque in sua corpora rursum,
Dissoluat natura neque ad nilum interemat res

·   ·   ·   ·   ·   ·   ·   ·   ·   ·

Quando alid ex alio reficit natura, nec ullam
Rem gigni patitur, nisi morte adiuta aliena."

[2] L. i. 543–548.   L. i. 215–265.

[3] L. i. 1021–1027. "Omne genus motus et cœtus *experiundo.*"

[4] This law, as *bearing upon the atomic theory,* may be thus stated:

chemistry and physics; and should we accept also his doctrine concerning body and void, I see not how there would remain anything in the material universe beyond the original ken of this poet-philosopher, nor anything for science to do but to verify by observation his metaphysical outline of nature and fill up its details. True, if we take what he calls "the *inane*" for absolute vacuum, some scientists would be at issue with Lucretius with their doctrine of a "luminiferous ether" filling all space and trembling with waves of light — what Roscoe calls an "elastic medium," [1] and Tyndall says "though more attenuated than any known gas, resembles jelly rather than air." [2] But Lucretius seems to mean by the

Each atom is a definite mass of matter, having a definite weight, and all atoms of the same substance have the same size and weight. Hence "when an atom of iron unites with an atom of sulphur to form a molecule of sulphide of iron, the union takes place in the proportion by weight of 56 to 32. When two atoms of hydrogen combine with one atom of oxygen to form a molecule of water, since each atom of oxygen weighs sixteen times as much as an atom of hydrogen, the two substances must combine in the proportion of $2:16$ or $1:8$. Further, the proportions of the different elementary substances which unite to form the various known compounds are so related that it is possible to find for each element a number, such that, in regard to the several numbers, it may be said that the elements always combine in the proportion by weight of these numbers or of some simple multiples of these numbers." See *The New Chemistry*, by Prof. J. P. Cooke, chap. v. Many chemists, though not all, accept the atomic theory as the best solution of this law of multiple proportions. To our estimate of Lucretius, the variation of meaning in the terms *molecule* and *atom*, as used in chemistry and in physics, is of no practical importance.

[1] "Light is due to the undulations of the elastic medium pervading all space to which physicists have given the name of luminiferous ether." Roscoe on *Spectrum Analysis*, p. 9.

[2] *Fragments of Science*, Essay I. "The Constitution of Nature." Reprinted from *Fortnightly Review*, vol. iii. p. 129.

Though this theory of a luminiferous ether seems to account satisfactorily for all the phenomena of light, there remain eminent phys-

inane, space in which there is no appreciable matter ; as
he expressly says " if it shall be intangible and unable
to hinder anything from passing through it on any side,
this you are to know will be that which we call empty
void." [1] This seems neither more nor less than what
philosophers have surmised, but not demonstrated, under
the name of ether.

Tennyson has finely phrased Lucretius' doctrine of the
void as the abode of the gods : —

> " The lucid interspace of world and world,
> Where never creeps a cloud or moves a wind,
> Nor ever falls the least white star of snow,
> Nor ever lowest roll of thunder moans,
> Nor sound of human sorrow mounts, to mar
> Their sacred everlasting calm."

We must pause here a moment to observe that, however in fact the universe was or is made, it was not first
constructed by the materialists of our day ; and if these

icists who reject it or hold themselves in suspense concerning it. The
path of Encke's comet as observed through the great equatorial at
Washington, seems to confirm von Asten's view that all the movements of this body could be accounted for by the disturbing attrac-
tions of the planets, without supposing a retarding influence from an
ethereal medium. The existence of such a medium is still an open
question.

Professor Challis, of Cambridge, regards the universe as made up
of atoms and ether. " The atoms are spheres, unalterable in magnitude, and endowed with inertia, but with no other property whatever. The ether is a perfect fluid, endowed with inertia, and exert-
ing a pressure proportional to its density. It is truly continuous (and
therefore does not consist of atoms), and it fills up all the interstices
of the atoms." Essay on the *Mathematical Principles of Physics.*
See *Nature*, vol. viii. p. 279. This ether of Challis is a modification
of the void of Lucretius. See again Helmholtz's incompressible frictionless fluid.

[1] " Sin intactile erit, nulla de parte quod ullam
    Rem prohibere queat per se transire meantem,
    Scilicet, hoc id erit, vacuum quod inane vocamus."
                                        L. i. 437—440.

gentlemen were better versed in the history of that philosophy which some of them affect to despise, they might grow wiser, if not more modest, in presence of the great masters of thought, whose shadows they are. For here observe in Lucretius, that it was *thinking*, and not seeing, that first penetrated the arcana of the universe. That Lucretius was familiar with the observations as well as the speculations of foregoing philosophers is evident ;[1] but his own theory of the universe, now confirmed at so many points by experiment, is a marvel of the deductive method. To the examples already given of his anticipation of modern discoveries I add two that alone should make him immortal among thinkers. Lucretius held that atoms " are of solid singleness," but that bodies as we see them are made up of atoms and void, and are solid or rare according to the proportions of body and void. This he illustrates by comparing a ball of wool with a lump of lead. Take now the beautiful experiment of packing the same globe with three kinds of vapor. A glass globe, with a capacity of one cubic foot, and containing one cubic inch of water, is exhausted of air, and then heated to the boiling point ; the water all evaporates, and the globe is filled with steam. If more water be added, the same temperature being kept up, not a particle of this will evaporate ; but if alcohol is introduced, " this immediately evaporates, and just as much alcohol-vapor will form as if no steam were present. The globe is filled with aqueous-vapor and alcohol-vapor at one and the same time, each acting, in all respects, as if it occupied the space alone. If now we add a quantity of ether, we shall have the same phenomena repeated ; the ether will expand, and fill the space with its vapor, and the globe will hold just as much ether-vapor as if neither of the other two were present. There is not here a chemical union

[1] See note, p. 262.

between the several vapors, and we cannot in any sense regard the space as filled with a compound of the three. We can give no satisfactory explanation of these phenomena except on the assumption that each substance is an aggregate of particles, or units, which, by the action of heat, become widely separated from each other, leaving very large intermolecular spaces, within which the particles of an almost indefinite number of other vapors may find place."[1] But Lucretius was just as sure that such must be the structure of bodies as if he had witnessed a thousand such experiments. One other point in which Lucretius anticipated the inductive and experimental science of modern times has elicited the special admiration of Sir William Thomson, himself a great authority upon the structure and properties of atoms. Lucretius, in his first book, vigorously contests the notion that the universe is compounded of four elements, — earth, water, air, and fire, — and especially the doctrine that fire is the source of all things; he refers all phenomena to the properties of atoms and their *kinetic* energy. As, for instance, "there are certain bodies whose clashing motions, order, position, and shapes, produce fires, and which, by *a change of order*, change the nature of the things."[2] Hence, according to Sir William, the recent methods of explaining heat, light, elasticity, diffusion, electricity, and magnetism, in gases, liquids, and solids, are "carrying out the grand conception of Lucretius, who admits no subtle ethers, no variety of elements with fiery, or watery, or light, or heavy principles; nor supposes light to be one thing, fire another, electricity a fluid, magnetism a vital principle, but treats all phenomena as mere properties or accidents of simple matter."[3]

[1] Cooke's *New Chemistry*: Lecture I.
[2] *Mutatoque ordine mutant naturam.* L. i. p. 685 *seq.*
[3] Address of Sir W. Thomson, LL. D., F. R. S., before the British Association, 1871; also *North British Review* on Lucretius, March, 1868.

Now, the point I make, and would insist upon, is that these were not lucky guesses or coincidences of Lucretius, but results of the *deductive* method to which scientific materialism is compelled to do homage by its own discoveries. But remarkable as are these correspondences of experimental physics and chemistry with the atomic theory, the atom itself is simply assumed. It never has been, and never can be brought within the range of the senses. The atomic theory is evidenced by experiments as to atomic weights, volume, heat, and combining capacity, and as to isomerism, and chemical molecules and homogeneity ; but the theory is still stoutly contested by some, and the very existence of the atom is disputed by others.[1] Yet we are called upon to accept the materialistic doctrine of the universe, and to receive nothing as *knowledge* which does not come to us through the senses, while forsooth the foundation of this sensible universe lies utterly beyond the senses, is not at all a physical fact that any one has seen or handled, but a theoretical deduction, an assumption of the mind to explain facts that are seen. Let the atomic theory have all due acceptance as an ingenious and subtile theory, but let it not be thrust upon us as a dogma by a hierarchy of physicists — which, in the name of human freedom, is as much to be resisted and detested as an ecclesiastical hierarchy. Most heartily and gratefully do I welcome all facts ascertained by physical science ; nor do I see, upon theistic grounds, any solid objection to the nebular hypothesis, the atomic theory, the doctrine of the correlation of forces, or of natural selection. But should all these be established upon the physical basis of experimental observation, I pray men of science to be honest enough to own that it was not

---

[1] See Essay of S. D. Tillman, *Nature*, vol. vi. p. 171 : E. J. Mills in *Philosophical Magazine*, xliii. p. 112; and Professor B. C. Brodie, *Journal of the Chemical Society*, London, p. xxi. p. 367.

physics but *metaphysics* that first suggested and sought
to demonstrate them, each and all. Materialism cannot
repudiate its own parentage; cannot steal the name of
Lucretius and scorn his method. Materialism was begotten not of nature, but of mind through metaphysics.

I accept the method of induction as the basis of scientific theorizing, but not to the exclusion of logic and imagination, — in one word, of metaphysical speculation.
Three hundred years have passed since Bacon gave us
the inductive method, and now that method is only beginning to give us results as to the physical universe,
which, nineteen hundred years ago, Lucretius, poet and
metaphysician, evolved from his own brain. In the
sphere of physics, speculation may require to be confirmed by observation, and speculation cannot stand
when positively contradicted by observation; but in the
conception of the universe there is a sphere for metaphysics as well as physics, and in which metaphysics may
be strong enough and clear enough to assert that the
seeming facts of physics are delusions and its deductions
fallacies. That which man *sees* is not all that *is*, nor all
that man knows or dare affirm.

Goethe, who might have been first among physicists
had he not been first among poets, said : " I want to
know what it is that impels every several portion of the
universe to seek out some other portion, either to rule or
to obey it, and qualifies some for the one part and some
for the other, according to a law innate in them all and
operating like a voluntary choice. But this is precisely
the point upon which the most perfect and universal silence prevails." [1]   And he puts into the mouth of Faust

---

[1] Conversation with Falk. Hegel quotes a like sentiment from
another poet : —

" In's Innere der Natur
Dringt kein erschaffner Geist,

that which we may take for at once the boast and the
confession of his own mind : —

> " I feel indeed that I have made the treasure
> Of human thought and knowledge mine in vain,
> And if I now sit down in restful leisure,
> No fount of newer strength is in my brain;
> I am no hair's-breadth more in height,
> Nor nearer to the infinite." [1]

*The knowledge of the Seen does not preclude the exist-
ence of the Unseen.* It is the failure to admit this simple
aphorism that has been the folly of materialists from
Lucretius to Haeckel. Lucretius says, " From the senses
first has proceeded the knowledge of the true, and the
senses cannot be refuted ; " [2] and he asks, " What surer
test can we have than the senses whereby to note truth
and falsehood — to what else shall we appeal? " [3] I
answer, to that Something within us that sits in judgment upon the senses and determines whether their testimony is true or false; which, for instance, when the
eye sees a ghost in the grave-yard, or a lake in the desert,
decides that this is but an illusion of the retina, or a
disease of the optic nerve.[4] When you look upon the

> Zu glücklich, wenn er nur
> Die äussere Schaale weis't."

To this Hegel adds the comment, " Rather should it be said, if the
essence of Nature is determined by any one as *inner*, in that very
determination he knows only the *outer* shell." *Encyklopädie der
philosophischen Wissenschaften.* § 140. *Die Lehre vom Wesen.*

[1] Bayard Taylor's translation.

[2] " Invenies primis ab sensibus esse creatam
Notitiem veri, neque sensus posse refelli."
L. iv. 475, 476.

[3] " Quo referemus enim? quid nobis certius ipsis
Sensibus esse potest, qui vera ac falsa notemus? "
L. i. 699, 700.

[4] Thus Macbeth, while intent upon the murder of Duncan, first
sees a dagger, then disputes his sight by his touch, then, when his
reason recovers from the bewilderment of his imagination, he passes

clever tricks of the juggler or the medium, you know
that you are being cheated, and do not see what you see,
nor hear what you hear. You judge your senses at the
time, and enjoy the conscious luxury of being hum-
bugged, or if misled for the moment by appearances,
when you think it over, you berate your senses for having fooled you. Our senses are not the final and sufficient judge upon all fact and truth. This crucial test of
Lucretius is unscientific in three particulars.

I. It would shut out the great body of mankind from
that knowledge which is necessary to just convictions
and beliefs, and to right action. It is not possible for the
body of mankind to make with their own senses those
observations of Nature upon which physicists base the
doctrine of the world and of life. Hence, in a matter of
such high concern as the order of things with which they
are related, mankind must put that *faith* in physicists

judgment both upon his senses and his fancy, and is himself again.
By italicizing a few words of his soliloquy the whole process becomes
plain : —

"Is this a dagger, which I see before me,
The handle toward my hand? Come, let me clutch thee; —
I *have* thee not, and yet I *see* thee still.
Art thou not, fatal vision, sensible
To feeling, as to sight? or art thou but
A *dagger of the mind :* a *false* creation,
Proceeding from the heat-oppressed brain?
I *see* thee yet, in form as palpable
As this which now I draw.

.   .   .   .

Mine *eyes* are made the fools o' the *other* senses,
Or else *worth all the rest :* I SEE thee *still :*
And on thy blade, and dudgeon, gouts of blood,
Which was not so before; — *There's no such thing :*
It is the *bloody business,* which informs
Thus to mine eyes."

Shakespeare made no mistake in making sense thus mislead, and
then refuting sense by reason.

which for themselves they contest and renounce. When the scientific materialist speaks *ex cathedrâ* there is nothing for the laity but implicit submission to his authority. If they venture an opinion, he tells them they have "no knowledge," they may feel or believe — but he *knows*.[1]

II. It is unscientific to assume that all things are discernible by the senses. No mortal has yet seen or handled that in the senses which discerns. No atomist has seen or felt an atom. No instrument has yet pierced or measured what lies in spaces that are ever and forever next beyond.

III. It is unscientific to attempt to account for man and the universe within the narrow range of man's external senses, leaving out of view that immeasurable reach and range of faculty by which he knows himself. to be other than a walking, seeing, feeling, eating brute. It was this unscientific limitation of knowledge to the vehicle of the senses that led Lucretius into the fallacy that "there is nothing which you can affirm to be at once separate from all bodies and quite distinct from void, which would, so to say, account for the discovery of a third nature,"[2] — that nothing exists or can exist in the universe beside void and bodies. For the constitution of a material universe, it is true that matter and space or body and void are alike essential, and so far as we know are all; but the question is, whether the material universe is all; and that question cannot be settled by purely physical observation upon the nature of bodies or the contents of space. That incessant striving of

---

[1] See Tyndall's reply to Martineau in *Fortnightly Review*, November, 1875.

[2] "Praeterea nil est quod possis dicere ab omni
Corpore seiunctum secretumque esse ab inani,
Quod quasi tertia sit numero natura'reperta."
L. i. 430–433.

man's nature after something above and beyond, — a
striving that grows the more impatient with his mastery
over nature and his accumulating stores of knowledge;
that mighty unrest in which a Prometheus, a Lucifer,
a Faust are but projected types of our inner selves; the
unrest that urges man on to think the unthinkable and
to know the unknowable; that makes poetry, philosophy, music, so much higher and worthier representations
of humanity than the recorded observation of phenom-
·ena, — what is this but an attestation of that "third
thing" that Lucretius could not feel nor see, but that
Paul had attained to when he spoke of "body, soul, and
spirit," and found not only a third element in the constitution of man and of the universe, but also a "third
heaven" in which spirit might abide?

But it is not my purpose here to discuss the world-
scheme of Lucretius or of Paul from a purely physical
point of view. As I have said, I would bring each system before you in the words and with the weight of these
great masters, and then leave you to test the materialism
of the one and the theism of the other by the needs and
aptitudes of your own nature. Lucretius lays it down as
his first principle "that nothing is ever gotten out of
nothing by divine power." [1] Hence matter, as to its essence, or what he terms the "first-beginnings," is eternal
and imperishable. Then, as to the forms of things, these
are due not to design nor intelligence, but to the conflicts
and combinations of atoms through motion and eternal
laws, so that everything exists as to its elements, and all
things are done, as to the manner of them, "without the
hand of the Gods." [2] Taking his illustration from the
minute bodies seen floating in a sunbeam in a dark chamber, he says: "For the first-beginnings of things move

[1] Nullam rem e nilo gigni divinitus umquam. L. i. 150.
[2] L. i. 157 and 1020 seq.

first of themselves ; next those bodies which form a small aggregate and come nearest so to say to the powers of the first-beginnings are impelled and set in movement by the unseen strokes of those first bodies, and they next in turn stir up bodies which are . a little larger. Thus motion mounts up from the first-beginnings, and step by step issues forth to our senses, so that those bodies also move which we can discern in the sunlight, though it is not clearly seen by what blows they so act." [1]

We must now keep in mind how strongly Lucretius insists that " from the senses first proceeded the knowledge of the true, and the senses cannot be refuted." Yet he here assumes several successive stages of motion by the impact of bodies before either body or motion becomes cognizable by the senses. That is, for the foundation of his atomic theory he reasons back from the seen to the unseen : the reasoning may be valid, but the existence of the atom is not attested by the senses. Yet nowadays, to reason from the seen to the unseen, from phenomena to cause, from adaptation to intelligence, is forsooth made an offense in the metaphysician, though Lucretius arrived at his atom by deduction, and then assumed the atom as the basis of his materialistic universe! Next, having inferred the motion of invisible atoms from the perceived motion of visible particles, he makes the bold assumption of self-originated motion for the first-beginnings. This is sheer assertion, since his senses had shown him only motion by impact, and neither the senses nor logic could derive from this motion without " blows " to start it. Newton has said that " the properties which we attribute to the least parts of matter must be consistent with those of which experiments on sensible bodies have made us cognizant." Now Lucretius admits that

[1] Prima moventur enim per se primordia rerum, etc. B. ii. 133 *seq.*

all bodies above the " first-beginnings " have the property
of inertia, and require to be " set in movement," " impelled," " stirred up " by " strokes and blows " from
without. But when he reaches his " first-beginnings "
he drops inertia and impact, and substitutes self-move-
ment, by a most gratuitous assumption. This is the
habit of his followers. On the materialistic principle
neither observation nor logic can begin the first-begin-
ning, nor start the first motion. At this point materialism begs the whole question. It gives no proof that the
universe is automatic.

But to proceed. From atoms and motion acting under
certain conditions, Lucretius produces organic life, so that
" whatever things we perceive to have sense are all composed of senseless first-beginnings ; " [1] and " Nature is
seen to do all things spontaneously of herself, without
the meddling of the Gods." [2] Nor does he stop with the
material origin of organic life, but teaches that " the nature of the mind and soul is bodily " — the directing and
governing principle of life being physically " no less part
of the man than hand and foot and eyes." [3] He even
goes so far as to describe the bodies, seeds, or atoms out
of which the mind is formed ; namely, that " these are
exceedingly small, smooth, and round, and inwoven
through the veins and flesh and sinews of the body ; the
proofs of which are the great velocity with which the
mind moves, and the fact that, at death, the " so-called
departure of the soul takes away none of the weight of
the body any more than a delicious aroma dispersed in
the air reduces the size or weight of the body that emits
it." [4] Hence he argues that in death the " cause of destruction is one and inseparable for both body and soul ; "
that the soul driven forth out of the body into the open

[1] L. ii. 865.   [3] L. iii. 94–162.
[2] L. ii. 1090.   [4] L. iii. 177–230.

air, "stripped of its covering, not only cannot continue through eternity, but is unable to hold together the smallest fraction of time." "The nature of the mind is mortal; therefore when the body has died, the soul itself has perished also" as to its individuality; the chain of self-consciousness is snapped asunder; and the elements of both body and soul are resolved into other material forms. "Immortal death takes away from both their mortal life." [1]

There, is a certain grandeur and beauty in these conceptions, and I confess that when first I had mastered Lucretius, I felt a touch of awe at the majesty of a soul thus blindly bowing to its fate, and, Samson-like, dragging down men and gods together in its own destruction. But as I looked upon such a universe, in which destruction is the ever-recurring law, and death alone is immortal, from this background of darkness and despair, I saw rise before me that marvelous vision of Wordsworth : —

> " In my mind's eye a temple, like a cloud
> Slowly surmounting some invidious hill,
> Rose out of darkness : the bright work stood still ;
> And might of its own beauty have been proud,
> But it was fashioned, and to God was vowed
> By virtues that diffused, in every part,
> Spirit divine through forms of human art ;
> Faith had her arch — her arch when winds blow loud,
> Into the consciousness of safety thrilled ;
> And Love her towers of dread foundation laid
> Under the grave of things ; Hope had her spire
> Star-high, and pointing still to something higher ;
> Trembling I gazed, but heard a voice, — it said,
> Hell-gates are powerless Phantoms when *we* build." [2]

This vision recalls us to the scheme of the universe as set forth by Paul, whom we mate with Lucretius as the greatest master of theistic thought. His foundation prin-

---

[1] L. iii. 632–867.　　　　[2] *Miscellaneous Sonnets,* xliv.

ciple is, "Every house is builded by some man, but He
that built all things is God."[1]　"Through faith we understand that the worlds were framed by the Word of
God; so that things which are seen were not made of
things which do appear."[2]　"For the invisible things of
Him from the creation of the world are clearly seen, being understood by the things that are made, even his
eternal power and godhead."[3]　Like Lucretius[4] seeking
to deliver men from superstition, but by satisfying that
feeling of devotion that is imperishable in man, Paul said
to the men of Lystra, "We preach unto you, that ye
should turn from these vanities unto the living God,
which made heaven and earth and the sea, and all things
that are therein.　He left not himself without witness in
that He did good; He gave us rain from heaven, and
fruitful seasons, filling our hearts with food and gladness."[5].　At Athens, this system of Paul came into direct
collision with the Epicurean system of Lucretius.　The
materialists of Athens, with the air of contempt that
their followers affect to-day, said, "What will this babbler say?"　What does he know of philosophy, of science,
of the universe?　And the "babbler," standing in the
place where Socrates was judged, with an eloquence that
Demosthenes might have envied, addressed himself to
their consciousness, to their understanding, to their moral
sense, to the dignity of their nature, appealed to their
reason, to their own poets, and to that irrepressible, insatiable yearning of their souls, which, overflowing all
boundaries of superstition, and all temples of human art,
went forth into the unmeasured void of Lucretius to seek
the Unknown.　"Ye men of Athens, I perceive that,

[1] Heb. iii. 4.　　　　　　　　　　[2] Heb. ii. 3.
[3] Rom. i. 20.
[4] See note at the end of this article.
[5] Acts xiv. 15–17.

above other peoples, ye are in every way given to religious reverence. For, as I passed through the city, and
looked over the objects of your devotion, I found an altar
with this inscription, — To an Unknown God. Him,
therefore, whom ye worship though ye know Him not —
Him do I set forth to you. God that made the world
and all things therein, seeing that He is Lord of heaven
and earth, dwelleth not in temples made with hands,
neither is worshiped with men's hands as though He
needed anything, seeing He giveth to all life and breath
and all things: and every nation of men — all alike of
one blood — He hath caused to dwell on all the face
of the earth, and hath determined the times before appointed and the bounds of their habitation ; that they
should seek the Lord, if haply they might feel after Him
and find Him, though He be not far from every one of
us : for in Him we live and move and have our being ;
as certain also of your own poets have said, For we are
also his offspring." [1]

As no materialistic philosopher of modern times has
improved upon Lucretius in his conception of the universe, so no theistic thinker has got beyond that " bab-
ble " of Paul at Athens ; and the question of to-day is,
to which system does your nature answer and which
teacher will your mind follow ? It is you then who are
to make the argument ; rather, it makes itself, as we ex-
hibit these two systems of the universe in the mirror of
your own nature.

I. The first test springs directly out of the day on
which and the purpose for which, we have come together.

---

[1] Acts xvii. 22 *seq.* It is to be hoped that the new English translation will restore this incomparable speech to its original beauty and
force of diction. Paul was an orator, a scholar, and a gentleman, and
did not open his speech by insulting his audience, and stirring their
prejudices, as represented in the English version.

In the words of the Proclamation by the President of the United States, " Amid the rich and free enjoyment of all our advantages, we should not forget the source from whence they are derived, and the extent of our obligations to the Father of all our mercies." And therefore, " in accordance with a practice at once wise and beautiful," and in sympathy with the millions of our countrymen, " we devote this occasion to the humble expression of our thanks to Almighty God for the ceaseless and distinguished benefits bestowed upon us as a nation, and for his mercies and protection during the closing year." But if the theory of Lucretius is true, it should shame you to be here, and should shame me still more to be speaking to you of such a theme. What then should we thank? the myriad atoms heaving, tossing, driving, mixing, without consciousness, without intelligence, without feeling as to whether they shall shape a mountain or a mole, a beast or a man? If the doctrine of Lucretius is true, this is no place and these are no acts for men of science or men of sense. We are no wiser, no better than the Africans at their fetich worship, though under another name. Thanksgiving is a superstition, and we of all people in the world should be free of superstition. And we are free of it. Our practical reasoning nature does not incline toward it. There is no background of superstition in our history, there are no legends, monuments, mythologies, ruins, for superstition to build upon. We have broken the yoke alike of political tradition and of ecclesiastical tyranny. We are free men of free thought. If we brought with us superstitions of our own, we have worked ourselves free of them by travel and study in foreign lands. Even that one amiable superstition that clings to the unsophisticated American, — that his is just about the biggest nation on the planet, — he gets ashamed of, when he sees what bigger fools other people can make of themselves by boasting their nation the centre of all wisdom, the source and end of all culture!

But if we are sometimes fools we are not hypocrites. No law, no form, no tradition, no regard for opinion compels our attendance here to-day. We are here because moved by one of the profoundest, noblest, holiest sentiments of our nature. In giving thanks to God, we do homage to that which is best and purest within ourselves. Man is as truly made for the exercise of gratitude as for the use of his physical senses. These are no more part of him than that. Nay, to be void of gratitude is worse than to be blind, deaf, or dumb. Mankind have stamped ingratitude as more execrable than any sin or crime. Æsop has branded it in the fable of the viper stinging him who had warmed it into life. In that tragedy that combines in itself more horrors than all dramas ever written for the stage,—the " Orestes " of Euripides,—though the matricide can plead in mitigation that his mother was an adultress and had murdered his father, and that the god Apollo had commanded him to slay her, yet the constant refrain of the chorus as they bewail his crime and of the people as they demand his punishment is, that he did not hold back the dagger when his mother bared to him the breasts that had suckled him : and in the torments of his madness, Orestes sees his father beseeching him not to slay her who bore him.[1]

The lowest deeps of his " Inferno," that he was powerless with terror to describe, Dante reserved for the infamy of ingratitude and treason. Shakespeare, holding before us the rent and bloody mantle of Cæsar, gives the

---

[1] Shakespeare has the same thought in *Lear*, act i. scene 4 : —
" Ingratitude ! thou marble-hearted fiend,
  More hideous, when thou show'st thee in a child,
  Than the sea-monster !
  How sharper than a serpent's tooth it is
  To have a thankless child ! "

final thrill of horror when he points to the wound of
Brutus's dagger: —

> " This was the most unkindest cut of all :
> For when the noble Cæsar saw him stab,
> Ingratitude, more strong than traitor's arms,
> Quite vanquished him ; then burst his mighty heart! "

And the greatest master of English style, South, has
said, " In the charge of ingratitude *omnia dixeris :* it is
one great blot upon all mortality: it is all in a word : it
says Amen to the black roll of sins : it gives comple-
tion and confirmation to them all." [1] How strong in
man must be that emotional texture, the rending of
which has filled the literature of all ages with sounds of
terror and of woe ! And now shall the materialist tell
me that I, who, when I receive anything of good feel
within me this swelling, bursting heart of gratitude and
praise, can find in the universe nothing worthy of myself
on which to bestow it ? nothing but atoms where I can
see, nothing but void where I cannot see ! Shall I consent to be stripped of this prerogative of love, of this
ecstasy of grateful praise, and be told that in the universe, amid its myriads of atoms, there is not one atom
of intelligence, of love, or good, that thinks or cares for
me ? What do I want from atoms like myself, grinding
on under the everlasting laws till our brief turn shall
come to be crushed and die? My heart is greater than
them all. My heart refuses to be satisfied with a universe that makes its finest, noblest sentiments of no account, because it has nothing for these to rest upon, —
aye that would put the heart itself into a crucible, and
reduce its divinest feelings to fantasies, — that would
make its love a folly and its gratitude a superstition !
Lucretius may puzzle my brain ; but when I cease to be
an automaton and feel myself a man, my heart rebounds

---

[1] Vol. i. Sermon 10.

at the voice of Paul, and I turn from these materialistic vanities "to the living God, which made heaven and earth and the sea, and all things that are therein, and fills our hearts with food and gladness." My whole nature rests in, and is satisfied with, the thought that "in Him we live and move and have our being; for we are his offspring."

Shall I be told that an appeal from human feelings can have no weight against the testimony of physical facts? I answer, first, that I do not array feelings against facts, but human nature against the narrow and exclusive inference that materialists would make from physical nature. And next, that I am dealing here not with modern materialists of one idea, — and that idea an atom, — but with the great master of materialism, whose brain was large enough to take in Mankind as well as Nature. Lucretius contemplated the nature of things as related to the conditions of man, and sought to relieve mankind of troubled feelings and fancies by teaching that they and all things are but a congeries of atoms. Hence it is a legitimate criticism upon his system that it fails completely of the end to which he sought to apply it. The materialist teaches that man himself is but a material product of means and agencies purely physical, and that at death he shall be resolved into primitive atoms. He is not at liberty, therefore, to set aside the feelings of man as having no relation to a physical system, and of no account as matter of knowledge. He is bound to account for the existence of such feelings, and to find some correlation of the universe to man as he is, and knows himself to be. It is a consistent, logical, and also a scientific objection to the materialistic scheme of the universe that it fails utterly to account for or respond to that which is noblest and best in man — his æsthetic and ethical nature, his spiritual longings and hopes. Far

be it from me to imply that materialists themselves are
wanting in these finer sentiments of our nature. Men
are often better than their systems, and a man's feeling
may show him better than his opinion or belief. Even
while one is employing his intellect to prove that he is
of the earth earthy, his moral nature may proclaim his
divine origin and his immortal destiny.[1] My argument
has to do not with men but with systems ; and I put it
to you personally, whether you would consent to stifle
your emotions of gratitude for any scientific dogma of
materialism, or whether that can be to you a scientific
and sufficient explication of the universe, which, by reducing it to mere matter and motion, leaves no place nor
object for the exercise of a part of your nature so tender,
so noble, so true, and so good ? Something in my heart
responds to the opening sentence of the proclamation
under which we meet to-day, that this custom of public
thanksgiving to Almighty God is "as wise as it is beautiful." What my æsthetic nature calls for, a universe
fit for me to live in, must respond to, through a spirit
of intelligence, beauty, and love.

---

[1] Professor Ernst Haeckel, of Jena, in the first chapter of his *History of Creation*, makes a proper distinction between *scientific* materialism and *moral* or *ethical* materialism, and justly protests against
the imputation of the belief and practice of the latter to those who
advocate the former, which he prefers to call *Monism.* Professor
Tyndall and Mr. Proctor likewise take pains to defend themselves
against the charge of moral delinquency in their scientific teachings.
It is a shame to the advocates of religion that there should be any
occasion for such a protest on the part of men of science. All personal imputation should be ruled out of a discussion which is of
equal import to science and religion. At the same time it would relieve the books and lectures of Tyndall and Proctor of a tiresome
element, if these gentlemen could be made to understand that their
personal faith or feeling upon subjects of which no one should sus-
pect them of "knowledge," is of very little consequence to the general public.

II. The second test to which I would subject the systems of Lucretius and Paul is the sentiment of patriotism. This also grows directly out of the occasion that has brought us together. This is the American Thanksgiving Day; and our gratitude grows more tender and sacred as we think to-day of that nation of which we are thankful, and in foreign lands — oh *so* thankful to be members!

For nothing am I more proud of my country than that she knows what she has to be thankful for; and from President to peasant dares to be thankful before a materialistic and gainsaying age. In America we respect the tenacity with which the German, though naturalized, clings to memories of his Fatherland; and the devotion with which the Frenchman, refusing to be naturalized, dreams of making his Paradise in *la belle France.* Even John Chinaman commands a tear of sympathy that he thinks the soil from which he digs his gold not good enough to lay his bones in, but provides that these shall be carried back to the Celestial Kingdom.

> " Breathes there the man with soul so dead
>   Who never to himself hath said,
>   This is my own, my native land ! "

But why a soul that itself consists of nothing but atoms, even though "these are exceedingly round and minute," [1] should have such a transcendent passion for coarser bodily atoms round about it, the atoms that compose my understanding are not "nimble" [2] enough to discern. Why do we foster with such reverent care the art, the literature, the monuments of a nation, identify ourselves with its past, and transmit this with ourselves to posterity? Whence the sentiment of national honor,

[1] Lucretius, l. iii. 179.
[2] Lucretius, l. iii. 186. See, also, Shakespeare, "nimble spirits," *Love's Labor's Lost,* iv. 3.

pride, humiliation, hope — all that goes to make the
moral personality of a nation, if we are but atoms
brought together by no intelligence, if at death these
atoms of our minds, like those of our bodies, are to be
used to manure the growth of plants and feed the life
of animals ? What place is there, then, for the patriotic
and historic sentiment in a nation ? It was with full
knowledge of nature and science that Du Bois Raymond
declared it absolutely and forever inconceivable that a
number of carbon, hydrogen, nitrogen, and oxygen atoms
should be otherwise than indifferent as to their own position and motion, past, present, or future. It is utterly
inconceivable how consciousness should result from their
joint action.[1] And it is still more inconceivable how
from any number of atomic structures, originated by
matter, consisting only of matter, exercising purely material functions, and then returning to matter, there
should arise that continuity of existence which is the
national life, that historic consciousness which is the
national soul.[2] If we are not the product of intelligence, is there aught of intelligence in that which we
produce ? is there any more of spirit in the printed word
than in the type that print it ? any more of skill in the
art of painter and sculptor than in the fortuitous forma-
tions of nature? Who or what shall determine this, if
mind and soul are bodily ? And what is there worth
preserving or transmitting where body, soul, and spirit,
nations, lands, and seas are all alike parts in the endless
flux and reflux of atoms ?

But on the spiritual system of the universe I can understand how minds can work together for the future,
how patriot spirits can labor for posterity, how the
thinkers of one generation can cherish the thoughts of

[1] Address at Leipzig, 1872.
[2] See, also, *Das Leben der Seele,* von Professor Dr. M. Lazarus.

the past, and add to their heritage for after ages, and do this with the feeling that there is a plan and purpose over nations; yes, with Paul's doctrine of men and things, I can even rise to his unrivaled utterance of self-sacrificing patriotism, "I could wish that myself were accursed from Christ for my brethren, my kinsmen according to the flesh: Who are Israelites, to whom pertaineth the adoption, and the glory, and the covenants, and the giving of the law, and the service of God, and the promises: Whose are the fathers, and of whom, as concerning the flesh, Christ came, who is over all, God blessed forever."[1] Yet patriotism is not the highest of the moral virtues; and a domineering antagonism, or a blind *Chauvinisme* too often abuse its name.

III. But in harmony with true patriotism, and, indeed, emerging out of it, is the spirit of philanthropy, — regard for mankind as having a community of rights and interests, and also in hopes and destiny. Nowhere in modern literature is this spirit more beautifully presented than by Goethe, in answer to the charge of lack of patriotism during the national movement of 1813–1814. In a conversation with Soret, in 1830, Goethe said, "National hatred is quite a peculiar thing. You will always find that it is strongest and fiercest in the lowest stages of culture. But there is also a stage where it entirely disappears, where one stands to some extent *above* the nations, and sympathizes with the weal or woe of a neighbor people as with that of one's own. This latter stage of culture suited my nature, and I had confirmed myself in it long before reaching my sixtieth year."

To this test of philanthropy I would now submit the systems of Lucretius and Paul. Their relations to this higher culture I can sum up in very few words. Lucretius laughed at the superstitions and miseries of man-

---

[1] Rom. ix. 1–5.

kind ; Paul pitied them. Lucretius wrapped himself
aloof from the world in pride; Paul took the whole
world to his heart in prayer. The contrast was not
merely personal; it lay in the systems, and is radical
and irreconcilable. Just what the philosophy of' Lucretius on " the nature of things " caused him to think of
his fellows, just how it made him feel toward them, himself has told us in the opening of his second book.

"It is sweet, when on the great sea the winds trouble
its waters, to behold from land another's deep distress ;
not that it is a pleasure and delight that any should be
afflicted, but because it is sweet to see from what evils
you are yourself exempt. It is sweet, also, to look upon
the mighty struggles of war arrayed along the plains
without sharing yourself in the danger. But nothing is
more welcome than to hold the lofty and serene positions
well fortified by the learning of the wise, from which
you may look down upon others, and see them wander-
ing all abroad and going astray in their search for the
path of life, — see the contest among them of intellect, the
rivalry of birth, the striving night and day with surpass-
ing effort to struggle up to the summit of power and be
masters of the world. O miserable minds of men! O
blinded breasts! in what darkness of life, and in how
great dangers is passed this term of life whatever its duration! not choose to see that Nature craves for herself
no more than this, that pain hold aloof from the body,
and she in mind enjoy a feeling of pleasure exempt from
care and fear." [1]

To recover ourselves from the shudder that this cold
scorn of humanity gives us, we must turn to Paul, a man
by nature as proud and fiery as Lucretius, and nursed
beyond exception in pride of race and religion, fed by
the flattery of teachers and rulers. Yet this " Hebrew

[1] L. ii. 1–20.

of the Hebrews," this "Pharisee of the Pharisees," this
free-born Roman, this petted pupil of Gamaliel, this
haughty commissioner of the Sanhedrim, this thinker and
orator, who, in the consciousness of his powers and his
cause, could refute judges, dispute with philosophers, ad-
monish kings, wrote to a little band of converted pagans
living in contempt at the capital, "I long to see you,
that I may impart unto you some spiritual gift; I am
debtor both to the Greeks and to the barbarians, both to
the wise and to the unwise."[1] Ah! my friends, nothing makes man so great and noble as the thought that
he is a child of God, and that all men share this parentage. It is the nature of an atom to agglomerate; it is
the nature of God to give. Some men have a talent
for the infinitely little, and it is well for the world there
are such minute investigators, and well for themselves,
when one knows how to connect the little with the
great. But it is bad for the vision to be always looking
through the microscope. There are men who spend
their lives in rolling atoms together as the beetle rolls its
ball, till they fancy that this ball they have rolled up is
the universe, and look down with swelling pride upon
the ants that it crushes as it rolls. Development through
the struggle for existence by the law of the strongest
tends to exclusiveness and selfish pride; but the possession of gifts bestowed from some higher source of life
and power inclines to a generous impartation to others:
"Freely ye have received, freely also give."[2] By so
much as Paul had received of the wisdom and knowledge of God, by so much did he feel himself a debtor
alike to the Greek who despised his race, and the barbarian whom his race despised. How patient he was of
human errors and infirmities, how sympathetic with human sorrows, "showing all meekness unto all men," that

---

[1] Rom. i. 14. [2] Matt. x. 8.

he might win them to the truth ; renouncing the honors and ambitions of his youth, working with his own hands, accepting bonds and stripes and imprisonment, that he might deliver men from the superstitions and errors that Lucretius made a mock of, and willing to brave shipwreck, that he might rescue the struggling mariners that Lucretius laughed at from his complacent footing on the shore. "We were gentle among you," Paul writes to the Thessalonians, " even as a nurse cherisheth her children ; so being affectionately desirous of you, we were willing to have imparted unto you, not the gospel of God only, but also our own souls, because ye were dear unto us."[1] It has been finely said that Christianity first wakened "an enthusiasm for humanity ; " and under the Roman Empire, in days of slavery and caste on the one hand, and conquest and colonization on the other, Paul gave the precepts, " Honor all men ; " " Owe no man anything, but to love one another."[2] The key to this all - embracing philanthropy was given in his speech at Athens : first the feeling of patriotism in the fact that God has assigned to each nation the bounds of its habitation, and furnished it with gifts and opportunities of its own ; and next the feeling of philanthropy in the fact that all these nations thus divinely parceled out are of one origin, children of one Father, their hearts beating with one blood. The highest motive for the love of man is given in the thought that this universe is our Father's house, and we are his offspring.

IV. To advance a step higher, let us test these two systems of the universe, in their adaptation to collective humanity, for its recovery or relief from the sorest evils with which it has always been oppressed. Though Lucretius mocked at human failures and miseries, in another mood he sought to mitigate them. The latter

---

[1] Thess. ii. 7, 8.　　　　[2] Rom. xiii. 8.

part of his third book, from v. 870, is devoted to this end.
It is almost impossible to condense his argument, or give
it fairly in modern forms of speech ; but if you will read
it attentively, I think you will agree with me that he
here falls quite below himself in the beggarly motives
that he presents for a noble and happy life. The sum
and substance of it all is, that the troubles and sorrows
of men either grow out of their superstitions or are
aggravated by these ; that the remedy is to learn the
nature of things, and adjust ourselves to the fact that
things always were, and always shall be, as they are —
that living and dying went on for ages before our birth,
and shall go on unendingly after our death, when we
shall sink into the sleep that knows no waking. He can
furnish us nothing higher nor stronger than this, where-
with to cope with " the ills that flesh is heir to." This
poverty of motive lies in his system. Materialism has
invented names and terms enough to fill a lexicon of its
own, but among these all you find no such words as recovery, restoration, redemption, applied to the world and
its needs. But how can any system cover humanity, or
even touch upon it, that fails of this ? I press this point
the more earnestly, as fatal to the materialistic scheme
of the universe. Tyndall tries to meet it, or rather to
evade it, by constantly asserting that all such questions
belong to the feelings, and are therefore outside the domain of knowledge and of science ; that the difficulties
they raise against the conclusions of " pure intellect " are
due to the fact that " reason is traversed by the emotions." If this were so, by what right does he assign to
" pure intellect " this exclusive preëminence over the
emotions as a part of the constitution of man to be satisfied in the constitution of nature ? He admits that
materialism cannot pretend " to be a complete philosophy
of the human mind," and that " what is really wanted is

the lifting power of an ideal element in human life." But shall this "ideal" power be a chimera of the feelings, a fantasy of the imagination, with no base of fact or knowledge? In what respect, then, would it be better than a superstition, which does not "lift up" but degrade? Haeckel tells us that "scientific materialism positively rejects every belief in the miraculous, and every conception, in whatever form it appears, of supernatural processes. Nowhere in the whole domain of human knowledge does it recognize real metaphysics, but throughout only physics." [1] And Tyndall says of the power manifested in the universe, "I dare not, save poetically, use the pronoun He regarding it; I dare not call it a mind; I refuse to call it even a cause." [2] Thus materialists claim a monopoly of the visible universe, and deny to men the conception of any other. But here is man in the universe, and of it, with most potent agencies of being, with most insatiable desires and needs, to which a materialistic universe utterly fails to respond. That cannot be a scientific account of the universe that is dumb to what is most vital and urgent in the chief known factor of the system — man.

Science has not solved that problem of moral evil that pervades the whole structure of society, and seems to be woven into the very texture of human life. Helpful as science has been, and promises yet to be, in the mitigation of outward forms of evil, and the possible avoidance of some evils in the future, it has not so much as furnished the elements for resolving that evil which the history, the legislation, and the conscience of mankind unite in stamping as moral, and therefore personal and responsible. Science multiplies its inventions, and the genius of destruction seizes upon these to make war more

---

[1] *History of Creation*, chap. 1.
[2] *Fortnightly Review*, Nov. 1, 1875.

sweeping, certain and terrible in its woes. Science pursues its analysis of nature to the molecules in which she had hidden her subtlest powers, and crime takes advantage of these to invent new means of fraud and murder, and to elude detection. Year by year, scientific associations, congresses for education, social science, law reform, meet for the advancement of mankind in knowledge and happiness — I rejoice in such gatherings, and meet with them ; — year by year they bring forth something for the advantage of society in health, in morals, and in peace ; but their processes are all too slow and too superficial for the healing of the world, that still sins and suffers, and suffers and sins, through the groaning ages. Development has not yet eradicated this root of evil ; natural selection has not yet secured the survival of the fittest in that moral sphere upon which human welfare depends ; social science has not lifted human nature to the point where it no more tends to go astray. Side by side with Bristol associations and Brighton congresses are Whitechapel murders and drunken brutes beating their wives ; so that every upward step in civilization seems contrasted by a lower deep of barbarism. The world cries out for redemption ; its soul complains, " I know there are evils without me, which the eternal strife of atoms has not worn away, and the grinding of the everlasting laws has not reduced to powder, but I find a deeper evil within, for which nature yields no remedy and no recompense." The heart in moments of agony cries out for relief ; but atoms piled mountain high only echo back its wail, and the laws that bind the universe together are walls of adamant to such a cry. In some hour of darkness, of fear, of despair, I lift up my voice, " Hear, O heavens, give ear O earth ! " but the heavens are brass over my head, the earth is iron unde- my feet ; but I now lift my voice to the Father in

Heaven, and the iron dissolves ; I am on the footstool of prayer ; the gates of brass burst asunder, and heaven and earth commingle in the light and air of love. All laws now bend before the supreme majesty of that law of love, which is God. I find myself in the higher universe of moral laws, and here, for fall is recovery, for sin is redemption, for death is life. And this system of the universe I feel to be true ; my needs confess it, my heart accepts it, my soul rejoices in it, and emancipated from the nature of things, I rise to the author of things, and join the triumphant doxology of Paul, "of Him, and to Him, and through Him are all things, to whom be glory forever."

V. We come now to the final test of these systems in their application to that feeling of hope which is native and imperishable in man, and to that cheerful and beneficent working that should realize the hopes of humanity. It may fitly characterize the system of Lucretius to say, there is no hope in it ; and it was a fitting commentary on such a system that he who framed it, seeing nothing to live for and nothing to hope for, should end his life by his own hand. Not that I would charge the suicide of Lucretius as a crime upon his system or himself. So far from being put under the ban of priestly superstition, or the more mercenary ban of life insurance companies, the suicide should be looked upon with a tender, even sacred pity, as the victim of mental or moral disease. Yet when Lucretius was so tempted, we find in his system nothing of the hope that could have restrained the hand which had written, " After death there will remain no self," — that is, no conscious personality, — and " no one wakes up upon whom the chill cessation of life has once come."[1] Thus we see this proud master of

---

[1] " Nec quisquam expergitus exstat,
Frigida quem semel est vitai pausa secuta."
L. iii. 927.

the material universe succumbing to the fate that befalls his atoms.

In that same capital where in the height of his fame Lucretius threw away his life, we see the aged Paul a prisoner in chains; of earthly toils, trials, conflicts, griefs, the labor and the weariness of life, he has had as much as any man could experience or bear; he knows that the end is near; in the feeble light of his dungeon, his hand chained to the guard; without, the sentry and the axe of the executioner, he writes these last words to his beloved Timothy: "I am now ready to be offered, and the time of my departure is at hand; I have fought a good fight, I have finished my course, I have kept the faith; henceforth there is laid up for me a crown of righteousness, which the Lord the righteous judge shall give me at that day, and (O great, loving, magnanimous heart of Paul!) not to me only, but unto all them also that love his appearing. The Lord shall deliver me from every evil work, and will preserve me unto his heavenly kingdom; to whom be glory forever and ever."[1] Who would not trample worlds of atoms under his feet to live in a universe of such hopes, such issues, such glorious rewards? Let the man that is within you answer which is the fitting universe for you. To all that Lucretius has said of "the nature of things," I oppose the nature of Man. That most self-sacrificing of patriots, gentlest of spirits, purest of men, Joseph Mazzini, once said to me, "These materialistic questions belong to the *kitchen* of humanity; it is the soul of humanity that I care for." All that is true in Darwin, Paul not only knew theoretically, but felt within himself. He knew how much of the animal he had inherited from his progenitors — that low materialistic untamed "law in his members" working ever toward sin and death — but he opposed to this "the law

[1] 2 Tim. iv. 6–9.

of the spirit of life ;" and in the struggle to be a man
secured the survival of the fittest, in the triumph of spirit
over matter. And from this personal experience, this in
ward *knowledge* of spiritual power, he held up the torch
of hope for humanity: " We are saved by hope. The
whole creation groaneth and travaileth in pain together
waiting for the manifestation of the sons of God," when
even the material creation "shall be delivered from the
bondage of corruption into the glorious liberty of the
children of God."[1] How grand the vista here opened
of the future of humanity, and not of man alone, but of
all nature, organic and inorganic, through the restitution
and perfection of humanity. These notes of hope and
triumph go sounding and echoing through the ages, like
the Fifth Symphony of Beethoven, that cannot loose its
hold upon the theme, but recovers it again and again,
and rising from gentlest cadences gathers in volume and
majesty, till it might rouse atoms to life and wake the
dead ; — so comprehensive, so inexhaustible is the
thought of Paul concerning man and the order of things
with which he is related.[2] But the scheme of Lucretius
admits of no expansion. It is shut down within its own
horizon : rather it is shut up within a cavern of endless
gloom, where those who enter must bid farewell to hope.
The scheme of Paul has made peoples wiser and better
in the degree that they have accepted it ; it wants but to
be accepted in its completeness, to fill the world with light
and peace and joy. It carries in itself the future of all
poetry and prophecy, and they who teach it are mes-
sengers of gladness and joy. But how can the followers

---

[1] Rom. viii. 19–25.

[2] Tyndall seems puzzled at "the wonderful plasticity of the theistic idea, which enables it to maintain, through many changes, its
hold upon superior minds." Has he never, then, read that "in Him
was *life*, and the life was the *light* of men ? "

of Lucretius exult in such a system ? Does the physician
put on airs of mirth and exultation when he tells his
patient there is no hope ? Yet this message of despair is
what the priests of materialism bring from the arcana of
nature. One would think they would go forth in sack-
cloth and ashes, with inverted torches, to the grave of all
things. Against a nature of such origin and end, I pit
my own manhood, and do not fear the issue. Would I
cherish the tender, graceful sentiment of gratitude? then
must I follow Paul, and not Lucretius. Would I yield
to the noble impulses of patriotism ? then must I follow
Paul, and not Lucretius. Would I rise to the magnanimous heights of philanthropy ? then must I follow Paul,
and not Lucretius. Would I help mankind in their sorrows, deliver them from their superstitions, raise them
from their sins ? then must I follow Paul, and not Lucretius. Would I lift myself and my race to immortal
hopes ? then must I drop Lucretius, and follow Paul to
the life everlasting.

That life is mine, by every title of nature and of spirit.
If I am the product of Nature's upward striving, I have
a right to demand that nature shall stand by her work,
and not burlesque her own laws. If her law be "the
survival of the fittest," then I, as the fittest, must and
will survive. Nature herself cannot reduce me to ob-
livion, and give immortality to atoms. With this conscious spiritual life I defy her power. Whatever its origin, whether struck out as a spark from flinty atoms, or
stolen from heaven, it is mine ; and not rock, chains,
nor vulture, not billows, tempest, nor thunderbolt of
Jove, not all the powers of nature, death, and hell
shall compel me to part with it. Nature may have the
atoms that encompass me, but cannot have ME.[1] And if

1 "You cannot satisfy the human understanding in its demand
for logical continuity between molecular processes and the phenom-

in this visible material universe there is no place where
this quickening, yearning, mounting, joying spirit of
mine can find its sphere, there is that within me that
will find or force its way out of such a universe to one
where the fittest do survive. But the way to that sphere
of spiritual and immortal powers is already open; though
tracked with tears and blood, made sure and bright for
us by the man our brother, who, passing through the
gates of death, has gone before — Him " who was dead,
but is alive forever more, and has the keys of hell and
death."[1] " Thanks be unto God, who giveth us the victory, through our Lord Jesus Christ."[2]

ena of consciousness. This is a rock on which materialism must in-
evitably split whenever it pretends to be a complete philosophy of
the human mind." — Tyndall, *Fortnightly Review*, November, 1875.
    [1] Rev. i. 18.   [2] 1 Cor. xv. 57.

NOTE TO PAGE 278.

It is the fashion with materialists to ridicule this mode of argument as having no basis of " knowledge." They mislead themselves
by assuming (1) that knowledge can only be objective. But when I
know a thing as an object, in the same instant I know the *fact* that
I know this thing. The knowing the thing requires simultaneously
these two other knowledges — the knowledge of Me and of My
knowing. If any one denies this, I can only apply to him the words
of Lucretius (l. iv. 468) : " If a man believe that nothing is known,
he knows not whether this even can be known, since he admits he
knows nothing. I will therefore decline to argue the case with him
who places himself with head where his feet should be."
    Materialists mislead themselves, also, by assuming that a convic-
tion based upon sensible phenomena is necessarily and always more
certain as a ground of action than a fact of consciousness or a conclusion or belief that rests upon moral evidence or metaphysical reasoning. Mankind act upon these latter in ten cases to one of objective knowledge. Professor Tyndall insists upon limiting knowledge
and certainty to facts perceived by the senses (*Fortnightly Review*,
November, 1875); and says : " The Power which I see manifested in
the universe I dare not, save poetically, use the pronoun He regard-

ing it; I dare not call it a mind; I refuse to call it even a cause."
Now, I have never seen Mr. Tyndall, but should he appear before
my eyes at this moment, could I be made a whit more certain of his
existence than I already am through his writings? Moreover, with
no disrespect to Mr. Tyndall or his atomic theory, the power which
I see manifested in these writings I dare not call a *mind ;* and, by
precisely the same method, the power that I see manifested in Tyndall himself I even dare call an intelligent cause.

Since Professor Tyndall cries out for "knowledge," I beg to direct his attention to some knowable things of which one marvels to
find him so oblivious. In his Belfast address he tells us that "the
merchant had rendered the philosopher possible. . . . In those regions where the commercial aristocracy of ancient Greece mingled
with its eastern neighbors, the sciences were born." Can it be possible that Professor Tyndall does not know what had been accomplished on the Nile, in mathematics, mechanics, astronomy, applied
chemistry, ages before Greece was born, and how the Greek philosophers owned their indebtedness to Egypt? Again in the *Fortnightly Review,* November, 1875, he speaks of the Mosaic cosmogony as finally abandoned. False interpretations of that cosmogony,
due to ignorance of Hebrew and to the realistic philosophy, have indeed been abandoned. But can it be possible Professor Tyndall
does not know that ages before geology was dreamed of, Augustine,
as a Hebrew scholar had said, "These are the ineffable days (*dies
ineffabiles*) of the infinite Jehovah." He also terms them *naturæ,*
natures, and *moræ,* pauses or delays (*De Genesi ad Literam,* l. ii. c. 14).
Surely Mr. Tyndall should know things within the reach of every
scholar, and not trust to the guidance of such an authority as Professor Draper. In teaching others, he should first find out what they
already know ; otherwise the originality of his *Fog Signals* may be
disputed.

XIII.

FINAL CAUSE; A CRITIQUE OF THE FAILURE OF PALEY AND THE FALLACY OF HUME.

(Read before the Victoria Institute, London, in 1879.)

In his "History of English Thought in the Eighteenth Century," Mr. Leslie Stephen pays an earnest and impartial tribute to the two writers of that period, who were the foremost disputants upon the doctrine of a final cause in nature as proving the existence of God, — David Hume and William Paley. Of Hume he says: "We have in his pages the ultimate expression of the acutest skepticism of the eighteenth century, — the one articulate statement of a philosophical judgment upon the central questions at issue."[1] And again: "Hume's skepticism completes the critical movement of Locke. It marks one of the great turning-points in the history of thought. From his writings we may date the definite abandonment of the philosophical conceptions of the preceding century, leading, in some cases, to an abandonment of the great questions as insoluble; and, in others, to an attempt to solve them by a new method. Hume did not destroy ontology or theology, but he destroyed the old ontology; and all later thinkers, who have not been content with the mere dead bones of extinct philosophy, have built up their systems upon entirely new lines."[2]

Of Paley Mr. Stephen says: "The natural theology

[1] Chap. vi. sec. 3.   [2] Chap. iii. sec. 43.

lays the basis of his whole system. The book, whatever its philosophical shortcomings, is a marvel of skillful statement. It states, with admirable clearness and in a most attractive form, the argument which has the greatest popular force, and which, duly etherealized, still passes muster with metaphysicians. Considered as the work of a man who had to cram himself for the purpose, it would be difficult to praise its literary merits too highly. The only fault in the book, considered as an instrument of persuasion, is that it is too conclusive. If there were no hidden flaw in the reasoning, it would be impossible to understand, not only how any should resist, but how any one should ever have overlooked, the demonstration." [1]

In the history of polemics there is hardly another instance of such collapse of popularity as has befallen the book, the style and method of which Mr. Stephen has here so justly praised. The argument of Paley was regarded by theologians of his time as invincible ; and his illustrations from nature were so attractive to youth that his " Natural Theology " was adopted as a text-book in colleges. Upon the basis of his famous axiom was built up the series of "Bridgewater Treatises," in which anatomy and physiology, astronomy, geology, and various branches of physics were brought to illustrate and establish the evidence of design in nature. So keen a logician as Archbishop Whately used his acumen to adapt Paley's reasoning to the later discoveries and developments of science ; and so careful a physicist as Dr. Whewell led his " Induction of the Physical Sciences " up to the same conclusion. Yet to the present generation, within less than eighty years from its first appearance, Paley's " Natural Theology " is already antiquated as to its once brilliant and conclusive demonstrations, and as an authority is well-nigh obsolete.

[2] Chap. viii. iv. 38.

Quite otherwise has been the fate of Hume. Mr. Stephen reminds us that "his first book fell dead-born from the press; few of his successors had a much better fate. The uneducated masses were, of course, beyond his reach; amongst the educated minority he had but few readers; and amongst the few readers still fewer who could appreciate his thoughts."[1] Add to this that Hume, though deeming himself a match for the philosophers and theologians of his time, had a secret dread of that religious pugnacity in the common people of Scotland, which is so quickly roused against an assailant of popular beliefs, and therefore kept back, to be published after his death, his "Dialogues on Natural Religion," — the book most fitted to provoke that acrimonious criticism which insures literary success. Now, however, within a century of its first appearance, we find this masterly product of Hume's dialectics still acknowledged as the standard treatise of philosophical skepticism. Scotch philosophers since his day have labored to reform philosophy in the light of Hume's criticism; Kant attempted to refute his skepticism; John Stuart Mill virtually built upon Hume; and he has lately been revived in Germany, with the honor of translation and the prestige of authority. His fame grows with time. This is due partly to the beauty of Hume's style, and the clearness and depth of his reasoning; due also to the decline of theological asperity, and the growth of a tolerant spirit among various schools of thought; and due not a little to the tone of audacity, — or what he himself styled "a certain boldness of temper," — with which Hume assailed convictions which had come to be accepted as axioms both in philosophy and in religion. And I am of opinion also that no small part of the favor which has accrued to Hume is due to the metaphysical fallacies which

[1] Chap. i. 1.

have sprung up side by side with the scientific facts which have discredited Paley. The whole history of science discloses a disposition to metaphysical speculation awakened by each new discovery in physical nature. With every fresh deposit of facts upon the borders of science comes a fresh brood of fallacies upon the adjacent borders of hypothesis; and the progenitors of these have a natural affinity for the greatest of skeptics, who was notably the dupe of his own fallacies. This phenomenon of the simultaneous generation of fact and fallacy is itself worthy of scientific investigation. But it is enough to note it here as showing that the failure of Paley's demonstration of God in nature should not drive us over to Hume's contradiction, which is demonstrably a fallacy.

Paley's statement of the doctrine of an end in nature was from the first open to these two objections.

(1.) Instead of formulating a proposition to be proved, or pointing to the sources from which the conviction of its truth arises in the mind, Paley tacitly assumed the thing in question, and wrapped this assumption in a self-repeating phrase which he sought to strengthen by multifarious illustrations.

(2.) Assuming that design or contrivance exists in the whole field of nature, Paley was betrayed into the use of illustrations, sometimes far-fetched, sometimes superficial or lacking confirmation, which wear the appearance of making out a case.

" There cannot be design without a designer, contrivance, without a contriver," was the axiom upon which Paley built up his treatise. He does not seem to have been aware — at least, he takes no notice of the fact — that Hume had assailed this axiom, and the very illustration of the watch by which Paley so triumphantly asserts it, at the one point at which it might be vulnerable, and if vulnerable, then worthless to Paley's end, namely, that the axiom rests solely upon experience, and holds only within the range of possible human action and observation. Though Hume's assertion is a fallacy, yet he had put it so plausibly that Paley could not afford to pass it by ; and by leaving his fundamental premise open to doubt and contradiction, Paley failed to establish the existence of a Supreme Being from traces of design in nature, however curious and multiplied. Indeed, he himself fell into the common fallacy of begging the question in the very statement of it.

That design implies a designer is as obvious as that thought implies a thinker; but the materialist denies personality to the thinking substance ; and to apply the term design to every hint of adaptation in nature, in the sense of an intelligence shaping matter to an end, is to *assume* the existence of God in the very form of proving it.

It was also an error of Paley that he sought to make out the *goodness* of the end, as part of the evidence of a supreme contriver; or at least to show the preponderance of good over evil in apparent ends. In this endeavor he was sometimes so unfortunate as to throw the weight of his illustration into the opposite scale. Thus, in asserting that " teeth were made to eat, not to ache," he failed to dispose of the fact that they do ache, as an objection to any ruling design in their structure and composition. Their aching is not always due to some violation of nature, since wild beasts in our zoölogical gardens sometime require dental surgery. It will not quiet the jumping tooth-ache, nor ease a neuralgic nerve, to assure the sufferer that teeth and nerves were not made for the purpose of giving pain. Indeed, it is quite a popular fancy that nerves are demons of evil. The *whence* and the *wherefore* of evil must be taken into view in forming an estimate of the end for which a thing was made, of unity and wisdom in its design, or of any purpose whatever in its existence. But the question of a final cause in things is not to be set aside by some single characteristic or quality of a thing which seems to mark it as useless or even injurious.

That every event argues a cause is an intuitive, not an experimental, conviction of the human mind. Whether the cause is intelligent and purposing, or is only a material or an accidental antecedent, is to be determined by observation and analysis of the thing itself in its place and its relations. Moral qualities or purposes, suggested by certain properties of a thing as inhering in the cause, — if cause there be, — do not necessarily enter into the proof of the existence of an intelligent cause, which might be either good or evil. Stripping Paley's statement of its verbal assumptions, and setting aside such of his illustrations as are crude or antiquated, his fundamental argument for the Creator as evinced by the traces of design in nature is not only tenable in face of the more recent discoveries of science, but is illustrated and con-firmed by a far richer array of natural phenomena than Paley had ever imagined. We may improve, however, upon his statement of the doctrine of final causes as follows: The perceived collocation or combination of phenomena or forces in nature toward a given result, produces in the mind the immediate conviction of an intelligent purpose behind such phenomena and forces. This statement, while it retains the essence of Paley's axiom, avoids his logical vice of including in the defini-tion the very term to be defined. A fixed series of events may be mechanical; but the *combination* of sev-eral independent series of phenomena toward a distinct-ive result must be referred to *Thought* purposing that event. Nature with all her forces and material has never produced a single thing that answers to the idea of an

20

invention. This is always the product of human intelligence applied to the powers and substances of nature. The contrivance seen in a machine instantly refers us to .the mind as its cause. Thus, electricity is a power everywhere present in nature ; yet electricity has never produced an electrical machine, an electric telegraph or telephone, or an electric light. But though nature cannot turn her own powers into a practical machine, and the least hint of an adaptation of these powers to the purposes of man suggests the intervention of the human intellect, yet the natural powers which man subordinates to his intelligent uses remain greater and more wonderful than the inventions to which they are applied. Are then the powers and substances of nature which stand, as it were, waiting for the touch of the inventor's genius to make them 'available wherever mind shall lead the way, themselves mere things of chance or products of material law with no *intent* in their existence? When made available do they proclaim intelligence, and yet is the marvelous property of *availability* only a meaningless phenomenon of matter? Hitherto the phraseology of the doctrine of design, and the illustrations of the doctrine, have had a certain coarseness of fibre, suggesting a mechanical universe turned out by what Cowper styles " the great *Artificer* of all that moves," and needing the constant oversight of the Maker to keep it in working order. The sublime personifications of the creation in the Bible have been literalized by our matter-of-fact philosophy, as though the differential calculus could measure the astronomy of Job or of the 19th Psalm. But science, by bringing us into nearer contact with what Tyndall has called the "subsensible world," has at once enlarged the sphere of our vision, and heightened its powers. Teleology addresses itself to some finer sense within. It widens its circle without changing its centre.

The mechanism of the universe drops away, and we find or feel the *Thought* of the Infinite Mind projecting itself in the actual through finite forms, and combining and comprehending the whole in an ever-unfolding purpose. Hence, we may say, with Von Baerenbach, "Darwin has not rendered teleology impossible under any and every form, but has conducted philosophical science to another and the true conception of design."[1] True, Von Baerenbach would find the solution of the universe in *Monism;* but his testimony, from a scientific point of view, shows that the question of causality will not be put down, and that, after all sciences, nature persistently demands the *wherefore* of her own phenomena.

Zeller, of Berlin, in his paper read before the Academy of Science, "upon the Teleological and the Mechanical Interpretations of Nature in their application to the Universe," seeks to combine the necessary in nature with the purposive in reason. "Since, on all sides, the investigation of nature, so far as it has been carried, shows us a firm linking together of cause and effect, we must assume from the coherence of all phenomena that the same holds also of those which have not yet been investigated and explained ; that everything in the world proceeds from its natural cause, according to natural laws ; and therefore nothing can here be brought in of the intervention of an active purpose bearing upon this fixed result, distinct from natural necessity. Yet we cannot consider these natural causes as barely mechanical ; for their effects reach far beyond that which can be explained by motion in space, or resolved into such motion. And if from these same causes along with inorganic nature, life also, and along with irrational life also conscious and rational existence have appeared, not as it were by mere

---

[1] *Gedanken ueber die Teleologie in der Natur*, von Friedrich von Baerenbach. Berlin, 1878, p. 5.

accident in course of time, but necessarily by virtue of
their natures, do proceed and ever have proceeded; if
the world never can have been without life and intelligence, since the same causes which now produce life and
reason must already from eternity have worked, and
therefore have produced these continually, so must we
call the world, as a whole, in spite of the natural necessity which rules in it, indeed, rather on account of this,
at the same time the work of absolute reason. That this
reason should have been guided in its action by proposed
ends is indeed not necessary. . . .

" Yet, inasmuch as it is one and the same cause from
which in the last analysis all effects spring, inasmuch as
all the laws of nature only show the art and manner in
which these causes, following the necessity of their existence, work toward many sides, so from the totality of
these operations must necessarily proceed a world harmonious in all its parts, a world complete in its way, and
arranged with absolute conformity to purpose." [1]

A point of still higher moment to the argument Zeller
has quite overlooked, namely, that in no case could the
mechanical theory be adequate to the solution of the universe. Motion, indeed, might account for all the phenomena of *physics*, with the exception of motion itself.
But, after all the facts of *mechanism* are disposed of,
there remain the facts and forces of *vitalism*, which refuse to be included under mechanism. Motion cannot
originate life, neither can chemistry create or evolve life.
We may analyze life into all its constituents and condi-

---

[1] It is a groundless assumption of Zeller that because life *is* it has
always been; an assumption not warranted by the law of scientific
induction. The rule of experience by which physicists would bind
us forbids such a generalization upon phenomena of which there is
no possible record. This is not scientific testimony, but speculative
hypothesis.

tions, but cannot detect the life itself. We may combine all the constituents and conditions of life, but cannot produce life. The living organism we know, but the mind demands the cause of life-organization, and sees that this does not lie in mechanism. The mechanism of the universe may be concluded within motion and the correlation of forces ; but force is a quality, not a cause, and motion demands an origin, and beyond both lie the immensities of vitalism and of intelligence.

Hume attempted to break down the teleological argument by assailing the conception of cause and effect. He maintained that "order, arrangement, or the adjustment of final causes, is not of itself any proof of design, but only so far as it has been experienced to proceed from that principle," and also, that our experience of design, from the operations of the human mind, cannot furnish ,an analogy for "the great universal mind," which we thus assume to be the author of nature. Hence, according to Hume, before we could infer "that an orderly universe must arise from some thought and act, like the human, it were requisite that we had experience of the origin of worlds, and it is not sufficient, surely, that we have seen ships and cities arise from human art and contrivance."

The first position of Hume is refuted by the universal consciousness of mankind. Most assuredly our belief that any particular object in which we perceive the adaptation of parts to each other, or of means to an end, must have proceeded from a designing cause, does not arise out of a previous observation or experience of such cause in objects of *the same class.* Of the millions of men who wear watches, how very few have ever seen the parts of a watch formed and put together ! Yet every possessor of a watch is sure that it had a maker ; and this conviction could not be strengthened by his going to Geneva and seeing watches made by hand, or to Waltham and seeing them made by machinery.

The first maker of a watch had no "experience" to follow. He used his own inventive skill. The watch existed in his mind before he shaped it in metal. And when the first watch was completed it testified *of itself*, to every observer, of the designing mind and the cunning hand which had produced it. And this because, as Hume himself says, "Throw several pieces of steel together without shape or form ; they will never arrange themselves so as to complete a watch." This is not an inference from the study of such a casual heap of steel, but is an immediate and irresistible cognition of the human mind. One does not need to trace the loose bits of steel from their entrance at one end of the factory to their emergence as a completed watch at the other, in order to be satisfied that, at some point of their course, a designing hand has adjusted them to each other. The perceived adjustment produces this conviction instantaneously ; and no amount of experience could render the conviction more certain. The conviction that a particular combination of means for an end is the product of a designing cause is not at all dependent upon the "experience" of such cause in *like* cases.

Neither does the conviction that adaptation proceeds from design rest upon "experience" in *any* case whatever. That the adaptation of means to an end proceeds from an intelligent and purposing foresight of that end is an intuitive conviction of the human mind. To be convinced of this casual connection the mind requires neither argument nor observation ; it could accept no other explanation of the existence of the event. The mind assumes this casual relation of intelligence to adaptation, in those very observations of nature or discoveries of inventive skill which Mr. Hume would include in the term "experience."

As the print of a human foot upon the sand gave to Robinson Crusoe the immediate conviction that there was another man upon what he had supposed to be his uninhabited island ; as the impressions of feet, talons, fins, vertebræ, embedded in rock, certify the geologist of extinct races ; so does the least token of adaptation at once articulate itself with the conception of design.

In the gravel-beds of the Somme were picked up at first a few flint stones, bearing rude marks of having been shaped for use. No human remains were associated with them. The beds in which they lay were hitherto supposed to antedate the appearance of man ; yet these shapen flints, produced in every observer the instantaneous conviction that man was there at the period of this formation. When once the eye had satisfied itself that these forms were not the result of natural attrition, were not worn but shaped, — that this flint, however rudely shaped, was *intended* for a knife or a hatchet, this block for a hammer, this pointed stone for a spear, — the mind at once pronounced it the work of man. The adaptation points to design, and the design points to a grade of human intelligence. It does not matter that we cannot divine the specific use of this or that implement ; if the object itself shows that it was shaped for *some* use, if it is not merely a stone but an implement, there springs up at sight of it the necessary conviction that this was the work of a designing cause. Hence Hume's appeal to "experience" is fallacious in the general as well as in the particular.

Equally fallacious is Hume's objection to the analogy from the products of human design to the works of a higher intelligence. The scale of the works, the vastness of the intelligence requisite to have conceived, and of the power to have executed them, have no place in the conviction of design. This arises from the single fact of *adaptation*, whether seen in the wheels of a watch or of a locomotive, in the point of a pin or the lever of a steam-engine, in the antennæ of an ant or the proboscis of an elephant. Could Lord Rosse's telescope itself be projected by a series of lenses to the farthest star within its field, this immensity of adaptation would no more exhaust the principle than does the actual size of the telescope as compared with the eye of a beetle. Size, number, magnitude, have no relation to the notion of adaptation, which in and of itself produces the conviction of design.

Moreover, the human mind is the only possible unit by which we may compute the operations of " the universal mind." If we drop the argument from design, and fall back upon ontology, still the finite mind which we know in consciousness is the only agent by which, through analogy, contrast, or negation, we can attain to a conception of the Infinite.

The very observations which Hume would classify under " experience " must be made and recorded by this self-same mind ; and no man has a higher confidence in the scope and the trustworthiness of its powers than the philosopher who attempts to account for the existence of nature without either a cause or an end. But as our conception of causality and of personality, derived from consciousness, is capable of being projected from ourselves into the infinite or " universal " mind, — just as we can project a mathematical line or circle into infinite space, — so adaptation seen in nature reflects our conception of design up to the highest heaven and back to the farthest eternity.

The mathematician does not pretend to comprehend the infinities or the infinitesimals which he nevertheless conceives of as quantities in his calculations. It would require his life-time to count up the billions which he handles so freely on a sheet of paper. The mind which can conceive of infinite number and of universal space without comprehending either, can also derive from itself the conception of a " universal mind." To do complete justice to Hume, I will now sum up his argument and my reply. In his essay on " Providence and a Future State " Hume says : —

" Man is a being whom we know by experience, whose motives and designs we are acquainted with, and whose projects and inclinations have a certain connection and coherence, according to the laws which nature has established for the government of such a creature. When, therefore, we find that any work has proceeded from the skill and industry of man, as we are otherwise acquainted with the nature of the animal, we can draw a hundred inferences concerning what may be expected from him ; and these inferences will all be founded in experience and observation." Hence, he concludes, we cannot " from the course of nature infer a particular intelligent cause, which first bestowed and still preserves order in the universe,"[1] inasmuch as we have had no experience of such a cause in nature upon which to ground this inference.

At least three oversights or misconceptions are apparent in this statement.

(1.) Mr. Hume overlooks the fact that each man is conscious of a designing faculty within himself, and does not need to be certified of the adaptation of means to ends through the observation of this faculty in other men. There was a time when a first man invented the first machine, or adapted something to his own ends ; and surely he had no experience of design in other men to create faith in himself as a designer. He put forth a conscious power ; his experience of what he could accomplish confirmed his conception of design, but did not

---

[1] *Prov. and Fut. State*, vol. iv. p. 168.

create it. So it is with us all. When we see adaptation
to an end, we say at once, Here was an intelligent cause,
and this not because we have observed that other men
have produced designs, but knowing ourselves as intelligent designing causes, we of course refer adaptation to
intelligence.

(2.) This points us to Hume's second oversight; he
fails to perceive that the single thing to which adaptation
refers us is *intelligence*. It is not man in general as a
being or an animal, but the *intelligent spirit* in man that
is immediately and indissolubly connected with the notion
of adaptation. Man does many things that are purely
animal; he eats, walks, sleeps, like other animals, by an
instinct or a law of his nature, and we never think of as-
cribing such acts to an intelligence superior to physical
laws and functions. But the adaptation of means to
ends we refer directly to such intelligence ; and it is this
thing of intelligence that differentiates such effects from
purely physical sequences by the nature of their causes.
Crunched bones on a desert island might suggest beasts
of prey, but a *cairn* suggests man. An approach to such
adaptation on the part of the beaver, the bee, the dog,
the ant, disposes us to clothe such animals with the attribute of reason. And on the same principle — that it
is intelligence and not man we think of directly we perceive adaptation — do we refer such adaptation in nature
to an intelligence higher than nature and higher than man.
It is intelligence that we associate with adaptation, and
we are not limited to intelligence as manifested by man
as an animal of skill and industry. In point of fact the
great advances of physical science in recent times have
been due more to the imaginative and inventive faculty
prompting investigation, than to inference from experience. Science itself looks forward, not backward. Its
spirit is inquisitive, and its discoveries spring from the

desire to know not only *what* is, but *why* it is, — to reach at once the first elements of things and their final cause.

And (3.) Hume has overlooked the fact that when once this idea of the connection between adaptation and intelligence has entered the mind, from whatever source, it does not require to be renewed, but remains always as an intuitive perception; no amount of experiences can strengthen or weaken it, and this for the reason that the conviction of a designing cause does not rest in observations or experiences, greater or less, of man and his contrivances, but lies in the thing of perceived adaptation; it does not require a knowledge of the cause or source of the adaptation. That wherever there is an adaptation of means to an end there must have been an intelligent cause is an intuition of the mind. This term intuition should not be confounded with the notion of *innate* ideas. An intuition is a self-evident truth; the mind may come to the knowledge of such a truth in various ways and by many processes; but when once it is perceived, it is seen to be true, as a proposition in and of itself, which no amount of reasoning or of evidence could make clearer or stronger than it is in its own simple statement. For example, the sum of all the parts is together equal to the whole. (A child may learn this, if you please, by trying it; but once gained it is *there*.) Everything that begins to be must have a cause; whatever exists must exist in time and in space. To this class of self-convincing truths belongs this also, that the adaptation of means to an end springs from an intelligent and designing cause. Under these criticisms of common sense and of universal consciousness Hume's elaborate structure falls to the ground.

I am aware that this reasoning involves the interminable controversy between sensation and consciousness as the originator of ideas. But it is clear that external phenomena do not and cannot impart to us the idea of a cause. We cannot see a cause, feel a cause, hear a cause. What we perceive in nature is never *cause* as a substantial entity, but only the sequence of phenomena. And yet the mind unhesitatingly affirms of every phenomenon which actually comes to pass, that it is not self-originated, but must have had a cause. Whence has the mind this conception of the necessary relation of an event to a cause? I answer that this is a necessary cognition of the human mind, given in and of the mind itself. The mind knows itself as a cause. It does not matter here whether this knowledge be spontaneous or the result of mental experiences. Of the first origin of cognitions in a child, the first realization of consciousness, we have no possibility of record. But this we know, that there comes to every mind a moment when it awakes to the feeling " I can " and " I will." It knows the Ego in consciousness, and clothes the Ego with volition and with causality. With the blow of a hammer I break a crystal. We say the blow is the cause of the fracture ; and this loose use of the term cause is sanctioned by usage. But where and what is the cause? In the hammer? Or in the contact of the hammer with the crystal ? Does it reside in the hammer? Or is it developed by the blow ? There is no sense nor instrument fine enough to detect it. We see the blow, we see the fracture, but not ten thousand such experiences would enable us to see the cause. The cause, you will say, is the force applied behind the hammer. But that force is not an entity ; it is only a quality of the cause, and that cause is the power which is in me put in action by my will. All force is but cause in action. And the sublime doctrine of universal force points of necessity to universal cause, and that cause intelligent. Having its sole idea of cause through the consciousness of itself as a cause, the mind intuitively refers every event to a cause adequate in power and wisdom to the result.

Even upon Hume's own principle, the thing which "experience" has taught us is, that the adaptation of means, or the collocation of materials *for an end*, must be referred to an intelligent designer purposing that end. And the world has grown so old in the infallibility of this so-called experience, that it accepts the principle as an axiom alike in its application to a watch and to a world. The principle being recognized, we are prepared to apply it more carefully than did Paley to the evidence of nature to a supreme intelligent cause.

Teleology is not an invention of Christian theology. In perceiving an end in nature, and from this assuming a divine author of nature, Plato and Aristotle anticipated Paul and Augustine; and we are all familiar with Cicero's reply to the Epicurean notion that the world was formed by a chance concourse of atoms. "He who believes this may as well believe that if a great quantity of the letters of the alphabet, made of gold or any other substance, were thrown upon the ground, they would fall into such order as legibly to form a book, say the 'Annals of Ennius.' I doubt whether chance could make a single line of them. . . . But if a concourse of atoms can make a world, why not a porch, a temple, a house, a city, which are works of less labor and difficulty?"

Many of the witnesses which Paley brought forward to establish the fact of design in nature have been discredited through the searching cross-examination of modern science; and some have even been so twisted and turned as to lean to the opposite side. But what then? This impeachment of testimony prejudices the jury, but cannot blind an impartial judge to the principles which underlie the case. Much the same has happened in geology. Many of the facts relied upon by earlier geologists have been modified in their meaning and their relations, or have been quite set aside by the research of

later times. Theories have changed with every new
master of the science, and the now-accepted theory of
Lyell may yet be modified by the results of deep-sea
soundings and of explorations in the Sierra Nevada.
But no one dreams of doubting that there is in the structure of the earth a foundation for a science of geology.
And so we may trace there a foundation for a science of
teleology, all the more clear, because the superficial
mechanism of design has been swept away. Indeed, the
very terms designer, contriver, smack of the mechanical,
the coarse, the vulgar. Professor Tyndall, who certainly
has no belief in final cause in the theological sense, is
already helping us to finer terms for teleology itself; and
these terms occur in examples best fitted to illustrate the
finer meanings and methods of this science. These examples are found in heat and in light.

There is even more of science than of poetry in the
saying that coal is "bottled sunlight." For what purpose was coal produced, but that it should serve for fuel ;
should be made to give back in practical and beneficial
uses the heat it had condensed from the sun ? And for
whose use intended but for man ? Nature in her operations has no service for this concentrated extract of ferns
and trees. No animal tribes in burrowing or foraging
had ever sought out the coal or applied it to their wants.
But when man had need of other fuel than the surface
of the earth could furnish him, there lay the beds of coal
ready to his hand. Can we resist the conviction that
coal was provided in anticipation of the coming of man
— stored, so to speak, in the cellar of his future abode?
If there were, indeed, such a purpose in the formation of
coal, the relation between the purpose and the result is
the more impressive because it was so long latent, and
required ages for its development. Not fact and form
alone, but idea and intent as well, are in process of de-

velopment. The plan in evolution is also the evolution of a plan. Professor Tyndall has given us the very term to characterize this phenomenon. " Wood and coal can burn ; whence come their heat, and the work producible by that heat? From the immeasurable reservoir of the sun, Nature has *proposed to herself* the task of storing up the light which streams earthward from the sun, and of casting into a permanent form the most fugitive of all powers. *To this end* she has overspread the earth with organisms which, while living, take in the solar light, and by its consumption generate forces of another kind. These organisms are plants. The vegetable world, indeed, constitutes the instrument whereby the wave-motion of the sun is changed into the rigid form of chemical tension, and thus prepared for future use. With this *prevision* the existence of the human race itself is inseparably connected." In the terms which I have italicized, teleology is so etherealized that nothing remains of the grossness of the old conception of the mechanism of the universe. *Prevision* is so much finer than design or contrivance ! We no longer require to see either the watch or the world in the process of making ; we no longer hear the starting of the machinery ; but as in Ezekiel's vision there is a spirit of life within the wheels, and they are borne on mighty wings.

The objection to this illustration, that if coal were intended for the use of man, it should have been evenly distributed over the globe, and upon the surface, seems too frivolous for a philosophical reply. But the reply is given in the whole nature of man, and in the totality of the ends of his existence. Man shall not live by coal alone. The distribution of the earth's products gives rise to that system of industries, to that development of energy, skill, foresight, and invention, and to that brotherhood of humanity which comes of widespread in-

tercourse, which render human existence so much higher
than that of brutes.

I am not strenuous, however, for this illustration. I
have adopted it because a leading man of science seems
driven to teleology to account for the fact of coal. Thus
teleology, as in Harvey's discovery of the circulation of
the blood, is often the guide of science to higher ends.

My object in this essay is not to prove the doctrine of
final causes, but to point out the lines of proof, — in the
true conception of causality, and in the wise interpretation of those more subtle phases of nature which science
now deals with, and which so transcend the mechanical
causes of Paley.

As with heat, so with light. To describe the web of
relations subsisting between solar light and the media
through which this passes to the human eye, Tyndall has
recourse to the same refinement of teleology.

" We have, in the first place, in solar light an agent of
exceeding complexity, composed of innumerable constituents refrangible in different degrees. We find, secondly,
the atoms and molecules of bodies gifted with the power
of sifting solar light in the most various ways, and producing by this sifting the colors observed in nature and
art. To do this they must possess a molecular structure
commensurate in complexity with that of light itself.
Thirdly, we have the human eye and brain, so organized
as to be able to take in and distinguish the multitude
of impressions thus generated. The light, therefore, at
starting, is complex ; to sift and select it as they do, natural bodies must be complex ; while to take in the impressions thus generated, the human eye and brain, however we may simplify our conceptions of their action,
must be highly complex. Whence this triple complexity ? If what are called material purposes were the only
end to be served, a much simpler mechanism would be

sufficient. But, instead of simplicity, we have prodigality of relation and *adaptation*, — and this apparently for the sole *purpose* of enabling us to see things robed in the splendor of color. Would it not seem that Nature *harbored the intention* of educating us for other enjoyments than those derivable from meat and drink? At all events, whatever Nature meant, — and it would be mere presumption to dogmatize as to what she meant, — we find ourselves here as the upshot of her operations, endowed with capacities to enjoy not only the materially useful, but endowed with others of indefinite scope and application, which deal alone with the beautiful and the true." [1]

In how many distinct forms and phrases in the two passages cited does Mr. Tyndall pay homage to the intuitive conviction of purpose, intention, design, as seen in the adaptations of Nature: "Nature has proposed to herself;" "to this end;" "with this prevision;" "atoms gifted with the power;" "prodigality of relation and adaptation;" "for the sole purpose;" "Nature harbored the intention;" "whatever Nature meant." Tyndall is a master of language, whether as the poet picturing the Alps, or as the philosopher analyzing and defining nature. In these passages he is the man of science upon his own ground, reporting his observations and experiments. And he tells us that in two of the most delicate, subtle, yet all-pervasive forces of nature, — heat and light, — he finds everywhere traces of intelligence, since only intelligence can harbor an intention, can have a meaning or purpose, or act with prevision for an end.

Two parallel incidents in geology will show that the scientific mind intuitively discriminates between nature and intelligence. (1.) In digging a well in Illinois, the workmen at a depth of several feet struck upon the

---

[1] Tyndall on *Light*, Lec. 1.

21

trunk of a tree, and under this upon a bit of copper ore
identical with that of Lake Superior. The inference
was that ages ago the copper had been washed from its
native bed, and lodged in the alluvium of the Mississippi
Valley, — perhaps that the great lakes then had an outlet through the Mississippi, — and over this deposit a
forest had grown, which in time was buried beneath the
ever-accumulating surface. The whole process was ascribed to natural causes, — the interest concentrating in
the question of time. (2.) In working the copper mines
of Lake Superior, the miner came upon traces of excava-
tion, of smelting, of rude implements of labor ; and the
immediate conviction was, *Man* has been here before us,
— probably that unknown race who built the mounds in
the Mississippi Valley had discovered and worked these
mines. How shall we account for the difference in these
judgments, — the one pointing to nature, the other to
man ? The judgment in each case was spontaneous, and
each judgment is accepted by science as correct. The
dividing line between them is, that perceived adaptation
to an end betokens an intelligent purpose directed to
that end. A corresponding instance is familiar to English geologists.

At a considerable depth in the delta of the Nile were
found remains of pottery. The immediate conviction
was that man was on the soil at the period of this formation. Beyond question the pottery was the work of man ;
and the geological age of the deposit would determine
how far back man existed on the borders of the Nile.
When it was suggested that the pottery bore marks of
Greek workmanship, the inference was that either by accident it had worked its way so deep, or the Nile deposit
had been more rapid than is commonly supposed. The
question recurs, how do we make this distinction between
man and nature, and the answer lies in the one fact of
adaptation to an end.

Now, Professor Tyndall assures us that in the single fact of light and vision " we have prodigality of relation and adaptation." From the point of view of physical science he cannot look beyond the bounds of nature, and hence he provides the intelligence which adaptation demands by *personifying* nature. I accept implicitly Tyndall's testimony to the wondrous fact ; and not being under the restriction which the pure scientist must observe, I accept the conviction of my own intelligence that *such* intelligence is above nature. The principle of teleology is thus attested by science itself in its most subtle and intricate investigations. Indeed, that principle becomes more patent the farther it is removed from the sensuous into the *sub*-sensible world. There we touch upon causes, first, mediate, and final. It does not matter that the relation of cause and effect is often obscure. Could we have looked upon our planet in the carboniferous era, who could have seen reflected in that murky atmosphere the coal-grate glowing in our dwellings, the furnace in our factories ? We are living in an unfinished system, an era of the evolution of phenomena, and, as I have said, the development of the ideas that lie at the back of phenomena.

Neither does it disparage teleology to point to the evil that is in the world. Moral evil is the product of man's free agency. But free will is the highest endowment of a rational creature. The power of moral choice makes man akin to the infinite and the absolute ; and moral evil is a perversion of this most illustrious attribute of being, and the possibility of perversion lies in the nature of free will, and gives to virtue its worth and its glory. Hence it may be that moral evil is incidental, in respect of divine prevention, to the best possible system.

As to physical evil, this is but partial and relative.

Our own experience testifies that this often serves to discipline the intellect of man, to put fibre into his will, and train him to noble and heroic action in subjugating nature to the service of the human family. The very doctrine of natural selection shows of how much worth to man is the struggle for existence as a moral element in the development of character.

Here, too, comes in the fact that the system is unfinished. Things that seem untoward because unknown may have a brighter end : "from seeming evil still educing good."

Science is teaching this, especially in chemistry, by transforming what once was feared as hurtful and hostile to man into some higher ministry of the beautiful and the useful, ordered by wisdom and beneficence. What serviceable dyes, what exquisite tints, are evolved from the noisome refuse of coal-tar !

And just this service should science render if teleology is true. For if there be a Creator, He must be spirit, and apprehensible only by spirit. Hence, the more we are developed in mind by science, and the more we penetrate through science to the silent, impalpable forces of nature, the nearer shall we come to Him who is invisible ; till with Dante, emerging into the light eternal, we can say : —

> " And now was turning my desire and will,
> Even as a wheel that equally is moved,
> The Love which moves the sun and the other stars."

APPENDIX TO THE LAST ESSAY.

Since the foregoing paper was read, Professor Huxley has published a "Life of Hume," with an analysis of his works, which in its cheap and attractive form may give a fresh impulse to the popularity of the Scotch philosopher. A review of Hume's philosophical system, as a whole, would here be out of place. Supposing Huxley's synopsis of it to be now at hand, I must restrict myself to the points raised in my paper — Cause, Power, Intuition. It is a hopeful sign that such a master in physics as Professor Huxley should invoke such a master in metaphysics as Hume (just as Professor Tyndall invokes Lucretius) in support of his own teachings; that science, which we have been told was the only knowledge — the knowledge of *things* by observation of the senses — should have recourse to philosophy to sift and classify phenomena under *ideas*, in order that they may have a place in the category of knowledge. The necessity for this I have endeavored to show in the article, "What is Science?" in the "British Quarterly Review" for January, 1879; and the recognition of this dependence of science upon philosophy for its own expression would put an end to much of the controversy over physics and metaphysics. As to ideal speculation, Professor Huxley goes quite far enough. On page 55 he says: "All science starts with hypotheses — in other words, with assumptions that are unproved, while they may be, and often are, erroneous; but which are better than nothing to the seeker after order in the maze of phenomena. And the historical progress of every science depends on the criticism of hypotheses, on the gradual stripping off, that is, of their untrue or superfluous parts, until there remains only that exact verbal expression of as much as we know of the fact, and no more, which constitutes a perfect scientific theory."

This statement of the way of attaining a scientific knowledge of external phenomena raises two questions, which must be answered before we can have any confidence in such knowledge. Who or what is it which makes that "criticism of hypotheses" upon which "the progress of every science depends?" And how do we "know a fact," or who are the WE who know a fact, so as to reduce it to its "exact verbal expression?"

Professor Huxley is not quite satisfied with Hume's negation of mind; that "what we call a mind is nothing but a heap or collection of different perceptions, united together by certain relations, and supposed, though falsely, to be endowed with a perfect simplicity and identity." Of this view, Huxley says: "He [Hume] may be right or wrong; but the most he, or anybody else, can prove in favor of his conclusion is, that we know nothing more of the mind than that it is a series of perceptions." Here, again, I ask, Who or what are the We, who know this, or anything else? Does a mere "series of perceptions," each of which gives place in turn to its successor, know itself as a series, and that this series is all that can be known of mind? Has a series of ever-changing, ever-vanishing impressions a continuity of consciousness, a power of retention as memory, and of discrimination as judgment? There can be no criticism without comparison, without remembrance, without selection, without discriminating judgment; and the question forces itself home to the school of Hume, If the mind "is nothing but a heap or collection of different perceptions," where or what is that faculty which examines and compares these impressions, and which reduces them to an "exact verbal expression" as fact or knowledge? The truth is that Mr. Hume and Professor Huxley necessarily assume a *something* within man which, though it cannot be known "by direct observation," yets knows itself, and knows other things. The existence of this something, which we call mind, is asserted by the consciousness of all mankind and in the language of every people. It is proved by the consciousness which every man has of personal identity and of individuality; by his exercise of memory and of will; and above all by his sense of right and wrong, and his spontaneous emotions in view of good or of evil. This something knows itself as a cause, as a power, and as possessing free will ; that is, in all actions having a moral quality it has power to choose a course of action, and also power to choose the contrary. Whatever the motive which finally determines its choice — say, if you please, the greatest *apparent* good — there is always the power of contrary choice. Every man knows these things to be true of himself. But it is absolutely impossible to predicate any of these things of a mere "series of perceptions." Though the existence and the properties of mind may "lie beyond the reach of observation," — as the term observation is applied to the study of nature, — yet the existence of mind is known in consciousness with a certainty as absolute as that which pertains to the phenomena of nature observed and reported through the senses. In either case the conviction of certainty is given in the mind, or it could not exist at all. How can I know anything if I do not first know the I who knows, so far as to have full confidence in the observations which *I* make, and in the judgments which *I* form ?

Now, there are also truths which the mind knows by intuition, of which it is as certain as of any fact ascertained by observation, and indeed as certain as of its own existence. Such truths do not depend upon experience, but are assumed in all experience. They could not be made a whit more clear or certain by reasoning or observation than they are seen to be by direct cognition. Of this class of truths are the axioms of mathematics. Hume admits that there are "necessary truths," but he would not class with these the axiom of causation, "That whatever event has a beginning must have a cause." Professor Huxley is more inclined to class causation with necessary truths, and this upon scientific grounds. Thus, on p. 121, he says : "The scientific investigator who notes a new phenomenon may be utterly ignorant of its cause, but he will, without hesitation, seek for that cause. If you ask him why he does so, he will probably say that it must have had a cause ; and thereby imply that his belief in causation is a necessary belief." What is true of the man of science is equally true of the human mind under all possible conditions. It is an intuitive conviction of a necessary truth, that every event must have a cause. It is absolutely impossible for the mind to conceive the contrary. Let any one conceive of absolute universal Nothingness, and he will find it impossible to conceive of anything as beginning to be! Either, then, we must have recourse to the unphilosophical conjecture of an infinite series, or we must believe in an eternal Creator of the universe.

In like manner, that adaptation points to a purposing intelligence is an intuitive cognition of the human mind. This does not arise from experience of adaptive power in other men; and though continually verified by experience, it does not rest in experience for its proof. Here, too, as above, it is impossible for the mind to conceive the contrary.

Having already exposed the fallacy of Hume on this point, and having traced the notions of causation and of power to their seat in the mind itself, I trust I have opened anew the way for the evidence of God in nature, which physics is more and more unveiling, for metaphysics to take note of and classify.

NOTE.

The reader who is interested in the preceding points of metaphysical inquiry, but who lacks facilities for studying German philosophy in the original, can put himself in communication with two of the greatest thinkers of Germany, by reading " A Critical Account of the Philosophy of Kant," by Professor Edward Caird, of the University of Glasgow; and " The Logic of Hegel," by William Wallace, M. A., Fellow of Merton College, Oxford. Kant was not satisfied with the argument from design, or as it is better called, the physico-theological argument for the being of God; and while controverting Hume on some points, he agreed with him that the existence of order in the universe could at most establish a *finite* cause. This point I have previously considered. But another form of reply presented by Professor Caird is so thoughtful and suggestive that I give the gist of it here, referring the reader to the full argument in his eighteenth chapter.

" Why do we seek in things, in the world, and in ourselves, a truth, a reality, which we do not find in their immediate aspect as phenomena of the sensible world ? It is because the sensible world, as such, is inconsistent with itself, and thus points to a higher reality. We believe in the infinite, not because of what the finite is, but quite as much because of what the finite *is not ;* and our first idea of the former is, therefore, simply that it is the negation of the latter. All religion springs out of the sense of the nothingness, unreality, transitoriness — in other words, of the essentially negative character of the finite world. Yet this negative relation of the mind to the finite is at the same time its first positive relation to the infinite. ' We are near waking when we dream that we dream,' and the consciousness of a limit is already at least the germinal consciousness of that which is beyond it. The extreme of despair and doubt can only exist as the obverse of the highest certitude, and is in fact necessary to it."

Hegel, who was fond of reducing every conception to the last possible analysis, says, " We must decidedly reject the *mechanical* mode of inquiry when it comes forward and arrogates to itself the place of rational cognition in general, and when it seeks to get mechanism accepted as an absolute category." He then shows how even the argument from design has been vitiated by a mechanical tone.[1]

" Generally speaking, the final cause is taken to mean nothing more than external design. In accordance with this view of it, things are supposed not to carry their vocation in themselves, but merely to be means employed and spent in realizing a purpose which lies outside of them. That may be said to be the point of view taken by utility, which once played a great part even in the sciences. Of late, however, utility has fallen into disrepute, now that people have begun to see that it failed to give a genuine insight into the nature of things. It is true that finite things as finite ought in justice to be viewed as non-ultimate, and as pointing beyond themselves. This negativity of finite things, however, is their own dialectic, and in order to ascertain it we must pay attention to their positive content.

[1] Pages 291 and 299.

" Teleological modes of investigation often proceed from a well-meant desire of displaying the wisdom of God, especially as it is revealed in nature. Now in thus trying to discover final causes, for which the things serve as means, we must remember that we are stopping short at the finite, and are liable to fall into trifling reflections. An instance of such triviality is seen when we first of all treat of the vine solely in reference to the well-known uses which it confers upon man, and then proceed to view the cork-tree in connection with the corks which are cut from its bark to put into the wine-bottles. Whole books used to be written in this spirit. It is easy to see that they promoted the genuine interest neither of religion nor of science. External design stands immediately in front of the idea: but what thus stands on the threshold often for that reason gives the least satisfaction."

The burden of my paper is to lead up through this external design to the idea that lies behind it. And here Hegel has given food for thought in his profound saying that " Objectivity contains the three forms of mechanism, chemism, and the *nexus* of design." This *nexus* holds the world and the universe together in our intuitive conception.

INDEX.

22

www.ingramcontent.com/pod-product-compliance
Lightning Source LLC
Chambersburg PA
CBHW021114270326
41929CB00009B/876